REVOLUTIONARY ROOTS

www.royalcollins.com

The CPC's Inspiring Legacy for Teens

REVOLUTIONARY ROOTS

Chen Jinlong

Revolutionary Roots: The CPC's Inspiring Legacy for Teens

Chen Jinlong
Translated by Ayinuer Yiganmu

First published in 2024 by Royal Collins Publishing Group Inc.
Groupe Publication Royal Collins Inc.
BKM Royalcollins Publishers Private Limited

Headquarters: 550-555 boul. René-Lévesque O Montréal (Québec) H2Z1B1 Canada
India office: 805 Hemkunt House, 8th Floor, Rajendra Place, New Delhi 110 008

10 9 8 7 6 5 4 3 2 1

ISBN: 978-1-4878-1167-9

To find out more about our publications, please visit www.royalcollins.com.

Contents

1921–1930

1931–1940

1941–1950

1951–1960

1961–1970

1971–1980

1981–1990

1991–2000

2001–2010

2011–2020

Preface

A hundred years ago, China, a semi-colonial and semi-feudal society, was like a fragmented country. The nation was bullied, and its sovereignty was constantly eroded. The suffering Chinese people looked forward to brightness in the dark. When the reformist experiments and the "Three People's Principles" could not save the terminally ill China, the Communist Party of China (CPC) was born in 1921. This epoch-making event has become a turning point in the destiny of the Chinese nation.

From 1921 to 2021, the 100-year struggle history of the CPC is the great history of the Chinese nation from decline to rejuvenation. One hundred years of history proves that only socialism can save China, and only socialism can develop China. Adherence to the leadership of the CPC is the fundamental guarantee of the success of the Chinese revolution and construction.

Today, 100 years later, when we look back on the glorious history of the CPC, the magnificent historical scenes are still in front of us. As a Chinese saying goes, "History, if not forgotten, can serve as a guide for the future," and we should not forget this history. On February 20, 2021, General Secretary Xi Jinping pointed out at the mobilization meeting of Party history learning and education, "Looking back at the past struggle and looking ahead, we must learn and summarize the Party's history well, and pass on and carry forward the Party's successful experience." "With the Party's struggle and great achievements to inspire morale and clear direction, with the Party's glorious tradition and excellent style to strengthen beliefs and cohesion, with the Party's practical creation and historical experience to enlighten wisdom and sharpen character."

The report of the 19th National Congress of the CPC states, "After a long period of effort, socialism with Chinese characteristics has entered a new era." Clarifying that socialism with Chinese characteristics has entered a new era is a major strategic consideration made by our Party based on scientifically grasping the profound changes in the world situation, in our country, and within our Party, which bears the overall situation. It further highlights the progressive nature of the CPC and the times and reflects high consciousness and self-confidence in grasping the laws and trends of history. The wheels of history roll on; the tides of the times are vast and mighty. The entry of socialism with Chinese characteristics into a new era is an inevitable result of China's social development and progress since the founding of the People's Republic of China (PRC), especially since the reform and opening-up. It is also an inevitable requirement for our Party to unite and lead the people of all ethnic groups to create a bright future.

Revolutionary Roots: The CPC's Inspiring Legacy for Teens is aimed at young readers. It represents the 100 years of struggle of the CPC with vivid stories. We hope that through reading this book, teenagers can further understand our great Party, love our great Party more, and love our great country more.

At the same time, we hope that it can be more profoundly understood that the leadership core position of the CPC in the cause of socialism with Chinese characteristics is unshakable. Only under the leadership of the CPC can the Chinese Dream of the great rejuvenation of the Chinese nation be realized.

In the long history, 100 years is only a drop in the ocean, but for the Chinese nation, these 100 years have carried too many dreams and glories, which are so majestic and heavy. Looking back on the past, countless Communists shed their blood for today's peaceful and happy life. As the hope of the motherland, young people should remember the past, cherish the present, cherish the future, establish lofty ideals from childhood, and become qualified successors to the socialist cause in the future.

没有共产党就没有新中国

1=A $\frac{2}{4}$

曹火星 词曲

1̇ 5 | 6 6 5·6 | 1̇ 1̇ 6 1̇ | 2̇ - | 3̇ 2̇ | 1̇ 3̇ 2̇·1̇ |
没 有 共 产 党 就 没 有 新 中 国， 没 有 共 产 党 就

6 2̇ 7 6 | 5 - | 1̇ 6 | 1̇ · 6 | 3 1̇ 6 5 |
没 有 新 中 国。 共 产 党 辛 劳 为 民

6 - | 3 1̇ | 6 · 5 | 2̇ 1̇ 6 5 | 6 - |
族， 共 产 党 他 一 心 救 中 国，

3 1̇ 1̇ 1̇ | 6 3 | 3 3 5 6 | 6 - | 3̇ 2̇ 1̇ |
他 指 给 了 人 民 解 放 的 道 路， 他 领 导

2̇ 5 | 6 1̇ 2̇ | 2̇ · 5 | 3 3 5 5 | 6 6 5 ∨6 |
中 国 走 向 光 明。 他 坚 持 抗 战 八 年 多，他

1̇ 1̇ 1̇ 6 2̇ | 7 6 5·∨6 | 2̇ 2̇ 2̇ 1̇ 2̇ | 3̇ 3̇ 2̇ ∨1̇ | 6 6 6 1̇ 1̇ |
改 善 了 人 民 生 活，他 建 设 了 敌 后 根 据 地，他 实 行 了 民 主

2̇ 1̇ 6 1̇ | 5 - | 1̇ 5 6 1̇ | 5 · 6 | 1̇ 1̇ 6 1̇ |
好 处 多。 没 有 共 产 党 就 没 有 新 中

2̇ - | 3̇ 2̇ 1̇ 3̇ | 2̇ · 3̇ | 5̇ 5̇ 3̇ 2̇ | 1̇ - ‖
国 没 有 共 产 党 就 没 有 新 中 国。

1921 The Red Boat on South Lake Welcomed the Founding of the Party

Keyword: the birth of the CPC

Beside the bank of the Yanyu Building on the island in the middle of the lake, there is an unusual and exquisite cruise ship, which is the world-famous Chinese revolutionary pilot ship. This ship frames the historical picture of the epoch-making event 100 years ago and represents the majestic years at the beginning of the founding of the CPC.

On July 23, 1921, the 1st National Congress of the CPC was secretly held in Shanghai. The domestic and Japanese party organizations sent 13 people to the conference: Li Da and Li Hanjun from Shanghai, Dong Biwu and Chen Tanqiu from Wuhan, Mao Zedong and He Shuheng from Changsha, Wang Jinmei and Deng Enming from Jinan, Zhang Guotao and Liu Renjing from Beijing, Chen Gongbo from Guangzhou, Zhou Fohai from Japan, and Bao Huisheng, a delegate appointed by Chen Duxiu. They represent more than 50 Party members. On the evening of July 30, when the delegates were having a meeting, a strange middle-aged man suddenly burst into the venue, looked around, and then left in a hurry.

Ma Lin, a representative of the Communist International with long-term experience in secret work, decided that this person was an enemy spy and proposed to suspend the meeting. At the suggestion of Wang Huiwu, wife of Shanghai delegate Li Da, the meeting was

Figure 1.
The Red Boat on South Lake

transferred to a boat on the South Lake in Jiaxing, Zhejiang Province.

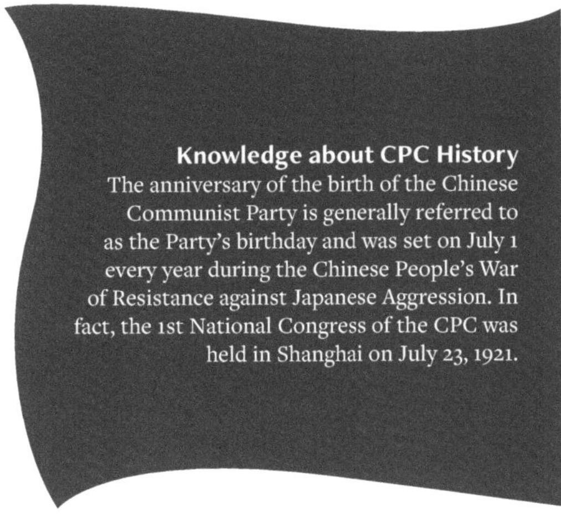

Knowledge about CPC History

The anniversary of the birth of the Chinese Communist Party is generally referred to as the Party's birthday and was set on July 1 every year during the Chinese People's War of Resistance against Japanese Aggression. In fact, the 1st National Congress of the CPC was held in Shanghai on July 23, 1921.

One day in early August, the delegates took the morning train from Shanghai North Railway Station to Jiaxing. Led by Wang Huiwu, they took a ferry to Huxin Island in the middle of the lake and then picked up by a small tugboat to Wang Huiwu's pre-rented meeting boat. The boat was about 16 meters long and 3 meters wide. Its bow was wide and flat. It had a front cabin, a middle cabin, a passenger's cabin, and a back cabin. The meeting was held in the middle cabin, while Wang Huiwu sat at the bow as sentry.

The meeting reviewed and adopted the first program and the first resolution of the CPC. By secret ballot, Chen Duxiu, Zhang Guotao, and Li Da were elected to form the national leading body of the Party, the Central Bureau. Chen Duxiu was the secretary of the Central Bureau, Zhang Guotao was in charge of the organization, and Li Da was in charge of publicity.

After six o'clock that afternoon, the meeting completed all the agendas and successfully closed, solemnly proclaiming the founding of the CPC. When the Congress closed, all the delegates softly called out the strongest voice of the times: "Long live the Communist Party! Long live the Third International! Long live communism—the liberator of mankind!" After the meeting, the delegates left the boat quietly and scattered that night to leave Jiaxing. They brought the spark of revolution to all parts of the country, and China's history has since written a new chapter.

In order to commemorate the significant historical event of the triumphant conclusion of the 1st National Congress of the CPC on the red boat on South Lake, the South Lake Revolutionary Memorial Hall was established in 1959. In 1985, Deng Xiaoping inscribed the name of the hall. In order to recreate the historical scene, the memorial hall made this memorial boat in the style of the boat rented for the meeting of the First Congress of the CPC, based on the memories of some delegates of the First Congress of the CPC, and moored it on the water of the southeast shore of the Huxin Island in front of the Yanyu Building, vividly showing the historical scene of the birth of the CPC.

This commemorative boat of the 1st National Congress of the CPC was affectionately called "The Red Boat on South Lake."

1922 The Revolutionary Program Set a Course

Keyword: the formulation of democratic revolutionary program in the 2nd National Congress of the CPC

July 16, 1922, was a day destined to be recorded in history. On this day, the streets of Shanghai were still full of traffic, and the crowds were in a hurry, a lively scene of a prosperous city. However, in an ordinary residential building, it was a different scene. A meeting of extraordinary significance would be held here. With the convening of the meeting, the storm of China's democratic revolution would sweep across the ancient land of China.

On that day, under the guidance and help of Communist International, the 2nd National Congress of the CPC was held at the home of Li Da in Fudeli, South Chengdu Road, Shanghai, attended by 12 delegates, including Chen Duxiu, Zhang Guotao, Li Da, Yang Mingzhai, and Cai Hesen. The delegates of the 2nd National Congress of the CPC reached a consensus on the future of the Chinese revolution and solved many problems left over by the 1st National Congress of the CPC. The meeting clearly put forward the party's democratic revolutionary

Figure 2.
The site of the 2nd National Congress of the CPC, at No. 30, Lane 7, Chengdu North Road, Shanghai

program and adopted the *Declaration of the 2nd National Congress of the CPC* and the *Constitution of the Communist Party of China*.

Knowledge about CPC History
New Youth is a comprehensive monthly cultural magazine. It was founded in Shanghai in September 1915, initially named *Youth Magazine*, and renamed *New Youth* in September 1916. It propagated democracy and science, advocated new literature and opposed old literature, and advocated vernacular Chinese and opposed classical Chinese. Later on, it propagated Marxism, and many of the founders of the CPC were influenced by the *New Youth*.

The significance of the 2nd National Congress of the CPC in the history of the CPC lies in the formulation of the Party's democratic revolutionary program. The declaration issued by the conference pointed out that, on the one hand, China was politically and economically oppressed by imperialism; it was still under the rule of warlord bureaucrats, which hindered the development of Chinese capitalism. Therefore, the highest program of the Party was to realize socialism and communism, but at that stage of democratic revolution, the revolutionary program was to overthrow the warlords, overthrow the oppression of international imperialism and unify China. Since modern times, an important reason for the repeated failures of the Chinese revolution is that the nature, object, and motive force of the revolution have not been clearly defined, and the revolutionary program against imperialism and feudalism has not been put forward. The formulation of the Party's democratic revolutionary program pointed out the direction of the Chinese revolution.

Mao Zedong's name did not appear on the list of participants in the 2nd National Congress of the CPC. There were various accounts of this. Fourteen years later, in 1936, Mao Zedong said in an interview with the American journalist Snow in Shaanxi that the Second Party Congress was held in Shanghai and he wanted to attend it, but he forgot the venue and could not find any comrades, so as a result, he did not attend. Mao Zedong always deeply regretted his absence from such an important meeting.

Since the meeting was held in secret, people did not know where the 2nd National Congress of the CPC was held after the founding of New China. On February 23, 1954, the Preparatory Office of the Shanghai Revolutionary History Memorial Hall received a letter from Li Da, a representative of the First and Second National Congresses of the CPC. In the letter, Li Da revealed that the first meeting of the 2nd National Congress of the CPC was not held on the West Lake in Hangzhou, as some people said, but at his home, No. 625 Fudeli, South Chengdu Road, Shanghai. In 1959, Fudeli No. 625 was officially hung with the Cultural Relics Protection Unit sign.

Time flies, and all the people who witnessed the Second Communist Party Congress have passed away. However, the democratic revolutionary program formulated at the meeting established the voyage of the development of China's democratic revolution and led the storm of China's democratic revolution to gallop along with irresistible force, deeply affecting the development of Chinese history.

1923 Beijing–Hankou Strike Showed Strength

Keyword: Beijing–Hankou railway workers' strike

On February 1, 1923, in Zhengzhou, it was freezing cold. However, in this cold and windy season, an "iron current" was surging. On that night, the executive committee of the General Union of Beijing–Hankou Railway held a secret meeting at the Zhengzhou Puleyuan Theater and held a general strike of the Beijing–Hankou Railway from February 4. In this way, the Beijing–Hankou Railway Workers' Strike, which shocked the world, began.

The Beijing–Hankou Railway ran through Hebei, Henan, and Hubei provinces. It was the transportation lifeline connecting North and Central China and was of important economic, political, and military significance. The revenue from the operation of the Beijing–Hankou railway was one of the main sources of military pay for warlord Wu Peifu. On February 1, 1923, the preparatory meeting of the General Union of Beijing–Hankou Railway under the leadership of the Party decided to hold the founding meeting in Zhengzhou. Nearly 300 representatives of various railway unions and student representatives from Beijing, Wuhan, and other places gathered in Zhengzhou to attend the meeting. The CPC Central Committee attached great importance to the meeting and sent Zhang Guotao, Chen Tanqiu, Luo Zhanglong, and others to attend the meeting.

On the morning of February 1, warlord Wu Peifu sent a large number of armed military and police officers to impose martial law in the whole city of Zhengzhou and ordered that

Figure 3.
Group photo of representatives at the founding meeting of the General Union of the Beijing–Hankou Railway

the founding meeting of the General Union of the Beijing–Hankou Railway be forbidden. However, the workers' representatives attending the meeting, regardless of their lives, broke through the heavy encirclement of the military and police and shouted slogans, such as "Long live the General Union of the Beijing–Hankou Railway" and "Long live the victory of the working class." The meeting lasted less than 15 minutes, and there was a conflict with the military police.

Knowledge about CPC History

After the 1st National Congress of the CPC was held, the Secretariat of China's Labor Union, which led the labor movement, was established. From January 1922 to February 1923, the first climax of China's labor movement was set off. Over 13 months, more than 100 strikes of various sizes took place throughout the country, involving 300,000 people.

From 9:00 a.m. on February 4, it took only three hours to realize the strike of tens of thousands of workers on the Beijing–Hankou Railway. All passenger cars, trucks, and military vehicles were stopped, and the Beijing–Hankou Railway was immediately paralyzed. Warlord Wu Peifu was genocidal and killed people. On February 7, on the pretext of mediating the strike, he tricked the union representatives to the Jiang'an union office to "negotiate." On their way there, the union representatives were shot. The unarmed workers' pickets were killed on the spot, with more than 30 people killed and 200 injured. The reactionary troops also broke into the workers' dormitories and carried out extensive raids, resulting in the "February 7 Massacre" that shocked China and the world.

After Lin Xiangqian, chairman of Jiang'an Branch and Communist Party member, was arrested, the reactionary army and police tied him to a telegraph pole and forced him with a knife to order the resumption of work. Lin Xiangqian shouted: "The head can be broken, the blood can flow, and the work cannot be restored!" He would rather die than surrender, and died heroically. Shi Yang, a member of the Communist Party and legal adviser to the General Union of the Beijing–Hankou Railway and the Hubei Federation of Labor Unions, was also brutally murdered. After the tragedy, although the reactionary warlords bound workers everywhere and forced them to return to work by terrorist means, the workers persisted in their struggle and resolutely refused to return to work until they were ordered to do so by the General Unions, and the local unions also refused to negotiate independently. The strike continued until February 9. In order to avoid unnecessary sacrifice and save strength to prepare for a larger-scale struggle in the future, the General Union of the Beijing–Hankou Railway and the Hubei Federation of Labor Unions painfully ordered the resumption of work, and the general strike was ended. In this struggle, more than 50 workers of the Beijing–Hankou railway from various places died, hundreds were injured, and more than 1,000 were arrested and forced into exile.

The Beijing–Hankou Railway Workers' Strike was the climax of the first labor movement led by the CPC. It further demonstrated the strength of the Chinese working class and expanded the influence of the Communist Party on the people of the country.

1924 The Climax of the KMT-CPC Cooperation Came

Keyword: the first KMT-CPC cooperation

After thousands of years of feudal autocracy, the once great country, the holy land of the East, which attracted the attention of the world, had become dilapidated. However, in modern times, the invasion of foreign powers and warlords had left ancient China devastated. In the bloody days, people were devastated by war and aggression. The country was no longer the country, and the family was no longer the family. "To overthrow the great powers and eradicate the warlords" had become the common aspiration of the people of the country.

Under such a revolutionary situation and historical appeal, the farsighted Chinese Communists believed that only when the Kuomintang (KMT) and the CPC worked together and sincerely cooperate to launch the Great Revolution could this tragic situation be changed as soon as possible. The Chinese Communists believed that Sun Yat-sen and the KMT under his leadership enjoyed high prestige in the minds of the people at that time and the KMT was a reliable revolutionary party. After many revolutions, Sun Yat-sen also deeply realized that it was difficult to make a revolution by relying on warlords. Therefore, KMT-CPC cooperation was the common aspiration of both parties.

Figure 4.
Sun Yat-sen (middle), Li Dazhao (middle left), and others stepped out of the 1st National Congress of the KMT.

In June 1923, the 3rd National Congress of the CPC was held in Guangzhou, which defined the policy of all Communist members joining the KMT in their own names and establishing a revolutionary united front with the KMT. From January 20 to 30, 1924, with the participation and help of the Chinese Communists, the 1st National Congress of the Chinese KMT was held in Guangzhou. The Congress adopted a declaration with anti-imperialism and anti-feudalism as its main content, which was drafted with the participation of the members of the CPC, reinterpreted the Three People's Principles, and determined the three major policies of alliance with Russia, the Communist Party and assistance to farmers and workers, thus developing the old Three People's Principles into the new Three People's Principles. In this way, the KMT began to transform from a bourgeois party into a revolutionary alliance formed by workers, peasants, the petty bourgeoisie, and the national bourgeoisie and became a united front organization of all revolutionary classes. The convening of the 1st National Congress of the KMT marked the formal establishment of the first KMT-CPC cooperation.

Knowledge about CPC History

On June 16, 1924, the Huangpu Military Academy was officially inaugurated, with Sun Yat-sen as its premier, Liao Zhongkai as its party representative, and Chiang Kai-shek as its president. Communists such as Zhou Enlai, Yun Daying, Xiao Chunü, Xiong Xiong, and Nie Rongzhen served as political instructors as well as other jobs at the military academy.

After the 1st National Congress of the KMT, with the joint efforts of the KMT and the CPC, the Chinese revolutionary movement further developed. The first civil revolutionary war hit the warlord forces with a devastating momentum, basically overthrew the reactionary rule of the Beiyang warlords, and also gave a powerful blow to the imperialist invasion forces; at the same time, it also publicized the program of CPC, expanded the influence of the Communist Party in the masses, and CPC began to master part of the revolutionary armed forces. The broad masses of the people were also baptized by the revolution, which laid the foundation for the Chinese revolution to continue to move forward.

However, as the revolutionary climax came, the struggle for leadership within the United Front intensified, especially after the death of Sun Yat-sen in March 1925, the right wing of the KMT became more and more rampant in usurping the leadership, coupled with the fact that the reactionary forces in China and abroad were too strong and united in strangling the revolutionary forces. The young CPC lacked sufficient theoretical preparation and practical experience, and the CPC Central Committee represented by Chen Duxiu and the representatives of the Communist International compromised with the right wing of the KMT and gave up the leadership of the revolution and the armed forces, and the first KMT-CPC cooperation ended in failure.

1925 May Thirtieth Heat Wave Swept China

Keyword: May Thirtieth Movement

On May 30, 1925, more than 2,000 students in Shanghai took to the streets to protest against the Japanese capitalists' suppression of the strike of the workers and the brutal killing of worker Gu Zhenghong. The concession authorities led by Britain sent out armed patrols to arrest students, and hundreds of students were arrested at Laozha police station alone. Students and citizens were extremely angry at the barbaric acts of imperialism. In the afternoon of that day, more than 10,000 people surrounded Laozha police station and demanded the release of the arrested students. The British police commander gave the order to shoot unarmed people. Dozens of foreign patrolmen shot together, killing 13 people, wounding dozens, and arresting more than 40. This was known as the May Thirtieth Massacre that shocked the whole world.

Gu Zhenghong, who was only 20 years old at that time, joined the workers' picket team and the strike agitation team, actively participated in the strike movement, and honorably joined the CPC. In the face of Japanese capitalists and their thugs with guns, he had no fear

Figure 5.
The scene of the May Thirtieth Movement

Knowledge about CPC History

On October 1, 1925, the National Revolutionary Army held its second Eastern Expedition. Chiang Kai-shek was the commander-in-chief of the Eastern Expedition Army, and Zhou Enlai was the director of the General Political Department. With the support of striking workers in Canton–Hong Kong strike and Dongjiang farmers, the Eastern Expeditionary Army quickly recaptured Chaozhou and Shantou. In early November, Dongjiang was recaptured, and the revolutionary base in Guangdong was basically unified.

and argued. The Japanese capitalist was so genocidal and enraged that he brutally shot Gu Zhenghong several times and he was shot to death. Gu Zhenghong was killed, which became the direct fuse of the May Thirtieth Movement.

After the tragedy, the Shanghai Federation of Industry and Commerce held an anti-imperialist demonstration with more than 200,000 participants and started workers' strikes, merchants' strikes, and students' strikes, calling for the abolition of all unequal treaties and the removal of all privileges of imperialism in China. The May Thirtieth Movement centered on Shanghai soon spread to the whole country, forming a nationwide anti-imperialist movement. Following the May Fourth Movement, this movement further awakened the anti-imperialist spirit and national consciousness of the Chinese people and became the prelude to the storm of the national revolution during the first domestic revolutionary war.

At that time, the United States, Britain, Japan, other imperialist countries, and warlords everywhere collaborated and competed, ruthlessly exploiting the Chinese people economically. They invested in China, set up factories, and plundered wealth. In 1924 alone, they took 2 billion silver dollars from China. The oppression of imperialism made the workers extremely angry and also aroused the great anger of the people all over the country, forming a protest movement of workers' strikes, students' strikes, and merchants' strikes. About 17 million people from all over the country participated in the movement. From commercial cities to remote towns, there were howls of "overthrowing imperialism" and "abolishing unequal treaties."

The May Thirtieth Movement became a struggle against imperialism with broad international influence, which dealt a heavy blow to the arrogance of imperialism, promoted the awakening of the Chinese nation and the development of the national revolutionary movement, and greatly improved the consciousness of the Chinese people. CPC was tempered in leading the May Thirtieth Movement, trained a large number of cadres, developed the Party organization, and accumulated experience in the anti-imperialist struggle, laying the foundation for the mass struggle led by the Party in the future.

1926 The Iron Army of the Northern Expedition Built a Monument

Keyword: the Northern Expedition

After the failure of the Revolution of 1911, the Beiyang government was corrupt and incompetent. The warlords had their own factions, each with their own troops so there were constant wars, and the people lived in dire straits.

In order to change this painful situation, on July 9, 1926, a massive Northern Expedition war was raging in South China. On this day, with the hope and sustenance of the people of the whole country, countless soldiers of the revolutionary army full of high morale marched northward in three ways. A revolutionary war was rapidly launched to overthrow the reactionary rule of the Beiyang warlords and strive for the independence, freedom, democracy, and reunification of the Chinese nation.

In February 1926, the CPC Central Committee held a special meeting in Beijing, pointing out that the Party's main political responsibility then was to prepare the Guangdong government for the Northern Expedition War from all sides, and that the political program of

Figure 6.
National Revolutionary Army Northern Expedition oath-taking military parade ceremony

the Northern Expedition must be based on solving the peasant problem as the mainstay. On July 1, the Guangzhou National Government issued the *Declaration of the Northern Expedition*. On July 9, the National Revolutionary Army swore its oath to the Northern Expedition.

Knowledge about CPC History

On March 20, 1926, Chiang Kai-shek staged the "Zhongshan Ship Incident" in Guangzhou, falsely claiming that the Communists were going to riot, using it as an excuse to declare martial law, send troops to arrest and monitor the Communists, and surround the Canton-Hongkong Strike Committee and the Soviet Adviser's Office. As Chen Duxiu, Zhang Guotao and representatives of the Communist International advocated compromise and concession, the Communists were forced to withdraw from the First Army of the National Revolutionary Army.

With the help of the Soviet Union's military advisers, the Northern Expedition Army formulated a correct policy of action, and first marched into Hunan and Hubei, which were dominated by warlord Wu Peifu. The Fourth Army Independent Regiment of the National Revolutionary Army, led by Ye Ting and composed of Communist Party members, was the pioneer of the Northern Expedition. With the support of the people from all walks of life, the Northern Expedition Army marched forward with flying colors. After entering Hubei, the Northern Expedition captured Tingsi Bridge and Hesheng Bridge, defeated Wu Peifu's main force, and captured Wuchang on October 10. In the battle, the Independent Regiment led by Ye Ting made outstanding achievements, and the Fourth Army of the National Revolutionary Army was known as the "Iron Army." At the same time, the Northern Expedition Army marched into Jiangxi, occupied Jiujiang and Nanchang in November, and wiped out the main force of the warlord Sun Chuanfang. The National Revolutionary Army had taken control of most southern provinces and regions only half a year after it swore to the Northern Expedition. On the way to the Northern Expedition, the CPC led workers and peasants at all levels in Guangdong, Hunan, Hubei, and other provinces to actively participate in transportation, rescue, publicity, and liaison, which provided a strong guarantee for the successful march of the Northern Expedition.

At a time when the national revolutionary situation was constantly rising, and the Northern Expedition was successfully marching, Chiang Kai-shek, Wang Jingwei, and other rightist forces of the KMT, with the support of imperialism, staged the "April 12" and "July 15" anti-revolutionary coups in Shanghai and Wuhan. At the same time, due to the influence of Chen Duxiu's Right opportunism and the wrong guidance of the Communist International, the CPC failed to take the correct measures to deal with emergencies. As a result, the Chiang Kai-shek group stole the fruits of the revolution, established a new warlord rule, and the spectacular Northern Expedition failed.

The Northern Expedition was a revolutionary and just war carried out jointly by the KMT and the CPC. In just one year, the Northern Expedition basically wiped out the armies of warlords Wu Peifu and Sun Chuanfang, severely damaged the armies of warlord Zhang Zuolin, severely attacked the rule of the Northern Warlords, and accelerated the historical process of the Chinese revolution. The lesson of this war's failure midway made the Chinese Communists and the Chinese people deeply realize the extreme importance of establishing a proletarian army and carrying out armed struggle.

1927 Nanchang Uprising Opened a New World

Keyword: Nanchang Uprising

On the night of August 1, 1927, the rain was coming in Nanchang, and it would be a sleepless night because an armed uprising was about to be staged here to create a new situation for China's democratic revolution.

When the loud gunfire broke the silence of the night sky, countless shouts echoed in Nanchang. Here was born the first people's army independently led by the CPC. This was an extraordinary army because it opened the prelude to the revolutionary armed struggle independently led by the CPC.

In 1927, because Chiang Kai-shek and Wang Jingwei rebelled one after another, the first domestic revolutionary war failed. In order to save the revolution, the CPC sent Li Lisan, Deng Zhongxia, and other comrades to Jiujiang, prepared to organize some of the Communist Party's forces in the National Revolutionary Army, and joined Zhang Fakui, the commander-in-chief of the Second Front Army, to return to Guangdong, establish a new revolutionary base, and carry out the agrarian revolution. However, Zhang Fakui had stood by Wang Jingwei

Figure 7.
Nanchang Uprising (oil painting)

at that time, making the original plan a failure. The CPC Central Committee decided to take independent military action, centralize the armed forces, hold an armed riot in Nanchang, and sent Zhou Enlai to Nanchang to lead the organization.

Knowledge about CPC History

On July 11, 1933, the Provisional Central Government of the Chinese Soviet Republic, on the recommendation of the Central Revolutionary Military Committee, decided that August 1 would be the anniversary of the founding of the Chinese Workers' and Peasants' Red Army. After the founding of the PRC, this commemorative day was renamed the "People's Liberation Army Day."

On July 27, Zhou Enlai arrived in Nanchang and held a meeting in Jiangxi Hotel, announcing the formal establishment of the former enemy committee of the CPC. Zhou Enlai was the committee secretary, and Li Lisan, Yun Daiying, and Peng Pai were the members. The meeting decided that He Long would be the commander-in-chief of the uprising, Ye Ting would be the former enemy commander-in-chief, and Liu Bocheng would be the chief of staff. The uprising was scheduled for the evening of July 30. Due to Zhang Guotao's obstruction, the uprising was postponed to 4:00 a.m. on August 1. However, due to the disclosure of the time of the uprising, the former enemy committee advanced the uprising to 2:00 a.m. on August 1. He Long, Ye Ting, Zhu De, Liu Bocheng, and others led an uprising with more than 20,000 troops under the direct control and influence of the CPC. After over four hours of fierce fighting, more than 3,000 enemies were killed, and the insurgent forces occupied Nanchang City.

At 9:00 a.m. on August 1, a joint meeting was held in Nanchang, attended by more than 40 leaders of the uprising and representatives of provinces, cities, and overseas Chinese. The Revolutionary Committee of the Chinese KMT, composed of 25 people, including Song Qingling, He Xiangning, Deng Yanda, He Long, and Zhou Enlai, was elected, and the presidium was composed of 7 people, including Song Qingling and Deng Yanda. The insurgent forces still used the Second Front Army of the National Revolutionary Army designation, with He Long as the acting commander-in-chief, Ye Ting as the acting commander-in-chief of the former enemy, and Liu Bocheng as the chief of staff.

After the Nanchang Uprising, Wang Jingwei ordered Zhang Fakui and Zhu Peide to attack Nanchang, and the insurgents moved southward according to the decision of the CPC Central Committee before the uprising. From August 3 to 5, the insurgent troops withdrew from Nanchang. However, the insurgents did not pay attention to the combination with the local peasant movement. By the end of September, powerful enemies besieged the insurgents in Chaoshan, Guangdong, and the uprising was declared a failure. Under the leadership of Zhu De and Chen Yi, some of the remaining insurgents moved to southern Hunan, while others moved to Hailufeng Area to continue their struggle.

Although the Nanchang Uprising failed, it fired the first shot of armed resistance against the KMT reactionaries, declared the CPC's firm position of carrying out the Chinese revolution to the end, and marked the beginning of the CPC's independent establishment of the revolutionary army and leadership of the revolutionary war.

1928 A Spark in Jinggang Mountain Would Start a Prairie Fire

Keyword: Zhu-Mao's Joining Forces

In Jinggang Mountain, a remote mountainous area in southern China, people witnessed a far-reaching historical event—"Zhu-Mao's Joining Forces" (also known as Joining Forces at Jinggang Mountain) 93 years ago. Over the turbulent history, the past of "Zhu-Mao's Joining Forces" is still familiar and enjoyed by the world. "Revolutionary heroes gathered at Jinggang Mountain and concentrated their strength to be stronger. After the Red Army's leadership was improved, the five sieges were broken to solidify the battlefield." This is a poem by Zhu De in 1957 to eulogize "Zhu-Mao's Joining Forces." It can be seen that the joining forces is a milestone for the Chinese Workers' and Peasants' Red Army and the Chinese revolution.

In 1927, Chiang Kai-shek and Wang Jingwei respectively launched the "April 12" and "July 15" anti-revolutionary coups, and the magnificent revolution failed. From March 1927 to the first half of 1928, more than 310,000 Communists and revolutionary masses were slaughtered by KMT reactionaries. As the *Bolshevik*, the CPC Central Committee journal, put it, "China is the most miserable country in the world in terms of white terror."

Figure 8.
Joining Forces at Jinggang Mountain (oil painting)

Knowledge about CPC History

From June 18 to July 11, 1928, with the help of Communist International, the 6th National Congress of the CPC was held in Moscow. 142 people attended the conference, including 84 official delegates. This is the only congress held abroad in the history of the CPC.

Among the Communists who continued to fight, there were two such great men. They held high the revolutionary banner, went through various hardships, firmly led the two failed troops after the uprising, moved and gathered toward the Hunan–Jiangxi border in the middle of the Luoxiao Mountains, and then developed rapidly. These two great men were Mao Zedong and Zhu De.

Mao Zedong was elected as an alternate Provisional Political Bureau of the CPC Central Committee member at the August 7 Meeting. At the critical moment when the revolution turned to the low tide, he was entrusted by the CPC Central Committee to lead the Autumn Harvest Uprising on the Hunan–Jiangxi border with full authority as a special commissioner of the CPC Central Committee and secretary of the former enemy committee. After the defeat of the uprising, he reviewed the situation and made a decisive decision. He led troops to Jinggang Mountain, lit the flames of the "armed independent regime of workers and peasants" at Jinggang Mountain, and became the main leader of the Jinggang Mountain Revolutionary Base.

After the main force of the Nanchang Uprising was defeated in Chaoshan, Zhu De withdrew to Sanheba and led the rest of the troops of the Nanchang Uprising to carry out guerrilla warfare on the border between Fujian, Guangdong, and Jiangxi. With the assistance of Chen Yi, after the "Three Rectifications in Southern Jiangxi," he led the uprising in southern Hunan. After the uprising was defeated, he led the rest of the troops of Nanchang Uprising and the rural army in southern Hunan to move toward Jinggang Mountain, becoming another important leader in consolidating and developing the Jinggang Mountain Revolutionary Base.

On April 24, 1928, the Autumn Harvest Uprising Army led by Mao Zedong and the rest of the Nanchang Uprising Army and the rural army in southern Hunan led by Zhu De successfully joined forces in Ningganglong City, known as "Zhu-Mao's Joining Forces" in history. The two great men, Zhu and Mao, met in the Wenxing Pavilion of Longjiang Academy and immediately had discussions on military building and the Chinese revolution. At that time, Mao Zedong was 35 years old and Zhu De was 42 years old. In order to share a common belief and goal, a man from Hunan and a man from Sichuan gathered along the Longjiang River and jointly occupied Jinggang Mountain, demonstrating the magnificent scenes of the Chinese revolution.

Since then, the Chinese revolution raised a new flag and started to gain ground. It can be said that without "Zhu-Mao's Joining Forces," there would not have been the creation of the Jinggang Moutain Road; without "Zhu-Mao's Joining Forces," there would not have been the breeding of the Jinggang Moutain Spirit. "Zhu-Mao's Joining Forces" profoundly impacted the struggle in Jinggang Moutain, the establishment and expansion of rural revolutionary bases, and the development of the national revolutionary cause.

1929 Military Discipline Rectification in Gutian

Keyword: the Gutian Conference

In December 1929, a cold wind blew in the small mountain area of western Fujian, and people seemed more willing to stay in their warm homes. However, in this cold winter, more than 120 representatives of the Fourth Red Army braved the cold and gathered at the west foot of Gutian Town to discuss the fate of the CPC. A charcoal fire was lit in the middle of the room, reflecting the faces of each participant, serious expressions, fierce arguments, firm eyes, and warm applause.

The Ninth Congress of the Fourth Red Army Party was held in Gutian Town, Shanghang County, Fujian Province, known as the "Gutian Conference" in history. The conference summarized the experience and lessons learned from the army building since the founding of the Fourth Red Army, established the basic principles of the people's army building, stipulated the nature, purpose, and tasks of the Red Army, and reaffirmed the principle of the Party's absolute leadership over the Red Army. The conference stressed the importance of opposing any pretext to weaken the Party's leadership of the Red Army and the need to make the Party a strong leader and unifying core in the army. This was a fundamental issue concerning the success or failure of the Party's cause.

After "Zhu-Mao's Joining Forces" in April 1928, the two uprising forces were combined into the Fourth Army of the Chinese Workers' and Peasants' Revolutionary Army, which

Figure 9.
Exterior view of the old site of Gutian Conference

Knowledge about CPC History

On December 11, 1929, Deng Xiaoping, Zhang Yunyi, and Wei Baqun, representatives of the CPC Central Committee, led the Fourth Brigade of Guangxi Police, the General Training Corps, and the Youjiang River Peasant Self-Defense Army under the control and influence of the Communist Party, held the Baise Uprising and established the Seventh Red Army, with Zhang Yunyi as the commander and Deng Xiaoping as the secretary and political committee member of the Front Committee, followed by the establishment of the Right River Soviet Government.

was renamed the Fourth Army of the Chinese Workers' and Peasants' Red Army in May, referred to as the "Fourth Red Army." Subsequently, under the leadership of Mao Zedong, Zhu De, Chen Yi, and others, the Fourth Red Army broke the enemy's repeated siege of the Jinggang Mountain Revolutionary Base and marched into southern Jiangxi and western Fujian from January 1929, creating revolutionary bases in southern Jiangxi and western Fujian and laying the foundation for the later Central Revolutionary Base.

With the development of the revolutionary situation and the expansion of the revolutionary ranks, a large number of comrades of peasant and other petty-bourgeois origins joined the Red Army and its party organizations, and with the treacherous environment, frequent battles, and hard life, the troops were not educated and trained in time. Therefore, such non-proletarian ideas as extreme democratization, emphasizing military over politics, roving bandits, and warlordism grew in the Fourth Red Army.

In late August 1929, Chen Yi arrived in Shanghai and truthfully reported the work of the Fourth Red Army to the CPC Central Committee. On August 29, the Political Bureau of the CPC Central Committee held a special meeting to hear Chen Yi's detailed report on the overall situation of the Fourth Red Army and decided to form a special committee composed of Li Lisan, Zhou Enlai, and Chen Yi to in-depth study and discuss the issue of the Fourth Red Army. After a month of discussion, a letter of instruction from the CPC Central Committee to the Front Committee of the Fourth Red Army, drafted by Chen Yi and approved by Zhou Enlai, was formed, namely the famous "September Letter." The "September Letter" affirmed the achievements and experience gained since the establishment of the Fourth Red Army, requested the Front Committee and all cadres and soldiers of the Fourth Red Army to uphold the leadership of Mao Zedong and Zhu De, improve the prestige of the guiding organ, and clearly pointed out that Mao Zedong was the Secretary of the Front Committee.

According to the spirit of the "September Letter" from the CPC Central Committee, the Ninth Congress of the Fourth Red Army Party was held in Gutian Town, Shanghang County, Fujian Province from December 28 to 29. At the conference, Mao Zedong gave a political report, Zhu De gave a military report, and Chen Yi conveyed the spirit of the CPC Central Committee's "September Letter." After a heated discussion, the conference unanimously passed the resolution of the Gutian Conference, whose central idea was to use proletarian ideology to build the army and the Party. At the conference, 11 people, including Mao Zedong, Zhu De, Chen Yi, and Tan Zhenlin, were elected as CPC Fourth Red Army Front Committee members. Mao Zedong was re-elected as the secretary of the Front Committee.

The resolution of the Gutian Conference is a programmatic document for the construction of the CPC and the Red Army, and its spirit still has important practical significance today.

1930 “Left League” Led the Way in Literature and Art

Keyword: the establishing of the League of Chinese Left-Wing Writers in Shanghai

It was an age full of bloody mist, and the white terror made the world urgently need rescue even worse. “Enduring seeing a friend become a new ghost, anger to the knife cluster to find a small poem.” On this dangerous wave, a group of intellectuals full of fighting spirit picked up their pens and began the revolutionary journey. They broke through the ideological shackles of autocratic rule, awakened the fighting spirit of the just people, and also opened a new chapter of the red revolution. These people are the League of Chinese Left-Wing Writers represented by the Five Martyrs of the “Left League.”

On March 2, 1930, the League of Chinese Left-Wing Writers was founded in Shanghai, referred to as the “Left League.” The founding of the “Left League” coincided with the failure of the first domestic revolutionary war. On the one hand, the KMT reactionaries carried out military encirclement and suppression of revolutionary bases; On the other hand, they

Figure 10.
The meeting place of the League of Chinese Left-Wing Writers, at No. 2, Lane 201, Duolun Road, Shanghai

carried out cultural "encirclement and suppression" in KMT-controlled areas. The situation at that time urged the left-wing writers in Shanghai to unite and fight against the KMT reactionaries. Under the leadership and support of the CPC, the "Left League" held its founding conference in Shanghai.

Knowledge about CPC History
In May 1930, in response to the dogmatic error tendency in the Fourth Red Army, Mao Zedong wrote the article "Oppose Book Worship," emphasizing that Marxist theory must be combined with the actual situation in China. This article discusses the basic ideas of seeking truth from facts, independence, and the mass line.

At the founding conference, Lu Xun made a speech entitled "Opinions on the League of Left-Wing Writers," which for the first time put forward the direction that literature and art should serve the masses of workers and peasants, and pointed out that left-wing writers and artists must contact with the actual social struggle.

After the League of Left-Wing Writers, the League of Left-Wing Social Scientists, the League of Dramatists, the League of Journalists, the League of Artists, the League of Educators, the League of Linguists, and the League of Musicians were also established one after another. At that time, they were known as the "Eight Leagues." In October 1930, all left-wing cultural groups jointly formed the General Alliance of Chinese Left-Wing Cultural Circles.

The "Left League" and other left-wing cultural groups successively founded the Left League and other left-wing cultural groups founded dozens of important publications, such as the *Sprout Monthly*, *Pathfinder*, *Culture Monthly*, *Beidou*, and *Literature*, and occupied cultural positions in the KMT-ruled areas. The KMT authorities brutally persecuted and suppressed the left-wing cultural movement. In the struggle against the reactionaries, Rou Shi, Yin Fu, and other writers were killed one after another. "Five Martyrs of the Left League" refers to five left-wing revolutionary writers, Li Weisen, Rou Shi, Hu Yepin, Yin Fu, and Feng Keng. Lu Xun successively wrote articles such as "Chinese Proletarian Revolutionary Literature and the Blood of the Precursors" and "For the Remembrance of Forgetting," deeply praising the revolutionary spirit and literary achievements of the martyrs.

At the beginning of 1936, in order to adapt to the new situation of resisting Japan and saving the nation from extinction, the "Left League" announced its dissolution. Although the history of the "Left League" was only six years, it has become a monument in the history of Chinese revolutionary literature with its great role at that time and far-reaching influence on later generations. Revolutionary writers published a large number of works in the journals of the "Left League" and other progressive publications. Lu Xun's "Old Tales Retold," Mao Dun's "Midnight," "The Shop of the Lin Family," and "Spring Silkworms," Jiang Guangci's "Roaring Land," novels by Ding Ling, Zhang Tianyi, Ye Zi, and others, plays by Tian Han, Hong Shen, Xia Yan, and others' plays, and the poems by the poets of the Chinese Poetry Association, all showed the achievements of left-wing literature and art with their new ideological and artistic expansions and had a wide and far-reaching impact on the development of Chinese literature and art.

1931 The "Founding Ceremony" in the Col Mountain

Keyword: the founding of the Soviet Republic of China

When mentioning the founding ceremony, people will naturally associate it with the unforgettable scene of the founding of the PRC on October 1, 1949. But few people know that this is not the first founding ceremony held by the Chinese Communists. On November 7, 1931, 18 years before the founding of the PRC, the Chinese Communists also held a lively "founding ceremony" of the Chinese Soviet Republic in Ruijin, a remote small town in southern Jiangxi.

As early as February 1930, the CPC Central Committee began to plan to establish the Soviet Republic. After more than a year of intense preparation, on September 28, 1931, Mao Zedong led the Soviet Central Bureau and the Red Army Headquarters to Ruijin from Yongfeng to speed up the preparation for the first national congress of the Chinese Soviet. At that time, although the CPC Central Committee decided to establish a Soviet Republic in the Soviet area, the specific location was still not determined. According to the original plan, the CPC Central Committee envisioned the establishment of the Chinese Soviet Republic

Figure 11.
Site of the 1st National Congress of the Chinese Soviet Union

with Changting, Fujian, as the center. However, when Mao Zedong and Zhu De arrived at Yeping Village of Ruijin, through a comprehensive analysis of the political, economic, and natural conditions of Ruijin, they believed that Ruijin in Jiangxi was more suitable for "capital building" than Changting in Fujian, so they decisively adjusted the original plan.

Knowledge about CPC History

On September 18, 1931, the Japanese Kwantung Army blew up a section of the South Manchurian Railway, falsely accused the Chinese army of sabotage, and used it as a pretext to raid Shenyang. The Northeast Army collapsed without fighting, and the military and political officers scattered to escape. Within a few months, Japanese troops occupied Liaoning, Jilin, and Heilongjiang provinces and began to attack Rehe. The September 18th Incident aroused the resistance against Japanese aggression anger of the Chinese people.

After the location of the 1st National Congress of the Chinese Soviet Union was determined, to ensure the safety of the Congress, Mao Zedong proposed to set up a fake venue for the Congress in Changting, Fujian and located the real venue in Yeping Village. On November 7, 1931, the 1st National Congress of the Chinese Soviet was held in Ruijin. Normally, the "Founding Ceremony" would have been held after the new government's inauguration, mostly during the day. However, the Red Army was in a dire military condition at that time, as it had no air force of its own, let alone air defense capability. In order to avoid bombing by KMT planes, the CPC Central Committee decided to hold the "founding ceremony" parade in the early morning of November 7. In the early morning of the same day, the Central Red Army corps representatives who would receive the inspection arrived at the Red Army Square in Yeping Village early in the morning. At around 6:00 a.m., amid the cheers of thousands of people, Mao Zedong, Zhu De, Xiang Ying, Wang Jiaxiang, Ren Bishi, Zeng Shan, and other party and government leaders boarded the reviewing platform. At 7:00 a.m., the parade began. Mao Zedong and others reviewed the heroic Red Army troops, and Peng Dehuai served as the general commander of the parade. Just after the military parade, more than ten KMT military planes flew directly to Ruijin County in an attempt to bomb the venue of the 1st National Congress of the Chinese Soviet Union. As all the soldiers and civilians on the Red Army Square had been evacuated and hidden, the plane did not find the venue target, but just dropped some bombs on the county and its suburbs, and then flew to Changting, Fujian. There, KMT planes finally found the fake meeting place there, so they dropped bombs and strafed at low altitudes, blowing up the fake meeting place. When people learned this news, they could not help admiring Mao Zedong for his thoughtful consideration.

In this way, with the wisdom of the Communists, the "founding ceremony" of the Soviet Republic of China was successfully held in the small mountain col of Yeping Village, Ruijin. The Chinese Soviet Republic became the first national democratic regime of workers and peasants in Chinese history.

1932 The Blow of the Northeast War Horn

Keyword: resistance against Japanese aggression in the Northeast

"This is a living hell, where death and displacement make people worry day and night, and since the fall of the provincial capital, there is only oppression, not freedom." This is a true portrayal of the daily state of Northeastern compatriots after the fall of the three eastern provinces. On February 5, 1932, Harbin fell, and all the great rivers and mountains in the three northeastern provinces fell into the hands of the Japanese aggressors. In March of the same year, Japan established the puppet regime of Manchukuo in Changchun and carried out military occupation, economic plundering, slavery education, and other means of aggression, leaving the people in the northeast in a state of deep suffering. However, in the face of the aggression and atrocities of Japanese imperialism, the national government led by Chiang Kai-shek ordered the Northeast army not to resist and placed hope on the mediation of the League of Nations, asking the people of the whole country to "bear with pain and indignation" and "temporarily adopt an attitude of resignation," which caused strong anger among the people. At a critical juncture for the nation's survival, the CPC took the lead in holding the banner of armed resistance against Japanese aggression and waged a long and arduous struggle against the Japanese aggressors in the Northeast.

To better organize the masses to fight against Japan, Party organizations in the Northeast actively carried out resistance against Japanese aggression propaganda. They scattered

Figure 12.
The Northeast United Resistance Army bombed Japanese trains.

leaflets in the Xiaojin Bridge clothing factory and put slogans on the walls and power poles of the prosperous Shenyang North Railway Station. By printing pamphlets, distributing leaflets, writing slogans, and other ways, local Party organizations not only publicized the Party's resistance against Japanese aggression ideas but also stimulated the people's resistance against Japanese aggression enthusiasm.

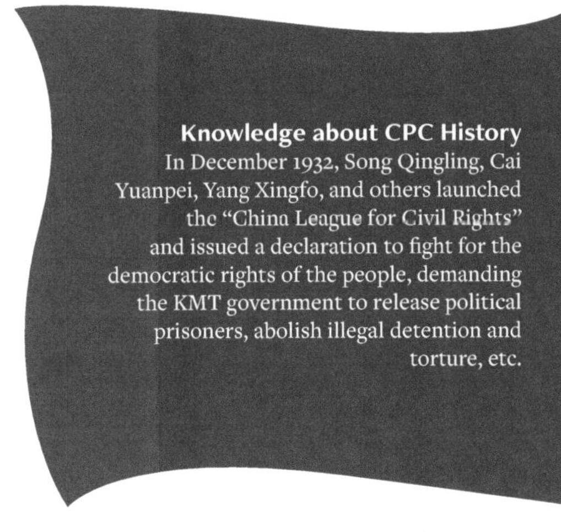

Party organizations throughout the Northeast widely mobilized the people to carry out armed struggle. On October 12, 1931, the CPC Central Committee issued instructions that requested local party organizations in the northeast to mobilize the masses of people to create northeast Counter-Japanese Guerrillas as soon as possible and sent comrades such as Tong Changrong, Yang Jingyu, and Zhao Shangzhi to the northeast to guide the work of local party organizations in creating counter-Japanese forces. Through arduous efforts, party organizations at all levels successively established counter-Japanese armed forces, such as the Liuhe Guerrillas, Hailong Workers and Peasants Volunteer Army, and Panshi Counter-Japanese Guerrillas. In 1932, counter-Japanese forces attacked important cities in Liaoning and Jilin provinces more than 30 times. Shenyang alone was attacked 11 times. Japanese airports in Shenyang and Harbin were burned down by counter-Japanese forces. Power plants in Fushun coal mines were also destroyed by counter-Japanese forces. Under the leadership of the CPC, guerrillas all over the country actively relied on the people, and carried out a protracted guerrilla war with the Japanese puppet army with a small number of personnel and backward weapons; their influence among the masses was growing.

At the same time, under the leadership of the Party organization, strikes of students and workers and demonstrations of various scales came one after another in various places, which dealt a heavy blow to the Japanese aggressors. In the fall of 1932, the people in northeast China under the occupation of Japanese imperialism lived in poverty and prices continued to rise. The CPC then used its strong organizational and mass basis among the electrical workers to lead the electrical workers in Harbin to strike. Later, Beining railway workers and Fengtian tobacco factory workers carried out several resistance against Japanese aggression strikes, which demonstrated the determination and strength of the Chinese people to fight against the Japanese aggressors and defend their sovereignty.

At the crisis moment of national subjugation and genocide, the counter-Japanese team led by the CPC bravely fought against Japan, which stimulated patriotic feelings and a sense of resistance in the people in the Northeast. Countless people with lofty ideals resolutely joined the counter-Japanese team, united around the CPC, and gradually became the core force of the counter-Japanese team in the Northeast.

1933 Luring the Enemy to Counter "Encirclement and Suppression"

Keyword: the fourth counter-encirclement and suppression campaign in the Central Soviet area

Since the CPC established the Soviet Republic in Ruijin, Jiangxi Province, the KMT reactionaries headed by Chiang Kai-shek had been unable to sit still. Since October 1930, they had been repeatedly "encircling and suppressing" the Central Revolutionary Base and the First Red Front Army in an attempt to strangle the young Red Army in its infancy. However, the Red Army, under the command of Mao Zedong and Zhu De, used its geographical advantages to win counter-encirclement and -suppression campaigns three times. More than 70,000 enemies were wiped out in three counter-encirclement and -suppression campaigns, more than 46,000 weapons were captured, and Zhang Huizan and others were captured alive. By the end of 1932, the KMT army had launched the fourth large-scale military "encirclement and suppression" campaign against the Red Army.

Because the Red Army repelled the first three "encirclement and suppression" campaigns, this time the KMT mobilized 400,000 troops and made careful arrangements: Chen Cheng commanded 160,000 soldiers to be the middle army, responsible for the main attack; Cai Tingkai commanded the Left Route Army, Yu Hanmou commanded the Right Route Army, and the Left and Right Route Army were responsible for the "clean-up and suppression."

Figure 13.
Huangpi Huoyuan, where the Central Red Army achieved the "Huangpi Victory" during the fourth counter-encirclement and -suppression

Knowledge about CPC History

On May 26, 1933, under the impetus and influence of the CPC, patriotic generals Feng Yuxiang, Ji Hongchang, and Fang Zhenwu established the Chahar People's Counter-Japanese Allied Army in Zhangjiakou, with Feng Yuxiang as commander-in-chief, Fang Zhenwu as commander-in-chief of the North Road Front, and Ji Hongchang as general director of the North Road Front, and sent a telegram to the whole country, advocating joint resistance to Japan and recovery of lost territories.

As for the Communist Party, after three victories against "encirclement and suppression," the base area had expanded, and the total number of Red Army had reached 70,000. But how to use 70,000 soldiers of the Red Army against 400,000 soldiers of the KMT army? Zhu De, the commander-in-chief of the First Red Front Army, and Zhou Enlai, the political commissar-in-chief, had their ingenious plans.

On the evening of February 12, 1933, the 3rd and 4th Legions of the First Red Front Army launched an attack on Nanfeng City, but Nanfeng City was firmly defended, and they failed to break through by the next morning. Chen Cheng, the commander of the middle KMT army stationed in Nanfeng City, knew the situation, ordered the garrison to defend the castle, and asked for help from the 24th KMT Army Division in the south to encircle the Red Army under Nanfeng City. This move was seen through by Zhu De and Zhou Enlai, who immediately decided to withdraw the Red Army that had besieged Nanfeng City. In the withdrawal process, the main force was quietly transferred to Dongshao and Luokou areas to wait. At the same time, the 10th Red Army was arranged to disguise its main force and confuse the enemy. The KMT generals did not distinguish between the true and the false. They were indeed confused by the Red Army and chased them all the way.

Such a deployment by the KMT army fell into the trap set by the Red Army. The so-called "luring the enemy in depth" is the most effective military strategy for weak forces to fight against strong forces in strategic defense. While waiting for the KMT army to enter the "trap," the First Red Army arranged for the left-wing team to gather in the Daping and Jiaohu areas; the right-wing team secretly gathered in the Huoyuan and Xiyuan areas. In this way, the KMT's 59th Division, chasing after them all the way, was like a dead pigeon, caught by the lurking Red Army. After two days of fierce fighting, most of the KMT army was wiped out, and Li Ming, commander of the 52nd Division, and Chen Shiji, commander of the 59th Division, were captured.

Because of this flexible strategy and tactics, the Red Army made surprise victories in the face of the dangerous enemy, beat them, and left them all at sea. In this battle, which lasted about three months, nearly three KMT divisions were wiped out, more than 10,000 people were captured, and more than 10,000 various guns were captured, creating an unprecedented example of large armies ambushing the enemy in the history of the Red Army.

1934 The Red Army Was Not Afraid of Expeditions

Keyword: Red Army's Long March

From 1930 to 1933, under the leadership of the Communist Party with Mao Zedong at its core, the Red Army adopted the policies of luring the enemy in deep and adapting measures to local conditions, and achieved four victories counter "encirclement and suppression." However, the development of the Red Army was not without twists and turns. By the end of 1934, the KMT army had launched the fifth large-scale military "encirclement and suppression" campaign in the central Soviet area. At that time, the leaders of the CPC Central Committee made the mistake of "Left" dogmatism and did not command the Red Army to fight according to the actual situation in the Soviet area, so the Central Red Army could not break the KMT army's fifth "encirclement and suppression." The young Red Army was in danger and was forced to withdraw from the Central Revolutionary Base in October 1934 and move west of the Xiang River, embarking on the Long March.

Around this time, the Red Army in other revolutionary base areas also made strategic shifts. The Sixth Red Army Corps left the Hunan–Jiangxi Base area in late July 1934 and moved westward. In October, it arrived in the northeast of Guizhou and joined the Second

Figure 14.
Jiajin Mountain, the first big snowy mountain the Red Army crossed

Red Army Corps. Later, it formed the Second Front Army of the Red Army to continue to move westward. In the name of the Second Advance Party of the Chinese Workers' and Peasants' Red Army against Japan in the North, the 25th Red Army left the base area of Hubei-Henan-Anhui in November 1934 and moved to southern Shaanxi.

Knowledge about CPC History

On November 7, 1934, the First Army of the Northeast People's Revolutionary Army was officially established. Yang Jingyu was the commander and political commissar. Since 1935, the Second, Third, and Sixth Armies of the Northeast People's Revolutionary Army, the Fourth Army of the Northeast Counter-Japanese Allied Army, the Fifth Army of the Northeast Counter-Japanese Allied Army, and the Tangyuan Guerrilla Corps had been established successively. These were the basic armed forces led by the CPC and later became the Northeast United Resistance Army.

In March 1935, the Fourth Front Red Army was ordered to withdraw from the Sichuan-Shaanxi Revolutionary Base and begin the Long March.

During the Long March, the Central Red Army first broke through Chiang Kai-shek's four blockade lines and entered the area in the west Xiang River. However, due to wrong commands, the number of troops dropped from more than 86,000 to more than 30,000. At the critical juncture, Mao Zedong proposed to march into Guizhou, where the enemy was weak. The Central Red Army, which had originally planned to go north, suddenly swung to the southwest, forcibly crossed the Wujiang River, and occupied Zunyi City. Since then, under the correct leadership of the new CPC Central Committee established at the Zunyi Conference, flexible strategies and tactics had been adopted to cross the Chishui River, Jinsha River, Dadu River, snowy mountains, and grassland. After going through thousands of difficulties and dangers, the Red Army successfully arrived at Wuqi Town, the Shaanxi–Gansu Revolutionary Base, on October 19, 1935. One year later, on October 22, 1936, the Second Front Army, the Fourth Front Army, and the Central Red Army of the Red Army, after a long journey, successfully joined forces in Huining, Gansu, and declared the end of the Long March of 25,000 *li*.

Mao Zedong wrote in his famous poem "The Long March": "Of the trying Long March the Red Army makes light; thousands of rivers and mountains are barriers slight. The five serpentine ridges outspread like rippling rills; the pompous Wumeng peaks tower but like mole-hills. Against warm cloudy cliffs beat waves of Golden Sand; with cold iron-chain bridge River Dadu is spanned. Glad to see the Min Range snow-clad for miles and miles, our warriors who have crossed it break into broad smiles."* The Red Army's Long March, which lasted for two years, continued the spark of the Chinese revolution. The victory of the Long March became the key to turning the corner of the Chinese revolution. The victory of the Long March shows that the CPC and the Chinese Workers' and Peasants' Red Army under its leadership have incomparably strong vitality and are an invincible force. The spirit of the Long March has become a powerful motivation for the Chinese Communists and the people's army to continue to move forward.

* Xu Yuanchong, *Xu Yuanchong's English Translation of Mao Zedong's Poems* (Beijing: China Translation & Publishing House, 2015), 48.

1935 The Zunyi Conference Shone Brightly

Keyword: the Zunyi Conference

There is a famous town in the north of Guizhou Province. A conference held here 86 years ago left a heavy mark on the modern history of China. It is Zunyi, an important town with red lights in the north of Guizhou.

The time goes back to 1934 when the Red Army began the Long March. At that time, Bo Gu, the leader of the CPC Central Committee, and others made the mistake of escapism in military affairs, which caused heavy losses to the Red Army. The number of Red Army troops, which was originally more than 86,000, fell sharply to more than 30,000. Suspicion and dissatisfaction grew among the Red Army officers and men, who also questioned the leadership of Bo Gu and others at that time. On December 18, 1934, the Political Bureau of the CPC Central Committee held a meeting in Liping and decided to give up the original plan of going north to meet the Second and Sixth Red Legions and accept Mao Zedong's proposal to open up a new base in Guizhou, where the enemy forces were relatively weak. On January 7, 1935, the Red Army occupied Zunyi, an important town in northern Guizhou.

Figure 15.
Site of Zunyi Conference

From January 15 to 17, 1935, the Political Bureau of the CPC Central Committee held an enlarged conference in Zunyi (i.e., the Zunyi Conference). The meeting was attended by the Political Bureau members Mao Zedong, Zhang Wentian, Zhou Enlai, Zhu De, Chen Yun, and Bo Gu, alternate members Wang Jiaxiang, Liu Shaoqi, Deng Fa, and He Kequan, the heads of the Red Army headquarters and corps Liu Bocheng, Li Fuchun, Lin Biao, Nie Rongzhen, Peng Dehuai, Yang Shangkun, and Li Zhuoran, as well as Deng Xiaoping, secretary general of the CPC Central Committee. Li De and Wu Xiuquan, the translators, also attended the meeting.

Knowledge about CPC History

On December 9, 1935, amid the deepening national crisis, thousands of patriotic students in Beiping (Beijing), under the leadership and organization of the Provisional Working Committee of the CPC in Beiping, held a powerful resistance against Japanese aggression demonstration to save the country, chanting slogans, such as "Oppose the North China Autonomous Movement," "Defeat Japanese imperialism," and "Stop the civil war and unite to against invaders." It is known as the "December 9 Movement" in history.

In Chen Yun's manuscript, some organizational changes made in the final resolution of the Zunyi Conference are recorded: first, Comrade Mao Zedong was elected as a member of the Standing Committee of the Political Bureau of the CPC Central Committee; second, Comrade Luo Fu was appointed to draft the resolution, entrusting the Standing Committee to review it and send it to the branch for discussion; third, an appropriate division of labor would be made among the Standing Committee members; fourth, the "three-member regiment" established before the Long March was abolished, with Zhu De and Zhou Enlai, the top military leaders, as the military commanders. The Zunyi Conference abolished the supreme military command of Bo Gu and Li De, ended the rule of "Left" dogmatism in the CPC Central Committee, and established Mao Zedong's leadership in the Central Committee and the Red Army. Later, the CPC Central Committee established a "three-member regiment" composed of Mao Zedong, Zhou Enlai, and Wang Jiaxiang. Zhou Enlai was the head of the regiment and was responsible for directing the military operations of the whole army.

Looking back on the tortuous development history of the CPC, the "Zunyi Conference" was considered a turning point of life and death. The Communists represented by Mao Zedong and Zhou Enlai solved the complicated problems within the Party with their own strength, which means that the CPC began to mature politically.

The Zunyi Conference opened magnificent historical pictures of "crossing Dadu River," "capturing Luding Bridge," and so on. The CPC was increasingly thriving in this eastern land.

1936 National Justice Would Last Forever

Keyword: Xi'an Incident

More than 80 years ago, an event that shocked the world happened in the ancient city of Xi'an. This event can be said to have changed the historical development of modern China.

The incident took place in 1936. Japanese imperialism had occupied Northeast China and other places, and more land would fall into the hands of Japanese aggressors. The CPC endeavored to safeguard the territorial integrity of the motherland and hoped to cooperate with the KMT again to fight against the Japanese army. However, the KMT refused to resistance against Japanese aggression and insisted on "suppressing the Communist Party."

On October 22, 1936, Chiang Kai-shek summoned Zhang Xueliang and Yang Hucheng respectively in Xi'an and coerced them to attack the Red Army. The two generals, who were well aware of the serious domestic situation, said that they should unite the Communist Party to resist Japan, but they were severely reprimanded by Chiang Kai-shek. At the same time, Chiang Kai-shek mobilized about 30 divisions of his direct troops to the Pinghan and Longhai railway lines with Zhengzhou as the center, readied to attack Shaanxi and Gansu and provoke civil war.

Figure 16.
Site of the Xi'an Incident

Knowledge about CPC History

On September 1, 1936, the CPC Central Committee issued the *Instruction on Forcing Chiang Kai-shek to Resistance against Japanese Aggression* to the Party, pointing out that "under the condition that Japanese imperialism continues to attack and the national revolutionary movement continues to develop, it is possible for all or a large part of Chiang's army to join the resistance against Japanese aggression. Our general policy should be to force Chiang to resist Japan," and prepare to send representatives to negotiate with the KMT.

At this critical moment, in the early morning of December 12, Zhang Xueliang and Yang Hucheng resolutely implemented "forced remonstration," put Chiang Kai-shek under house arrest, and wired the whole country to put forward eight propositions centering on "stopping all civil wars." Zhang and Yang said, "We hold justice and have no regrets. Our only hope is to seek the realization of these policies and to contribute to the country. Let the compatriots of the nation judge our merits and demerits!" This is the "Xi'an Incident" that shocked the world.

After the Xi'an Incident, the attitudes of all parties in China were complicated. Within the Nanjing National Government, the pro-Japanese faction headed by He Yingqin advocated a solution by force, ignoring Chiang Kai-shek's life and death. Song Meiling, Song Ziwen, Kong Xiangxi, Sun Ke, and others advocated the peaceful settlement of the Xi'an Incident and lobbied to rescue Chiang Kai-shek. Among the local military leaders of the KMT and many centrists, only a few people expressed their full support for Zhang and Yang. Most people favored resistance against Japanese aggression, but they were worried that Zhang and Yang's actions would lead to a larger civil war, so they did not support them.

After the Xi'an Incident, the CPC, proceeding from the interests of the whole nation, advocated a peaceful settlement and joined Chiang Kai-shek in resistance against Japanese aggression. On the 17th, Zhou Enlai, the representative of the CPC Central Committee arrived in Xi'an and discussed with Zhang Xueliang how to correctly solve the Xi'an Incident. On the 18th, the CPC Central Committee called the KMT and proposed to convene the resistance against Japanese aggression and National Salvation Conference to peacefully resolve the Xi'an Incident. and National Salvation Conference to peacefully resolve the Xi'an Incident. The next day, the CPC clearly advocated "freeing Chiang Kai-shek" and negotiated with him to stop the civil war and unite resistance against Japanese aggression.

The peaceful settlement of the Xi'an Incident opened the prelude from the civil war to the joint resistance against Japanese aggression between the KMT and the CPC and became the key to turning the situation around. From then on, the ten-year civil war basically ceased, and the resistance against Japanese aggression national united front was initially formed. As Zhou Enlai said, the righteous acts of General Zhang and General Yang "contributed greatly to the cause of the war of resistance against Japanese aggression" and are the "heroes of the Chinese nation for thousands of years."

1937 Gunfire Started at Lugou Bridge

Keyword: the full-scale outbreak of the War of Resistance against Japanese Aggression

In 1937, in the traditional Chinese lunar calendar, it was the Year of the Ox. Looking at the long history of the world, it seems that this is not a special year, but it is by no means an ordinary year for Chinese history and all Chinese people. In order to occupy the whole of China, Japan launched a large-scale war of aggression against China that year.

Since May 1937, Japanese troops stationed in Fengtai frequently conducted military exercises. In May and June, the headquarters of the Japanese Kwantung Army and the headquarters of the Chinese garrison in Tianjin held frequent meetings to intensify planning for a large-scale war of aggression against China. At 10:00 p.m. on July 7, 1937, the Japanese troops carried out a military exercise near the Lugou Bridge, more than 10 kilometers from Peiping, to provoke the Chinese garrison.

In the process, the Japanese army falsely claimed that a soldier was missing and asked to enter Wanping County near the bridge to search. Of course, the Chinese authorities did not agree with their unreasonable request. After being refused, the Japanese army finally tore off

Figure 17. Lugou Bridge

Knowledge about CPC History

On September 22, 1937, the Central News Agency of the KMT issued the *Declaration of the CPC Central Committee for the Announcement of the KMT-CPC Cooperation*. On the 23rd, Chiang Kai-shek made a report, which actually recognized the legitimate status of the CPC. The release of the *Declaration of the CPC Central Committee for the Announcement of the KMT-CPC Cooperation* and Chiang Kai-shek's talk announced the realization of the second KMT-CPC cooperation, marking the formal formation of the resistance against Japanese aggression national united front with KMT-CPC cooperation as the main body.

its disguise and attacked the Chinese garrison to encircle Wanping County. At that time, the officers and soldiers of the Chinese 29th Army stationed in Wanping County rose to resist, and the commander, Ji Xingwen, went to the front line and commanded the battle. According to the memories of the retired veteran who later experienced the war, a soldier killed and wounded 13 Japanese soldiers with a broadsword and died a martyr. And a company of soldiers stationed on the north side of the Lugou Bridge fought to the end with only four men left. This incident was called the July 7 Incident, also known as the Lugou Bridge Incident.

After the Japanese army launched the July 7 Incident, it aroused strong repercussions throughout the country. On July 8, the CPC Central Committee sent a telegram to the whole country, pointing out that the only way out for China was to carry out a national war of resistance. The slogans of "Pingjin is in danger! Northern China is in peril! The Chinese nation is in danger!," "Do not let Japan occupy China," and "Bleed for the defense of the country" spread all over China. After the Lugou Bridge Incident, the Japanese government decided to increase its troops in North China and expand the war of aggression. This situation forced the KMT government to change its attitude toward Japan to a certain extent. On July 17, Chiang Kai-shek delivered a report in Lushan, proposing the minimum conditions for resolving the incident and expressing the Chinese government's determination to fight the war of resistance.

The outbreak of the July 7 Incident marked the beginning of Japan's all-out invasion of China and the beginning of China's national war of resistance. Its great historical significance lies in promoting the awakening of the whole nation and condensing the strength of the resistance against Japanese aggression of all Chinese people. The roar of the guns at Lugou Bridge became the clarion call for the general mobilization of the Chinese nation against the war, and the entire Chinese land was filled with the fury of resistance against Japanese aggression. This overwhelming force awakened the sleeping national soul. Now, the smoke of war has gone away, and the sonorous sound of "the broadsword cuts the devil's head" still echoes in the land of China for a long time. On the square of the Memorial Hall of the Chinese People's War of Resistance against Japanese Aggression, the large-scale sculpture "Lugou Rising Lion," which symbolizes the awakening of the Chinese nation, stands tall.

1938 A Magic Weapon for Victory in the War of Resistance against Japanese Aggression

Keyword: the publication of *On Protracted War*

In the world-famous military academy, the United States Military Academy at West Point, two Chinese military books are regarded as books students must read. One is Sun Tzu's *Art of War*, famous at home and abroad since ancient times, and the other is *On Protracted War*. Speaking of *On Protracted War*, the time can be traced back to 1938. The nation's war of resistance against Japan in China lasted nearly a year. At that time, there were two domestic opinions about whether China could win the war of Resistance against Japanese Aggression.

One was the theory of "quick victory." Many people believed that by relying on the regular army of the KMT, China's War of Resistance against Japanese Aggression would soon be won; the other was the theory of "national subjugation," which held that it was difficult for China to win the War of Resistance against Japanese Aggression in the face of strong Japanese imperialism. However, 10 months after the national war of resistance, neither of these statements was verified. Where would China's War of Resistance against Japanese Aggression go? Mao Zedong's *On Protracted War* answered this question.

Figure 18.
In 1938, Mao Zedong wrote *On Protracted War* in his Yan'an cave-dwelling.

It is said that Mao Zedong wrote *On Protracted War* in less than ten days from the beginning of May 1938. The famous Western scholar Ross Trier described the process of Mao Zedong's writing of *On Protracted War* in *The Biography of Mao Zedong* as follows:

Knowledge about CPC History

From September 29 to November 6, 1938, the CPC held an enlarged Sixth Plenary Session of the 6th CPC Central Committee in Yan'an. Mao Zedong made a political report entitled "On the New Stage" and summarized the meeting, demanding that the whole Party shoulder the major responsibility of leading the War of Resistance against Japanese Aggression. The Plenary approved the line of the Political Bureau of the CPC Central Committee, represented by Mao Zedong, and put forward the proposition of "localization of Marxism in China."

> Mao sat at the desk in the cave, and the faint candlelight shone on his pale face. He didn't sleep for two days and only ate a little. There was a stone beside his notebook. When Mao's arm was sore, he held the stone tightly to loosen his fingers. Five days later, there was a pile of paper full of Mao's unruly and unique cursive characters, but Mao's body weight was reduced, and his eyes were bloodshot. On the seventh day, Mao jumped up because of pain. The fire burned the shoe on his right foot in the brazier, and he was still thinking. He drank a glass of Baijiu and tried to finish the last part of On Protracted War. However, he had a bad headache on the eighth day and fainted for a while. After the doctor diagnosed his illness, he continued to write. On the ninth day, he finally finished this 50,000-word paper.

In *On Protracted War*, Mao Zedong elaborated on four basic characteristics of China and Japan, that was, the enemy was strong, and the Chinese side was weak; the enemy was small, and the Chinese side was big; the enemy retreated, and the Chinese side advanced; and the enemy got little help while the Chinese side got a lot of that. At the same time, Mao Zedong concluded that China would not die, nor would it win quickly. As long as the Chinese people persevered in the arduous and protracted war of resistance, the final victory must belong to China. At the same time, Mao Zedong stressed that the foundation of a protracted war was laid in the broad masses of the people.

After the publication of *On Protracted War*, it won a great response. Not only did the Communist Party agree with Mao Zedong's judgment, but also KMT members Chiang Kai-shek and Bai Chongxi agreed. After that, the domestic people read this article one after another, which improved the morale of the Chinese People's War of Resistance against Japanese Aggression. More importantly, *On Protracted War* provided the correct strategic guidance for China to achieve a final victory in the Chinese People's War of Resistance against Japanese Aggression. In fact, the War of Resistance against Japanese Aggression developed exactly as Mao Zedong predicted in *On Protracted War*. After three stages of strategic defense, strategic stalemate, and strategic counter-offensive, the Chinese people finally defeated the Japanese aggressors and won the War of Resistance against Japanese Aggression.

1939 Party Building Opened a New Chapter

Keyword: the publication of *How to Be a Good Communist*

In Huaming Building, Ningxiang County, Hunan Province, there is a memorial hall covering an area of 34,000 square meters, which was built in memory of Liu Shaoqi, the founding father of the PRC. In Liu Shaoqi Memorial Hall, there is a pamphlet *How to Be a Good Communist*, which reflects Liu Shaoqi's concern and thinking about the Party building in the war environment.

In March 1938, the CPC Central Committee made a *Resolution on the Mass Development of Party Members*, calling for the mass and tenfold recruitment of Party members throughout the Party. After this resolution was issued, local Party organizations took many measures to develop themselves and recruit new members. A large number of young patriots, progressive youth, and intellectuals were absorbed into the Party, and the number of Party members increased rapidly. Under this circumstance, the ideological situation of the whole Party became active. At the same time, the situation within the Party became more complex. If the Party could not timely strengthen the education and guidance of new Party members,

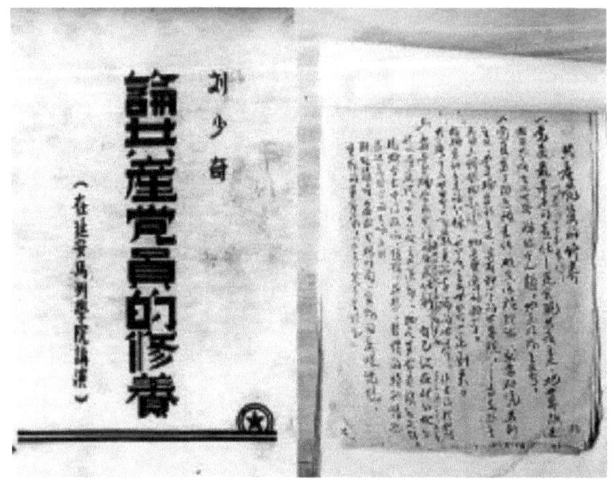

Figure 19.
How to Be a Good Communist

correct their thinking, and establish a correct outlook on life and the world, it was bound to affect the healthy growth of the Party members, and thus affect the development and expansion of the cause of the Party. So, what kind of norm should Party members used to retrain themselves? How should the Party carry forward its fine revolutionary tradition? This became an important issue for the whole Party at that time.

Knowledge about CPC History

On January 16, 1939, the Southern Bureau of the CPC Central Committee was officially established in Chongqing. Zhou Enlai, Bo Gu, He Kequan, Wu Kejian, Ye Jianying, and Dong Biwu were six standing members, of whom Zhou Enlai was the secretary. The Southern Bureau successively set up ten institutions, including the Organization Department, the Publicity Department, the Social Department, the United Front Committee, the Cultural Affairs Committee, and the International Studies Office.

Liu Shaoqi's *How to Be a Good Communist* was written to answer this question. Starting from the reality of the CPC itself, he creatively and systematically put forward the cultivation theory of Communist party members by applying Marxist principles and combining the excellent traditional culture of China and profoundly expounded that the Communist party members should strive to transform their subjective world and strengthen their self-cultivation in all aspects while transforming the society and the objective world. The book also points out the close relationship between self-cultivation and practice and theoretical learning and emphasizes the importance of practice and theoretical learning for the cultivation of Communist Party members.

How to Be a Good Communist is a classic work on the construction of the Party. For this important work, Deng Xiaoping gave such evaluation at the memorial meeting for Liu Shaoqi: "His book *How to Be a Good Communist* and other works on party building have educated all party members and are a valuable spiritual wealth of our party." Mao Zedong repeatedly praised *How to Be a Good Communist* as a very useful book, believing that the book was very thorough about the relationship between Party members and the Party, the cultivation of Communist ideology, and other issues. At that time, all the new and old cadres in Yan'an had the book in their hands. They studied it carefully and used it to check themselves against it.

How to Be a Good Communist became a must-read for every young person who pursued progress and yearned for truth since the day of its birth. It has educated generations of Communists and progressive young people, and today it is still essential reading material for every Party member.

1940 The Hundred-Regiment Campaign Shook North China

Keyword: Hundred-Regiment Campaign

With the development and expansion of the resistance against Japanese aggression base areas, they were increasingly threatening the rear of the Japanese invaders in China. In order to destroy the resistance against Japanese aggression base areas and consolidate their occupied areas, the Japanese army implemented the "Cage Policy" in North China in 1939, successively establishing more than 3,000 strongholds, more than 10,000 blockhouses, more than 5,000 kilometers of railways, and more than 30,000 kilometers of roads so that the resistance against Japanese aggression bases and other areas and bases were isolated from each other. The Eighth Route Army was blockaded in remote areas, and its survival and development were extremely difficult. In this regard, the CPC hoped to break the "Cage Policy." Small-scale guerrilla warfare would definitely not work. A large-scale campaign must be fought to completely solve this problem.

From the issuance of the preparatory order on July 22, 1940, to the final issuance of the operational order, the headquarters of the Eighth Route Army deployed 22 regiments

Figure 20.
Monument to the Hundred-Regiment Campaign

Knowledge about CPC History

Before the Hundred-Regiment Campaign, the headquarters of the Eighth Route Army stipulated that the number of troops participating in the battle should not be less than 22 regiments. However, after the launch of the campaign, because the commanders and fighters of the Eighth Route Army and the people in the resistance against Japanese aggression base areas hated the Japanese army's "Cage Policy" and were highly motivated to participate in the crackdown, the ministries invested a large number of troops, 105 regiments in total, more than 200,000 people, and many local guerrillas and militias participated in the war.

to participate in the battle of the Zhengtai Railway, the most important transportation hub in North China. However, on August 22, when the headquarters of the Eighth Route Army made a comprehensive analysis of the war situation, Peng Dehuai and Zuoquan found that 105 regiments had participated in the battle. In other words, 85 regiments took the initiative to fight. What was more exciting was that there were guerrillas and militias equivalent to or more than the regular troops of the Eighth Route Army participated in the Hundred-Regiment Campaign, and at least 200,000 people participated. On August 20, the Eighth Route Army launched an attack at the same time in a vast area centered on the Zhengtai Railway. The vast majority of Japanese strongholds, railways, roads, bridges, and telegraph poles in the theater of operation became the targets of the Eighth Route Army, guerrillas, and the masses. The Japanese army was in chaos, and more and more troops participated in the War of Resistance against Japanese Aggression.

At first, the headquarters of the Eighth Route Army did not specify the war period for the Hundred-Regiment Campaign, but only required in the preparatory order to prepare food for one month from the date of the troops' dispatch, which can be roughly interpreted as about a week of combat. Finally, the Hundred-Regiment Campaign lasted for half a year. Within a few days after the start of the battle, the Japanese troops in the theater operation were completely passive. The victory in the early stage of the Hundred-Regiment Campaign gave Peng Dehuai the idea of launching the second stage of fighting. On the night of September 20, the second stage of the Hundred-Regiment Campaign began. On December 22, 1940, Mao Zedong, Zhu De, and Wang Jiaxiang called Peng Dehuai from Yan'an and said: "The Hundred-Regiment Campaign should not be declared over. Chiang Kai-shek is launching an anti-Communist campaign. We still need to use the momentum of the Hundred-Regiment Campaign to oppose him." The Japanese army deployed a "War of Destruction" at the end of September 1940, with up to 5 divisions, 10 independent mixed brigades, and a cavalry brigade in the battle sequence, sending about 150,000 troops to try to retaliate against the Eighth Route Army. All the Eighth Route Army ministries continued to fight against "mopping-up." On December 5, 1940, the Hundred-Regiment Campaign ended with a brilliant victory for the Eighth Route Army.

The Hundred-Regiment Campaign inspired the confidence of the whole country's army and people in fighting for victory in the War of Resistance against Japanese Aggression, refuted the slander of the KMT stubborn faction against the Communist Party and the Eighth Route Army for "touring but not striking," and also restrained the strength of the Japanese army, delayed the Japanese "southern advance," and was a support to the frontal battlefield.

1941 Incredible Grievances in Southern Anhui

Keyword: the Southern Anhui Incident

With the beginning of the whole nation's War of Resistance against Japanese Aggression, the CPC and its army became increasingly powerful, which aroused extreme dissatisfaction and concern among the KMT. At that time, the KMT and the CPC were still in the period of resistance against Japanese aggression cooperation, but those who were anti-communist and Communist-phobic within the KMT had begun to be ready to stifle the power of the CPC. On October 19, 1940, He Yingqin and Bai Chongxi, in the name of the Military Commission of the National Government, forced the New Fourth Army and the Eighth Route Army in the south of the Yellow River to withdraw to the north of the Yellow River within one month. The CPC promised to transfer the New Fourth Army from southern Anhui from the perspective of maintaining the overall situation of the war, but this was the beginning of a tragedy.

On the night of January 4, 1941, more than 9,000 troops of the New Fourth Army headquarters and southern Anhui troops were ordered to move northward. They set out from the Yunling station and prepared to move to the north of the Yangtze River through southern Jiangsu. On the 5th, when the troops arrived in the Maolin area of Jing County, they were surrounded and attacked by the army led by Gu Zhutong without warning. On the 6th, under the order of Chiang Kai-shek, Gu Zhutong and Shangguan Yunxiang led more

Figure 21. Southern Anhui Incident Martyrs Cemetery

than 80,000 troops from the 52nd and 40th Divisions of the 32nd Group Army in the Third Theater Operation to launch a general offensive against the New Fourth Army, and "purge them completely." On January 7, the New Fourth Army arrived at the Xingtan area to the north of Jingde and was stopped by KMT troops. Ye Ting, the commander of the New Fourth Army, was determined to forcibly attack the Xingtan and kill a bloody road to continue the advance. However, it was a pity that this opinion was not adopted and the opportunity was missed, forcing them to return to the west of Yunling by the same route. On the 8th, Shangguan Yunxiang's headquarters launched a crazy attack on the New Fourth Army with its overwhelming strength and weapons. Shangguan Yunxiang also conveyed Chiang Kai-shek's handwritten order: 100,000 yuan for the capture of Ye Ting alive and 50,000 yuan each for Xiang Ying and Yuan Guoping. On the evening of January 12, Ye Ting personally organized a breakthrough in Shijingkeng. The two sides clashed in the line of fire for seven days and seven nights, and the New Fourth Army was trapped in a desperate situation because of its weak strength. In order to preserve the army, Ye Ting, according to the opinion of Rao Shushi, Deputy Secretary of the Southeast Bureau of the CPC Central Committee, wrote a letter to Shangguan Yunxiang, accusing him of "treachery" and expressing his willingness to go to Shangguan Yunxiang's headquarters for consultation. On the 14th, Ye Ting was detained as soon as he arrived at the headquarters of Shangguan Yunxiang, Yuan Guoping, the director of the Political Department of the New Fourth Army, was killed in action during the breakout, and Xiang Ying, the deputy army commander, was killed by traitors during the breakout. The Maolin position of the New Fourth Army was completely occupied. Of the entire army of about 9,000 men, most were captured, separated, or killed in action, except about 2,000 who broke out under the leadership of Huang Huoxing and Fu Qiutao. On January 17, Chiang Kai-shek slandered the New Fourth Army's "rebellion," announced the cancellation of the New Fourth Army's designation, and claimed that Ye Ting would be handed over to a "military justice trial."

Knowledge about CPC History

On May 1, 1941, the *Xinhua Daily* published the "Program of Governance for the Shaanxi-Gansu-Ningxia Border Region" approved by the Political Bureau of the CPC Central Committee, stipulating that the "3 3" principle should be applied to the distribution of personnel in the public opinion organs and government of the border region, with Communist Party members accounting for roughly one-third, leftist progressives for roughly one-third, and centrists and other elements for roughly one-third. Communists must cooperate democratically with non-Party people and not go alone and control the overall arrangements.

This event, which happened in the south of Anhui, is known as the "Southern Anhui Incident" in history. The New Fourth Army suffered heavy losses in this incident. Communist soldiers who should have gone to the battlefield to fight the Japanese army and kill the Japanese aggressors died at the gunpoint of KMT troops who were also Chinese.

After learning about the Southern Anhui Incident, Zhou Enlai angrily wrote a poem in the *Xinhua Daily*, saying, "What an incredible injustice it is for Ye Ting and those who were cruelly injured or killed! What is the rush to kill the brothers under the same roof as you?" The Southern Anhui Incident was a tragedy for both the Chinese Communists and the Chinese nation.

1942 Seeking Truth from Facts and Cultivating Integrity

Keyword: the Yan'an Rectification Movement

During the Yan'an period, the CPC launched a large-scale rectification movement, which profoundly impacted the later CPC and the Chinese revolution. But why did this movement happen? How did it happen?

Marked by the convening of the First Congress of the CPC, the birth of the CPC was officially announced. However, the Chinese revolution did not run smoothly with the birth of the CPC. Before the young political party could consider how to build the party ideologically and theoretically, it led the people into the fierce Chinese revolution. During the Agrarian Revolution, the "Left" and Right mistakes made by the CPC made the Chinese revolution suffer serious setbacks. After the outbreak of the whole nation's War of Resistance against Japanese Aggression, the "Left" opportunism and dogmatism represented by Wang Ming had not been eliminated, and there were still problems in the Party's style of work, style of study, and style of writing. More and more people in the Party realized that the Communist Party needed to seriously consider how to build the Party and rectify its style of work.

Figure 22.
Mao Zedong's report on rectification for senior cadres in Yan'an

It was against this background that in May 1941 and February 1942, Mao Zedong respectively made reports on "Rectifying Our Study," "Rectifying the Party's Style of Work," and "Opposing Stereotypical Party Writing," calling on the whole Party to oppose subjectivism to rectify the style of study, oppose sectarianism to rectify the Party's style of work and oppose Party stereotyped writing to rectify the style of writing.

Knowledge about CPC History

The Yan'an period refers to the almost 13 years from the time when the CPC Central Committee arrived at Wuqi Town in northern Shaanxi with the Long March of the Central Red Army in 1935, to the time when Mao Zedong, Zhou Enlai, and Ren Bishi crossed the Yellow River eastward in Wubao County in northern Shaanxi in 1948 to meet the dawn of revolutionary victory. During this period, the CPC Central Committee led and directed the War of Resistance against Japanese Aggression and the War of Liberation, laying the foundation and bright prospects for the Party to win the victory of the New Democratic Revolution in the country.

After these reports were published, the Yan'an Rectification Movement began. The central problem to be solved in the Yan'an Rectification Movement was to oppose dogmatism. At that time, some comrades in the Party believed that everything would be all right as long as they followed the practices in books, regardless of their own environment and conditions. Undoubtedly, this was absurd. The Yan'an Rectification was precisely to solve the situation of "turning books and theories into dogmas, thinking rigidly, and starting from definitions and formulas." So, what should be the starting point and basis for doing things? Mao Zedong gave a clear answer: we must proceed from reality and combine Marxist theory with practice. For those comrades who have made mistakes, we should adopt the principles of "learning from past mistakes to avoid future ones and curing the sickness to save the patient" and "unity-criticism-unity." Each party member should seriously carry out criticism and self-criticism. For those comrades who have made mistakes, we should not focus on investigating their personal responsibility but focus on analyzing the environment and reasons for their mistakes, to achieve the goal of "not only making clear about their minds but also uniting with comrades."

The Yan'an Rectification Movement lasted more than three years from February 1942 to the spring of 1945. The rectification movement is not only a Marxist ideological education movement within the whole Party but also an ideological liberation movement that breaks the wrong tendency of the Party to dogmatize Marxism and sanctify the resolutions of the Communist International and the Soviet experience. It is also a successful practice and a great initiative for the Party's construction. Through this rectification movement, the whole Party has achieved unprecedented unity.

1943 Ode to Northern Shaanxi—as Good as Southern China

Keyword: the Production Campaign

"I come to Nanniwan, and it is a pleasant place with beautiful scenery ..." This well-known "Nanniwan" is a folk song of northern Shaanxi and a classic revolutionary song. It has inspired countless people. Even today, when we listen to this song again, we still feel its joy and excitement.

In order to support the long-term War of Resistance against Japanese Aggression, the CPC Central Committee held a production mobilization conference in Yan'an in February 1939. Mao Zedong called on the army and the people in the Shaanxi–Gansu–Ningxia Border Region to "draw on our own labor to supply ourselves with adequate food and clothing," and required the troops to participate in the production campaign without hindering the war. Later, the Central Military Commission issued *Instructions on Carrying out the Production Movement* to the whole army.

Nanniwan is located 45 kilometers southeast of Yan'an City. It is desolate, but the soil is fertile. In the spring of 1941, because the KMT reactionaries at that time imposed an economic blockade on the Shaanxi–Gansu–Ningxia Border Region and the resistance against Japanese aggression base area, goods and materials outside could not be transported. The

Figure 23.
The officers and soldiers of the 359th Brigade of the Eighth Route Army opened up the wasteland in Nanniwan.

Knowledge about CPC History

On May 15, 1943, the Presidium of the Executive Committee of the Communist International, in order to meet the needs of the anti-fascist war, made the *Decision on the Proposed Dissolution of the Communist International*, to which the CPC Central Committee expressed its full agreement. After the official dissolution of the Communist International on June 10, the CPC relieved itself from its obligations to the articles of association and resolutions of the Communist International and completely got rid of its influence.

CPC Central Committee ordered the 359th Brigade of the Eighth Route Army to enter Nanniwan to open up the land for cultivation and help themselves in production. If they had no houses, they dug their own caves. If they had no vegetables, they dug wild vegetables to eat; if they had no tools, they made their own hoes and shovels. They planted crops in the wild mountains with amazing perseverance. In just three years, the 359th Brigade led by Brigadier Wang Zhen carried forward the revolutionary spirit of "self-reliance and hard struggle" and turned Nanniwan, which was full of thorns and desolate, into "a place as good as southern China in northern Shaanxi" with a scene of "crops are everywhere, cattle and sheep are everywhere." In the autumn of 1943, the 359th Brigade of the Eighth Route Army, which "did not want any grain, any inch of cloth or any cent of money from the public," handed over public grain to the government of the Shaanxi–Gansu–Ningxia Border Region, completely breaking the economic blockade of the KMT reactionaries. The 359th Brigade became a banner of the whole army in the production campaign.

Since 1942, the earth-shaking changes in Nanniwan had attracted many famous people, who came there to visit and write many poems. The famous patriotic general Xu Fanting's poem "Ode to Nanniwan," the famous poet Xiao San's poem "I Came to Nanniwan Twice," and the poet He Qifang's prose "Remembering General Wang Zhen" all spoke highly of the achievements of reclamation in Nanniwan.

In the Spring Festival of 1943, the Yangko team of the Yan'an Lu Xun Art Institute came to Nanniwan and presented the newly compiled Yangko dance "Picking Flower Basket" to the heroes of the 359th Brigade. "Nanniwan" was one of the episodes. This song, whose lyrics were written by He Jingzhi and composed by Ma Ke, has a beautiful and lyrical melody. It sings about Nanniwan's transformation from a barren mountain to "a place as good as southern China" and enthusiastically praises the Eighth Route Army soldiers who pioneered wasteland production and established meritorious deeds. The whole song can be divided into two parts with contrast. The first half of the tune is soft and euphemistic, and the second half is happy and dynamic. Finally, the whole tune ends with a five-degree upward swing. The song absorbs the tones and rhythms of folk songs and dances and combines the performance forms of lyricism and dance, which integrates lyricism and dance, making it more vivid and touching.

The 359th Brigade stationed in Nanniwan became a national "model," as the song said. The cultivation spirit inherited by this team has influenced generations.

1944 Red Journey of Chinese and Foreign Journalists

Keyword: Chinese and foreign reporters' northwestern tour group visiting Yan'an

In 1944, the situation of the Second World War had undergone major changes. The fascist parties of Germany, Italy, and Japan had collapsed, and the whole anti-fascist front had been frequently reported with success. However, in China, on the one hand, the frontal battlefield saw the horrific routs in Henan, Hunan, and Guangxi; on the other hand, the Communist-led resistance against Japanese aggression base areas, where the revolutionary enthusiasm of the general public was high, and the will of the people was united, showed a promising scene of flourishing and invincible victory everywhere. This formed a sharp contrast between the two. Red Yan'an, a mysterious place, aroused the curiosity and yearning eyes of the whole world. On June 9, 1944, a delegation of 21 Chinese and foreign journalists from the northwest arrived in Yan'an and began their red journey.

Figure 24.
Foreign journalists who had in-depth interviews in northwest Shanxi

Knowledge about CPC History

September 15, 1944, Lin Boqu, the representative of the CPC, proposed to abolish the one-party dictatorship of the KMT, convene a meeting of all parties, and establish a democratic coalition government at the Third Session of the 3rd National Political Conference held in Chongqing. Later, the CPC submitted a written proposal for a democratic coalition government to the KMT authorities.

On the afternoon of June 9, Ye Jianying, Chief of Staff of the Central Military Commission, held a banquet for Chinese and foreign journalists. In the early morning of the 12th, all the members of the Chinese and foreign journalists visiting group received a light red invitation sent by Mao Zedong. At 3:00 p.m. on the 12th, Mao Zedong met 21 Chinese and foreign journalists in the Yangjialing Central Auditorium in Yan'an. The reporters were curious and fresh about everything in Yan'an and raised many questions in the conversation with Mao Zedong.

At the meeting, Mao Zedong quickly summarized the questions raised by the reporters into three main issues and elaborated on them in his report: first, the KMT-CPC negotiations. Mao Zedong hoped that the negotiations would make progress and achieve results, but there was no comment yet on the details of the negotiations. The second was about the second battlefield. Mao Zedong believed that Hitler could not be defeated without opening a second front, which would directly affect Europe, as well as the Pacific and China. However, China's problems still depended on the efforts of the Chinese themselves. The improvement of the situation abroad alone could not solve the problem. Mao Zedong focused on the third issue, which was democracy and reunification in China. He said that there would be no real unity without democracy. The fundamental solution to China's problems lay in the implementation of a democratic system, which required not only political freedom of report, publishing, assembly, and association, but also military, economic, and cultural democracy. This was an urgent demand at that time, demanding the legitimate status of the Communist Party and other political parties.

The journalists were fascinated by Mao Zedong's eloquence. His keen vision, careful thinking, original opinions, and straight-to-the-point conversational style captivated them. In the following days, Mao Zedong also received separate interviews with foreign journalists Stein, Forman, and others in turn. Later, these journalists wrote many books and articles reflecting the real situation of the Liberated Areas. Foreman's *Report from Red China*, Stein's *The Challenge to Red China*, and Epstein's comments received extensive attention. Even Father Shanahan, a member of the journalists' delegation who had always been hostile to communist ideas, believed that the Border Region was good.

This red trip of the Chinese and foreign journalists' delegation to the northwest swept away the KMT's distorted propaganda about the image of the Central Republic's Shaanxi–Gansu–Ningxia Border Region, and let the world see the shining light of this red-hot land.

1945

Stabilization Gained by the Bloody Fight in the War of Resistance against Japanese Aggression

Keyword: victory in the War of Resistance against Japanese Aggression

On September 2, 1945, on the American battleship "Missouri" in Tokyo Bay, Japanese Foreign Minister Mamora Shigemitsu and Japanese Chief of Staff Yoshijiro Umezu signed the instrument of surrender on behalf of the Emperor of Japan, the Japanese Government and the Japanese Imperial Base. The signing ceremony was very grand. So far, the Chinese nation's War of Resistance against Japanese Aggression ended with complete victory, and the Second World War came to a heavy end. Therefore, China set September 3 as the victory memorial day for the War of Resistance against Japanese Aggression. The whole country celebrated for three consecutive days, during which the sirens were blaring, salutes were fired, and people were rushing to tell each other the news with tears in their eyes. China was the second country, after the United States, to sign the Japanese Instrument of Surrender. Zhu Qiping, a journalist from *Ta Kung Pao*, wrote a paragraph: "This signature has washed away the great humiliation of the Chinese nation for 70 years. This scene is simple, solemn, and unforgettable." This famous piece of journalism, "Sunset," which has been recited to this day,

Figure 25.
He Yingqin, commander-in-chief of the Chinese Army, accepted the instrument of surrender submitted by the Chief of General Staff of the Japanese Invading Army, Asasaburo Kobayashi.

> **Knowledge about CPC History**
> On August 28, 1945, Mao Zedong, Zhou Enlai, and Wang Ruofei, accompanied by KMT representative Zhang Zhizhong and American Ambassador Hurley, flew to Chongqing from Yan'an to negotiate with the KMT. After 43 days of negotiations, on October 10, representatives of the KMT and the CPC signed the *Summary of Conversations Between the Government and Representatives of the Chinese Communist Party*, namely the *Double Tenth Agreement*.

concludes with ten Chinese characters of great power, which means "The old shame has been cleaned up and China should be reborn."

On August 15, Emperor Hirohito of Japan issued the *Imperial Rescript on the End of War*, declaring Japan's unconditional surrender to the world. China's war zones were divided into 15 surrender zones, with He Yingqin as the plenipotentiary. The first surrender zone was located in Hanoi, Vietnam, and the commander of the First Front Army, Lu Han, was the chief officer of the first surrender zone. The surrender troops to Vietnam under the command of Lu Han were 200,000 Yunnan troops. They arrived in Hanoi in a mighty manner, eliminated the Japanese roving bandits, successfully accepted the surrender of the Japanese, and made a good start for the Chinese theater to accept the surrender of Japan.

In the War of Resistance against Japanese Aggression, China made great national sacrifices. The total number of military and civilian casualties in China exceeded 35 million, with direct economic losses exceeding 100 billion US dollars and indirect economic losses exceeding 500 billion US dollars.

China's War of Resistance against Japanese Aggression won the world's respect and became an important part of the world's anti-fascist war. During the War of Resistance against Japanese Aggression, more than 200 major battles and nearly 200,000 battles of various sizes were fought in backstage and center-stage battles, annihilating more than 1.5 million Japanese troops and 1.18 million pseudo-armies.

The victory of the War of Resistance against Japanese Aggression is inseparable from the bloody struggle of all the Chinese people. In the face of the enemy, the KMT-CPC Cooperation opened the prelude to victory in the War. In particular, the CPC adhered to the independent guerrilla war against Japan, established several resistance against Japanese aggression base areas, such as Shaanxi-Gansu-Ningxia, Shanxi-Chahar-Hebei, Shanxi-Suiyuan, Shanxi-Hebei-Henan, and opened up the battlefield behind the enemy, mobilized all the forces that could be mobilized to join the flood of the War of Resistance against Japanese Aggression, and became the mainstay of the War of Resistance against Japanese Aggression.

China's War of Resistance against Japanese Aggression is the first national liberation war that won a complete victory against foreign invasion since modern times. It promoted the awakening of the Chinese nation and laid an important foundation for the CPC to lead the Chinese people to achieve complete national independence and people's liberation. China opened up the eastern battlefield of the world's anti-fascist war and made important contributions to the victory of the world's anti-fascist war.

1946 Land to Peasants

Keyword: the release of the *May 4 Directive*

On May 4, 1946, the CPC Central Committee issued the *Directive on Liquidation of Rent Reduction and Land Issues*, also known as the *May 4 Directive*. Once released, this document was welcomed by the farmers. Why on earth should the *May 4 Directive* be welcomed by farmers? Why was it released at this time?

The *May 4 Directive* was issued in a complex struggle situation. On the one hand, the War of Resistance against Japanese Aggression had just ended, and the contradiction between the KMT and the Communist Party was increasingly prominent; on the other hand, the policy of "rich peasant landlords pay rent and interest, peasants pay less rent and interest" implemented by the CPC during the War of Resistance against Japanese Aggression also gradually failed to meet the requirements of the majority of farmers. The CPC Central Committee believed that to overthrow the reactionary rule of the KMT, it was necessary to win the broad masses of the people to come to the side of the Communist Party. To get support from them, the peasants must be given tangible benefits. Only by using force to distribute to the peasants the land occupied by the landlords in the liberated areas could the peasants really lead a good life.

Figure 26.
The *May 4 Directive* was welcomed by farmers in the liberated areas after its release.

Knowledge about CPC History

On November 21, 1946, the CPC Central Committee held a meeting in Yan'an. Zhou Enlai reported on the negotiations between the KMT and the CPC over the past year, and Mao Zedong analyzed the national situation. The meeting decided to use "overthrow Chiang Kai-shek" as the final policy to solve domestic problems. The establishment of this policy transformed the war of self-defense of the People's Liberation Army into a national war of liberation.

Against this background, the *May 4 Directive* decided to transform the policy of rent and interest reduction implemented since the War of Resistance against Japanese Aggression into the policy of "land to the peasants." The way to solve the land problem was not to confiscate the land of all landlords unconditionally, but to enable farmers to obtain land from landlords mainly through liquidation, rent reduction, and land donation, in addition to confiscating and distributing the land of a few big traitors; plus, there should be some differences between the treatment of ordinary rich peasants, small and medium-sized landlords and that of big landlords, local tyrants, evil gentry and bullies; we should unite with the middle peasants and use all means to attract them to participate in the movement, and the interests of the middle peasants must not be violated. Those enlightened gentlemen and small and medium-sized landlords who had cooperated with us should be handled with caution and given due consideration. The issuance of this instruction marked the official start of land reform in the liberated areas.

After the *May 4 Directive* was issued, the liberated areas took prompt action. The first step was to mobilize the masses and establish peasant associations. In the propaganda, in order to let the farmers really understand the land reform policy, various localities sent art troupes to perform the opera *White-Haired Girl* to improve the farmers' awareness, and then established peasant associations on the basis of improved awareness. The second step was to confiscate the landlords' excess land, houses, livestock, farming tools, and grain, and to expropriate the rich peasants' excess land and distribute it to peasants who had little land or no land in accordance with the land reform policy. By February 1947, two-thirds of the liberated areas had solved the land problem. It was such a greatly popular land policy that greatly consolidated the liberated areas and won the support of the people in the liberated areas for the War of Liberation.

Since ancient times, the majority of Chinese farmers had depended on the land for survival, and they had been looking forward to getting their own land one day. This wish and expectation became a reality at that moment; thus it can be imagined how happy they were. Later historical development proved that victory in the War of Liberation was impossible without the support of hundreds of millions of peasants who had obtained land.

1947 March into the Dabie Mountains

Keyword: strategic counterattack

In June 1946, the KMT troops attacked the central plains liberated areas on a large scale and then launched a comprehensive attack on the liberated areas. A nationwide civil war broke out. At that time, the total strength of the KMT army was 4.3 million, while the people's army led by the CPC was only 1.27 million. One year later, more than 1.1 million regular KMT troops were wiped out, the number of KMT troops dropped sharply to more than 3.2 million, and the number of the people's army led by the CPC increased to 1.9 million. The development of the situation forced the KMT army to change the all-around attack into a key attack: a total of 200,000 people from 31 brigades were deployed on the northern Shaanxi battlefield, and a total of 400,000 people from 56 brigades were deployed on the Shandong battlefield.

On June 30, 1947, Liu Bo Cheng and Deng Xiaoping led the main force of the Shanxi-Hebei-Shandong-Henan Field Army (i.e., the "Liu-Deng Army") with more than 120,000 men to break through the Yellow River and win the Campaign of Southwest Shandong; without resting, they advanced into the Dabie Mountains at the end of August, completing a special form of offensive action characterized by a long drive into the enemy's strategic depths without rear support. This attack was like a sharp knife straight into the heart of the KMT's

Figure 27.
Troops led by Liu-Deng Army marched into the Dabie Mountains on the self-made wooden bridge.

ruling area, which opened the prelude to the strategic counter-offensive of the People's Liberation War.

Knowledge about CPC History

On October 27, 1947, the CPC Central Committee issued an instruction that the revolution must be carried out to the end. The CPC Central Committee instructed to expose the political conspiracy of the U.S. and Chiang reactionaries to instigate "peaceful reunification," to do a good job of fighting to educate and unite all democratic parties, and to oppose all incomplete bourgeois compromise ideas or reformist political platforms.

From the map, it can be seen that the Dabie Mountains are the watershed between the Yangtze River and the Huai River, spanning Hubei, Henan, and Anhui, just like an arched natural barrier. The changes in the mountains affect the situations of the three provinces, which also determined that this place was destined to be a place of opportunity. Deng Xiaoping once pointed out that the Dabie Mountains was a good base for advancing strategically. They were close to the Yangtze River and reached Nanjing and Shanghai in the east, and Hankou in the southwest. They were an important springboard for crossing the Yangtze River. On August 31, 1947, the 53rd Regiment of the 18th Brigade of the 6th Column of Liu-Deng Army marched along the line of Dahepu and Chengmagang from Jingfu (now Xin County, Henan Province) and occupied Macheng County. This time, Liu-Deng Army occupied Macheng without firing a single shot. Because there were no regular KMT troops in Macheng County at that time, Luo Weilang, the head of the County from KMT, heard of the arrival of Liu-Deng Army and fled in a panic with the County's self-defense force. After entering eastern Hubei, Liu-Deng Army controlled more than 300 kilometers of the north bank of the Yangtze River through arduous fighting. At that time, Chiang Kai-shek, who was in Lu Mountain, was so frightened that Liu-Deng Army might cross the Yangtze River that he ordered five KMT infantry regiments to stop them. In October 1947, Liu-Deng Army skillfully used favorable terrain to plan "pocket tactics" in the Gaoshanpu of Qingshui River in Qichun with 17 regiments, lured the enemy in, annihilated 12,600 people of the other side, and cut off the "tail" that chased the Communist army, laying the foundation for realizing the "best strategic future" that Mao Zedong hoped to advance into Dabie Mountains and stand firm. The battle of Gaoshanpu was also the biggest battle of Liu-Deng Army in the Dabie Mountains.

It can be said that without the victory of the battle in the Dabie Mountains, it would have been difficult to win the National War of Liberation. By the end of 1947, the KMT army had been forced to change from a strategic offensive to a comprehensive defense, thus ending the strategic defensive posture of the people's army in the revolutionary war for a long time, marking the arrival of a new climax of the Chinese revolution.

1948 Strategic Armageddon

Keyword: Liaoshen Campaign

In the autumn of 1948, as the War of Liberation entered its third year, the country's political, economic, and military situation changed significantly, which was more beneficial to the CPC than to the enemy. The total strength of the People's Liberation Army (PLA) had increased from 1.27 million at the beginning of the war to 2.8 million, and its equipment had been greatly improved. Its ability to tackle difficult problems had been significantly improved, while the total strength of the KMT army had decreased from 4.3 million at the beginning of the war to 3.65 million. In the Northeast battlefield, although the total force of the KMT Weilihuang Group was 550,000, it was divided into three isolated areas, Changchun, Shenyang, and Jinzhou, and was in a very difficult situation. On the contrary, the army of the CPC had reached 700,000 people in the northeast, and with the local troops, its total strength exceeded 1 million. The liberated areas accounted for 97% of the Northeast, and had more than 86% of the population, making the War of Liberation obtain inexhaustible human and material support. Among the five major battlefields in China, the Northeast battlefield was the only one where the economic strength and military strength of the CPC exceeded those of the enemies', and had already met the conditions for a strategic decisive battle with the enemy.

Under such circumstances, the CPC Central Committee held an enlarged meeting of the Political Bureau in Xibaipo from September 8 to 13, 1948, to carry out a strategic decisive

Figure 28. Memorial Hall of the Liaoshen Campaign

Knowledge about CPC History
The Huaihai Campaign was launched on November 6, 1948, and ended on January 10, 1949. It took 66 days to wipe out 555,000 KMT troops. This campaign basically liberated East China and Central Plains to the north of the Yangtze River, creating extremely favorable conditions for the PLA to cross the river.

battle between the PLA and the KMT army and to make important preparations ideologically, politically and organizationally for the final defeat of Chiang Kai-shek and for the planned and step-by-step victory of the New Democratic Revolution nationwide.

Mao Zedong drafted the *Operational Guidelines for the Liaoshen Campaign* for the Central Military Commission, which defined the policy of conducting a strategic decisive battle with the KMT army in the northeast. On September 12, Lin Biao, the commander of the Northeast Field Army, and Luo Ronghuan, the political commissar, followed the instructions of the Central Military Commission and mobilized the main forces from Changchun, Siping, and other places to the Beining Line to launch the Liaoshen Campaign.

The Liaoshen Campaign lasted 52 days, wiped out more than 470,000 KMT troops and liberated the northeast. There were reasons for the victory of the CPC army and the failure of the KMT army in the Liaoshen Campaign. Both Chiang Kai-shek and Mao Zedong, the supreme commanders of the KMT and the CPC, saw the key move in Jinzhou almost at the same time. However, Chiang Kai-shek and his Northeast generals disagreed, so they hesitated and delayed the fight. Chiang Kai-shek later made a fatal strategic mistake, that was, he stubbornly fought a decisive battle with the PLA, regardless of the actual situation of the strength and growth of the Northeast PLA at that time, which eventually led to the destruction of hundreds of thousands of elite troops in the Northeast. The strength of the army of the CPC, including local troops, was almost twice that of the KMT army, and the equipment of the Northeast Field Army of the CPC was the strongest among the four major field armies. If the KMT army retreated to the Shanhaiguan Pass quickly, it might have been able to change the fate of being completely wiped out by the CPC army. In contrast, the strategy and tactics of the Chinese PLA were relatively successful. Mao Zedong believed that the best policy was to attack Jinzhou first and close the way for the KMT troops to escape from the border and to "close the door and beat the dog." After the fall of Jinzhou, the KMT troops were closed in the northeast, trapped in isolation, and could not escape by land. When attacking Changchun, the commanders of the Northeast Field Army strengthened their political offensive, so that the KMT troops took the initiative to revolt and surrender, and the Northeast Field Army won Changchun without bloodshed, avoiding casualties. Later, although the Northeast Field Army disrupted its organizational system and marched into Shenyang, the army finally liberated Shenyang because of its clear targets.

Since then, the Northeast had become a solid base of the PLA, and the Northeast Field Army had become a powerful strategic mobile force of the PLA, ready to be deployed on other battlefields. The Liaoshen Campaign was recorded in history as the first battle of strategic decisive battle between the Chinese PLA and the KMT army.

1949 The Chinese People Have Stood Up

Keyword: the founding of the PRC

October 1 is of special significance to every Chinese. It is the birthday of the motherland. On October 1, 1949, Mao Zedong solemnly declared to the world: "The Central People's Government of the PRC is established today!" Since then, the Chinese people have stood up proudly. Looking back on the magnificent scene of the founding ceremony in 1949, people are still excited.

On October 1 at 2:00 p.m., the Central People's Government Committee elected by the First Plenary Session of the Chinese People's Political Consultative Conference (CPPCC), held its first meeting in the Palace of Qinzheng. Chairman Mao Zedong, Vice Chairmen Zhu De, Liu Shaoqi, Song Qingling, Li Jishen, Zhang Lan, Gao Gang, Zhou Enlai, and the other 56 members of the Central People's Government Committee announced their inauguration. The Conference unanimously resolved to proclaim the establishment of the Central People's Government of the PRC, accept the *Common Program of the CPPCC* as the policy of governance, declare to all governments that the Central People's Government of the PRC was the sole legitimate government of China and was willing to establish diplomatic relations with any foreign government that abided by the principles of equality, mutual benefit and mutual

Figure 29.
On October 1, 1949, at 3:00 p.m., the founding ceremony of the PRC was held in Beijing Tiananmen Square.

respect for territorial sovereignty. After the conference, the Chairman, Vice Chairman, and members of the Central People's Government set out collectively to take a bus out of the East Gate of Zhongnanhai and go to the Tiananmen Gate Tower to attend the founding ceremony. At this time, 300,000 soldiers and civilians from Beijing who participated in the founding ceremony gathered in Tiananmen Square, looking forward to the arrival of the great historic moment.

Knowledge about CPC History

In September 1949, the first plenary session of the CPPCC unanimously voted that the capital of the PRC was set in Beiping and would be renamed Beijing from then on; the calendar year of the PRC adopted the AD calendar year; before the national anthem of the PRC was formally formulated, the "March of the Volunteers" was used as the national anthem; the national flag of the PRC was a five-star red flag, symbolizing the great unity of the Chinese revolutionary people.

At 3:00 p.m., Mao Zedong announced in his loud voice with a Hunan accent: "The Central People's Government of the PRC is established today!" This simple but meaningful sentence opened the gate for people to cheer. It was difficult for everyone to express their excitement in words, but only to use smiles and cheers instead of words. In the magnificent melody of the "March of the Volunteers," China's first five-star red flag was rising slowly. After that, 54 cannons fired 28 salutes on the square, symbolizing the 28 years of glorious struggle of the CPC leading the people of all nationalities. Then a grand military parade was held. Commander-in-chief Zhu De, accompanied by parade commander-in-chief Nie Rongzhen, reviewed the troops by open-topped car. The parade lasted nearly three hours, and when it was already late and the lights were on in Chang'an Street, the mass parade began. Groups of marchers held up red flags and red lights to enjoy the first night of New China.

China, the great oriental country, woke up like a sleeping lion on October 1, 1949. The founding of the PRC marked the great victory of China's new democratic revolution and the beginning of a new era in Chinese history. After more than 100 years of heroic struggle, the Chinese people finally overthrew the rule of imperialism, feudalism, and bureaucrat capitalism; China truly became an independent country, and the Chinese people, who accounted for one-fourth of the total number of mankind, stood up since then. The founding of New China strengthened the power of world peace, democracy, and socialism.

1950 Resist US Aggression and Aid Korea to Defend the Motherland

Keyword: the War to Resist US Aggression and Aid Korea

After the founding of New China, the development was not all smooth. Internationally, the Western countries led by the United States adopted policies of political isolation, military encirclement, and economic blockade and embargo against New China. In June 1950, the Korean War broke out, and the United States sent the Seventh Fleet to invade the Taiwan Strait of China when it intervened in the Korean Civil War. On June 28, Mao Zedong delivered a speech at the eighth meeting of the Central People's Government Committee, calling on people all over the country and the world to unite and make full preparations to defeat any provocation of American imperialism. On the same day, Zhou Enlai, on behalf of the Chinese government, issued a statement strongly condemning the US aggression against Korea and Taiwan (China) and its interference in Asian affairs.

On October 8, 1950, Mao Zedong issued an order to reorganize the Northeast Border Guard Army of the Chinese PLA into the Chinese People's Volunteers (CPV), appointed Peng Dehuai as the commander and political commissar of the CPV, and ordered it to stand by for

Figure 30.
The volunteer army launched a countercharge against the US military in Sanggamryong.

Knowledge about CPC History

On April 13, 1950, the Central People's Government Committee held its seventh meeting and considered and adopted the *Marriage Law of the People's Republic of China*, which abolished the feudal marriage system of arranged and forced marriage, male superiority over females, and disregard for the interests of children, and implemented the new marriage system of freedom of marriage between men and women and protection of the legitimate interests of women and children. This is the first basic law formulated by New China.

deployment. On October 19, the CPV, in accordance with the scheduled plan, crossed the Yalu River from Andong (now Dandong), Changdian Hekou, and Ji'an, and entered Korea to fight in the war, which began the War to Resist US Aggression and Aid Korea. From October 25 to December 24, the CPV, together with the Korean People's Army, carried out two campaigns in a row, killing more than 50,000 enemies, recaptured Pyongyang on December 6, and drove the enemy back to the vicinity of the 38th parallel, initially reversing the tide of war in Korea. Later, the CPV launched three campaigns from December 1950 to June 1951, wiping out more than 100,000 enemy troops. On April 11, 1951, General MacArthur, the commander-in-chief of the "United Nations Army," was removed from his post and replaced by General Ridgway, the commander of the Eighth Army of the US Army, invading Korea.

Later, the US military launched a "summer offensive" on the Korean battlefield and spread a large number of animals and insects with plague, cholera, typhoid fever, and other infectious diseases in northern Korea and northeast China, launching a "bacterial war." The series of actions did not achieve their expected goals, but they were resisted by the CPV and the Korean army and people, and the international community condemned the bad acts of the United States.

In order to redeem the defeat and force China and Korea to accept the negotiation conditions of the US, Clark, the commander-in-chief of the United States Far East Army and the "United Nations Army," launched the Sanggamryong Campaign on October 14, 1952. The US military successively invested more than 60,000 troops, dispatched 3,000 aircraft and over 170 tanks, and used 18 artillery battalions to attack the Sanggamryong position, less than 3.7 square kilometers. In the 44-day fierce battle, the US military fired 2 million shells and 5,000 bombs at Sanggamryong and launched more than 900 charges. However, the volunteer soldiers held their ground. In this campaign, the volunteer army wiped out 25,000 enemies. From mid-May to mid-June 1953, the CPV launched two offensive operations in conjunction with the armistice negotiations, destroying more than 40,000 enemy troops. On July 13, the Chinese and Korean people's armies launched the Kimsong Campaign, killing more than 50,000 enemies and recovering 178 square kilometers of land.

Under the more unfavorable situation, the United States signed the "Korean Armistice Agreement" with the representatives of China and Korea in Panmunjom on July 27, 1953. The Korean War, which lasted three years and 32 days, ended. The Chinese and Korean armies wiped out more than one million enemies, including 390,000 US troops, shot down and injured more than 12,200 enemy aircraft, sank and injured 257 enemy ships, and destroyed and captured countless enemy combat materials.

1951 Spring on the Snow-Covered Plateau

Keyword: peaceful liberation of Xizang

On the southwest border of China, on the Qinghai–Xizang Plateau, there is a magical and beautiful land, Xizang. However, more than 70 years ago, people there lived under feudal serfdom and lived a miserable life.

After the founding of the PRC, the Central People's Government officially announced the abolition of national oppression, and the PLA successfully entered the Changdu area, where it implemented the Party's ethnic policies. At this time, the long-suppressed patriotism of the people in Xizang began to burst out; the 10th Panchen Lama Erdeni expressed his support for the Central People's Government; the 14th Dalai Lama expressed his acceptance of the people's government's proposal for the peaceful liberation of Xizang. These were the bases on which negotiations could proceed.

Figure 31.
Monument to the Peaceful Liberation of Xizang

> **Knowledge about CPC History**
> In October 1951, the first volume of *Selected Works of Mao Zedong* was published. Since then, there has been an upsurge in learning Mao Zedong's works throughout the country. The second and third volumes of *Selected Works of Mao Zedong* were also published in April 1952 and April 1953.

In April 1951, five plenipotentiaries sent by the Xizang local government, including Ngapoi Ngawang Jigme, arrived in Beijing and held talks with plenipotentiaries Li Weihan and Zhang Jingwu of the Central People's Government. After negotiations, the plenipotentiaries of the Central People's Government and the Xizang local government reached an agreement on the peaceful liberation of Xizang. On May 23, 1951, the *Agreement of the Central People's Government and the Local Government of Xizang on Measures for the Peaceful Liberation of Xizang* (hereinafter referred to as the *Agreement*) was officially signed in Beijing. The signing ceremony was presided over by Zhu De and Li Jishen, Vice Chairmen of the Central People's Government, and Chen Yun, Vice Premier of the Council of the Central People's Government. The main contents of the *Agreement* were as follows:

> The Tibetan is one of the ethnic groups with a long history in China and a part of the motherland family; the religious beliefs of the people in Xizang are guaranteed; imperialist aggressive forces are expelled from Xizang, and the people in Xizang return to the family of the PRC; the local government of Xizang actively assists the PLA in entering Xizang to consolidate national defense; under the unified leadership of the Central People's Government, Xizang implements regional ethnic autonomy; to achieve unity within the people in Xizang, gradually develop agriculture, animal husbandry, industry, commerce, culture and education in Xizang in accordance with the actual situation of Xizang, and improve people's lives; all matters concerning foreign affairs in Xizang shall be handled by the Central People's Government in a unified manner; the Central People's Government establishes a military and political committee and a military region command in Xizang.

On October 26 of the same year, the PLA entered Lhasa in accordance with the provisions of the *Agreement*.

The peaceful liberation of Xizang shattered the dream of "Tibet Independence" planned by the imperialists and a small number of separatists in the upper class of Xizang, put an end to Xizang's long history of being borderless, and safeguarded China's sovereignty and territorial integrity. The peaceful liberation of Xizang is an important turning point from darkness to light, from separation to unity, and from backwardness to progress. Since then, Xizang has entered a new period of historical development.

After the peaceful liberation of Xizang, democratic reforms were carried out in Xizang, and the decadent and dark feudal serfdom was abolished. Millions of serfs and slaves were liberated. They were no longer the personal property of serf owners, were no longer forced to work by serf owners, and gained a series of human rights such as personal freedom. This was a great epoch-making change.

1952 First Case of Anti-corruption

Keyword: public trials of major embezzlers Liu Qingshan and Zhang Zishan

After the Third Plenary Session of the Seventh CPC Central Committee was held in June 1950, the CPC Central Committee and the Central People's Government took a series of measures to restore the national economy. One of them was to adjust industry and commerce so that capitalist industry and commerce developed rapidly. However, the lawbreakers among the capitalists were not satisfied with making general profits in the normal way; they were as pervasive as moths, bribing and corrupting state employees for profiteering. In the face of such a situation, the CPC Central Committee called for movements against the "three evils" of corruption, waste, and bureaucracy among Party and government officials and against the "five evils" of bribery, tax evasion, theft of state property, cheating on government contracts, and stealing of economic information among private businessmen. In 1952, the movement reached its climax when the public trial of the major embezzlers Liu Qingshan and Zhang Zishan took place.

On February 10, 1952, in Baoding, the capital of Hebei Province, there was light snow in the sky. Just after 9:00 a.m., people from all directions poured into the municipal stadium. The

Figure 32. Liu Qingshan and Zhang Zishan underwent a public trial.

Knowledge about CPC History
In the early days of the founding of the PRC, under the leadership of the CPC, government organs, schools, organizations, the military, and political parties at all levels launched a movement against the "three evils" of corruption, waste, and bureaucracy. And among private businessmen, there was a movement against the "five evils" of bribery, tax evasion, theft of state property, cheating on government contracts, and stealing of economic information.

public trial of the major embezzlers Liu Qingshan and Zhang Zishan would be held here. At that time, more than 20,000 people attended the meeting. The People's Court of Hebei Province, in accordance with the instructions of the Supreme People's Court of the Central People's Government, formed a temporary court to give a public trial and sentence to Liu Qingshan and Zhang Zishan. As the two villains of the first anti-corruption case of the Republic, they were firmly nailed to the pillar of shame in history.

Liu Qingshan, the secretary of the CPC Tianjin Prefectural Committee, was the deputy secretary of the CPC Shijiazhuang Municipal Committee before his arrest. Zhang Zishan, the deputy secretary of the CPC Tianjin Prefectural Committee and the commissioner of the Tianjin Special Zone, was the secretary of the CPC Tianjin Prefectural Committee before his arrest. Under the white terror of the KMT, Liu and Zhang made many achievements in the arduous War of Resistance against Japanese Aggression and the War of Liberation. However, in a peaceful environment after the national victory, they could not withstand the erosion and inducement by the bourgeoisie and degenerated. They used their authority to embezzle airport construction funds, shipbuilding loans, and river management funds for flood relief, embezzle relief grain for cadres' families and local grain, exploit civilian workers by withholding their grain supplies, defraud bank loans, etc. The total amount was 17,162,720,000 RMB (old currency), the first set of RMB issued by the People's Bank of China from December 1, 1948, and its ratio to today's RMB was 10,000:1.1, that is, equivalent to 1,716,272,000 yuan of today's RMB. According to the currency system standard and market price index at that time, 17.1 billion yuan could buy nearly a ton of gold, which is now worth 400 million yuan. In November 1951, the corruption case of Liu and Zhang was exposed. On December 4, the CPC Hebei Provincial Committee expelled them from the CPC and arrested them according to law. In view of the seriousness of the crime, the Provisional Court of the Hebei Provincial People's Court, by order of the Supreme People's Court, sentenced the two men to death and immediate execution and confiscated all their property.

Before the public trial of Liu and Zhang, someone asked whether they could tell Mao Zedong not to shoot them but give them a chance to mend their ways. The opinion reached Mao Zedong, who said, "It is because of their high status, great merit, and influence that the two of them should be executed with determination. Only by executing them can we save 20,200, 2,000, even 20,000 cadres who have made mistakes to varying degrees."

History, if not forgotten, can serve as a guide for the future. More than 60 years ago, this case taught the state employees to think about the people rather than seek personal interests since they were in important positions. In today's anti-corruption campaign, the outcome of Liu Qingshan and Zhang Zishan still has a profound warning effect.

1953 The First Step of Economic Construction

Keyword: the implementation of the 1st Five-Year Plan in China

After the founding of New China, the economy improved after three years of recovery. But objectively speaking, China was still a backward agricultural country at that time, and its industrial level was far behind that of developed countries in Europe and the United States. As Mao Zedong said at the time, "What can we build now? We can make tables and chairs, we can make tea bowls and teapots, we can grow food, we can grind it into flour, and we can make paper, but we can't make a car, an airplane, a tank, or a tractor." Because of this, a national economic plan centered on the realization of socialist industrialization and the 1st Five-Year Plan came into being.

The 1st Five-Year Plan started in 1953 and was completed ahead of schedule in 1957. The 1st Five-Year Plan draft was formulated under the direct leadership of the CPC Central Committee and presided over by Zhou Enlai, Chen Yun, Li Fuchun, and others. This draft plan was started in 1951. It was developed and compiled at the same time. After nearly four

Figure 33.
Workers from all walks of life devoted great enthusiasm to the realization of the 1st Five-Year Plan.

years of supplementation and revision, it was finally formally adopted at the Second Session of the First National People's Congress in July 1955. The basic tasks of the 1st Five-Year Plan were to concentrate major forces on developing heavy industry and to establish the preliminary foundations for national industrialization and modernization of national defense; to develop transportation, light industry, agriculture, and commerce accordingly; to train construction talents accordingly; to promote the cooperative transformation of agriculture and handicrafts and the socialist transformation of capitalist industry and commerce step by step; to ensure that the proportion of the socialist sector of the national economy increases steadily and that individual agriculture, handicrafts, and capitalist industry and commerce play a correct role; and to ensure that the people's material and cultural living standards were gradually improved based on developing production.

Knowledge about CPC History

On June 15, 1953, Mao Zedong made a relatively complete statement on the content of the Party's general guideline in the transitional period for the first time at the enlarged meeting of the Political Bureau of the CPC Central Committee, that was, in 10 to 15 years or more, the country's industrialization and the socialist transformation of agriculture, handicrafts, and capitalist industry and commerce should be basically completed.

The formulation and implementation of the 1st Five-Year Plan were supported and assisted by the Soviet government. The 156 projects that the Soviet Union helped China build laid a preliminary foundation for China's socialist industrialization. With the joint efforts of the whole Party and the people of the country, the 1st Five-Year Plan was successfully implemented. On December 26, 1953, the commencement ceremony of the three major projects of Anshan Iron and Steel Company-Large Steel Rolling Plant, Seamless Steel Tube Plant, and No. 7 Ironmaking Furnace was held, which was the first batch of important projects put into operation in heavy industrial construction. At the same time, Baotou Iron and Steel Company and Wuhan Iron and Steel Company also officially started work, starting the establishment of large iron and steel bases on the mainland. By 1956, China's first heavy truck manufacturing plant, Changchun First Automobile Factory, was completed and put into operation. China's first aircraft manufacturing plant succeeded in piloting China's first jet aircraft. China's first machine tool manufacturing plant, Shenyang First Machine Tool Factory, was completed and put into operation. The Wuhan Yangtze River Bridge was under construction. At the same time, transportation, light industry, agriculture, commerce, culture and education, and other undertakings had been developed accordingly, and people's lives had been greatly improved.

By the end of 1957, the indicators of the 1st Five-Year construction plan had been substantially exceeded, thus greatly changing the backward outlook of the country's economic development and effectively strengthening the country's economic strength.

1954 All Power Belongs to the People

Keyword: the birth of the *Constitution of the People's Republic of China*

On September 15, 1954, the First Session of the First National People's Congress was solemnly opened in Beijing. The meeting lasted 14 days (with a two-day break) and ended successfully on September 28 after completing its historical tasks.

The meeting was attended by 1,226 delegates. The delegates included model workers from various industries, heroic figures from the army, famous literary, artistic, scientific, and educational workers, and representatives from business and religious circles. Among them were 178 delegates from ethnic minorities and 147 women delegates.

At this meeting, several major events were completed: the formulation of the Constitution; the enactment of several important laws; the hearing and consideration of the government work report; and the election of new national leaders. Among them, the formulation of the *Constitution of the People's Republic of China* was of extraordinary significance.

At 4:00 p.m. on September 15, the First Session of the First National People's Congress was held. After the adoption of the agenda of the meeting, the meeting immediately entered the first agenda and listened to the report on the *Draft Constitution of the People's Republic of*

Figure 34.
After the First Session of the First National People's Congress voted to adopt the *Constitution of the People's Republic of China*, all the delegates stood up and applauded warmly.

China made by Liu Shaoqi on behalf of the Constitution Drafting Committee. Liu Shaoqi's report lasted more than three hours. After that, the delegates had a heated discussion on the report and the draft constitution.

According to the opinions put forward by the delegates during the discussion, Mao Zedong presided over a meeting of the Central People's Government Committee, at which he said, "This is a relatively complete constitution. It was first drafted by the CPC Central Committee, then it was discussed by more than 500 senior cadres in Beijing and more than 8,000 people nationwide, and then it was discussed by all the Chinese people, and this time it is discussed again by more than 1,000 delegates to the National People's Congress in three months. The Constitution was carefully drafted, and every article and word was carefully worked on, but it need not be said to be flawless and seamless."

At 3:00 p.m. on September 20, a plenary session of the First National People's Congress was held. The full text of the finalized *Draft Constitution of the People's Republic of China*, as amended and adopted by the Central People's Government Committee, was read out. After the reading, the audience applauded warmly, and the Executive Chairman immediately announced that the final text would be voted on. The constitutional vote was carried out by secret ballot, and each delegate received a light red "vote to pass the *Constitution of the People's Republic of China*" printed in four languages: Han, Mongolian, Tibetan, and Uyghur. Delegate seats were divided into eight voting areas according to seats, and each area was equipped with a ballot box. The delegates began to vote at 4:50 p.m. At 5:55 p.m., the Executive Chairman announced the voting results of the *Constitution of the People's Republic of China* according to the report of the vote counters and scrutineers: the total number of votes cast was 1,197, with 1,197 votes in favor. At this time, the whole audience stood up and applauded and cheered for five minutes. Then, the Executive Chairman solemnly announced that the *Constitution of the People's Republic of China* had been adopted at the first session of the First National People's Congress on September 20, 1954. The whole audience stood up again, and the storm-like applause and cheers lasted for a long time.

The adoption and promulgation of the *Constitution of the People's Republic of China* pointed out a clear and definite road to socialism for the people of the whole country, mobilized the enthusiasm of the broad masses of the people to build socialism, and was a good start for China to move toward socialist democracy and legal construction.

1955 Planting the Friendship Tree in Bandung

Keyword: Zhou Enlai attending the Bandung Conference

In the 1950s, Asia and Africa, which had been bullied by foreign invaders for a long time, got rid of the oppression of colonists and gained national independence. But how would Asia and Africa develop in the future? This was a common problem puzzling Asian and African countries. On December 29, 1954, Myanmar, Ceylon (now Sri Lanka), India, Indonesia, and Pakistan jointly launched a meeting attended by 29 Asian and African countries. The meeting was held from April 18 to 24, 1955, in Bandung City, Indonesia. Therefore, the meeting was also called the "Bandung Conference."

China was one of the participating countries in this conference. In April 1955, Zhou Enlai led the Chinese delegation to the beautiful city of Bandung surrounded by mountains.

Due to the long-term colonial rule and the influence of some historical disputes and political prejudices left by colonial rule, it was difficult to avoid some misunderstandings and estrangement between the participating countries. Imperialist and colonial countries that were not eligible to participate in the meeting also expected that there would be quarrels at the meeting and nothing would be achieved. Zhou Enlai held high the banner of peace, unity, anti-imperialism, anti-colonialism, and friendly cooperation with a broad vision and

Figure 35.
On April 19, 1955, Zhou Enlai addressed the Bandung Conference.

broad-mindedness as a statesman. In his report at the conference, Zhou Enlai clarified the position and policies of the Chinese government, and put forward the policy of "seeking common ground while shelving differences." He hoped that all countries could resolve conflicts, remove obstacles, and win friends. This view was widely accepted by all countries and made an important contribution to the success of the Conference under extremely complex circumstances.

Knowledge about CPC History

After the founding of New China, the Soviet Union took the lead in establishing diplomatic relations with New China. From October 1949 to January of the following year, New China established diplomatic relations with ten people's democratic countries, namely, Bulgaria, Romania, Hungary, North Korea, Czechoslovakia, Poland, Mongolia, the German Democratic Republic, Albania, and the Democratic Republic of Vietnam.

On the afternoon of April 24, amid prolonged applause and cheers, the Conference unanimously adopted the *Final Communiqué of the Asia-Africa Conference*, which contained a wide range of elements on economic cooperation, cultural cooperation, human rights, and self-determination, issues concerning the peoples of affiliated countries, and on the promotion of world peace and cooperation. In the *Declaration on Promoting World Peace and Cooperation*, the conference proposed the famous "Ten Principles of the Bandung Conference," which was the extension and development of the Five Principles of Peaceful Coexistence proposed by our country.

The Bandung Conference is the first international conference sponsored by Asian and African countries and on their own initiative. Based on the principles of seeking common ground while shelving differences and equal consultation, the Conference established a series of guidelines for the international community to handle international relations. The spirit of solidarity among Asian and African people, anti-imperialism and anti-colonialism, striving for national independence, maintaining world peace, and developing friendly cooperation among countries embodied in this meeting was called "Bandung Spirit" and went down in history. Participation in the Asian-African Conference was an important milestone in the process of New China's entering the international political arena. The Chinese delegation headed by Zhou Enlai made universally recognized contributions to the success of the Conference. The success of the Bandung Conference marked the awakening and unity of the Asian and African peoples, showed that Asian and African countries, as an important political force in the post-war world, had begun to step onto the international stage, and also meant that China had opened the door to extensive exchanges with Asian and African countries.

1956 Striding Forward to Socialism

Keyword: completion of the Socialist Transformation

On January 15, 1956, more than 200,000 people from all walks of life in Beijing gathered in Tiananmen Square to celebrate the victory of socialist transformation. Mao Zedong and other central leaders attended the conference. Peng Zhen, the then mayor of Beijing, announced at the conference that our capital had entered a socialist society. On January 21, Shanghai and Chongqing held a rally and parade to celebrate their entry into the socialist society. For a moment, the whole land of China was decorated with lanterns and colored silks, and gongs and drums were played to celebrate the successful completion of the socialist transformation.

After the founding of New China, after several years of exploration, the CPC Central Committee formally proposed the general guidelines for the transition period in 1953. Under the guidance of the general line, the socialist transformation began. Agriculture generally went through several stages, including mutual aid groups, primary agricultural production cooperatives, and senior agricultural production cooperatives, and completed the transformation from individual agriculture to collective agriculture. The handicraft industry generally went through several stages, including production cooperation groups, handicraft supply and marketing cooperatives, handicraft production cooperatives, and completed the

Figure 36.
Shanghai held a parade celebrating its entry into the socialist society.

socialist transformation. With regard to capitalist industry and commerce, the Party and the government implemented the policy of "restriction, utilization, and transformation," which generally went through the development process from the form of low-level state capitalism (exclusive purchase and marketing, processing and ordering) to the form of high level state capitalism (public-private partnership). In this process, the Party and the government creatively realized the peaceful redemption of the means of production possessed by the capitalists, which Marx and Lenin had envisaged.

Knowledge about CPC History

On April 25, 1956, Mao Zedong made a report on "On the Ten Major Relations" at an enlarged meeting of the Political Bureau of the CPC Central Committee. The report summarized the experience of China's socialist construction, put forward the basic policy of mobilizing all positive factors to serve the cause of socialist construction, and made a preliminary exploration of the road of socialist construction suitable for China's situation.

In the process of and after the completion of the socialist transformation, the state successively paid more money to private businessmen than their original total assets in the form of "dividing the profits of the enterprises into four parts" and fixed interest payment as the price of peaceful redemption. This practice won the support of the national bourgeoisie. Rong Yiren, who had 24 textile, printing and dyeing, flour and machinery factories in eight major cities in China, said that "For me, what I have lost is some of my personal gains from exploitation ... What I have gained is a socialist country where everyone is rich, prosperous, and strong."

By the end of 1956, the number of farmers who joined the cooperatives had reached 96.3% of the total number of farmers in China, of whom 87.8% were farmers who joined the senior cooperatives; the handicraft workers who participated in the cooperatives accounted for 91.7% of the total handicraft workers; 99% of the private industrial households and 82.2% of the private commercial households in China had been incorporated into the track of public-private partnerships or cooperatives respectively. So far, the socialist transformation of China's agriculture, handicrafts, and capitalist industry and commerce had been basically completed.

With the establishment of a new economic foundation in which public ownership of the means of production had an absolute advantage, the socialist economic system, the political system, and the educational, scientific, and cultural system had basically taken shape. All aspects of economic construction and national work had been developed and improved to adapt to and serve the establishment of the socialist economic system.

Although in the late period of the socialist transformation, there were problems, such as being too urgent in requirements, too rough in work, too fast in changes, and too simple and uniform in forms, on the whole, in a large country with hundreds of millions of people, such complex, difficult and profound social changes were relatively smoothly achieved, which promoted the development of the entire national economy. It was indeed a great historic victory. The establishment of the basic socialist system laid the institutional foundation for all development and progress in contemporary China.

1957 Great Gathering of the Socialist Camp

Keyword: Mao Zedong leading a delegation to visit the Soviet Union

In November 1957, the October Revolution of the Soviet Union ushered in its 40th-anniversary celebration. Delegations of the Communist Party and the Workers' Party of 64 countries, totaling 15,000 people, participated in the celebration meeting held at the Luzhniki Stadium in Moscow on November 6. On November 2, 1957, Mao Zedong led the Chinese delegation to leave Beijing by special plane to participate in the celebration.

Mao Zedong's plane landed at 3:20 p.m. Moscow time (8:20 p.m. Beijing time) at Vnukov Airport, 30 kilometers southwest of the Moscow suburbs. He delivered a speech at the airport and pointed out:

> I visited the Soviet Union at the end of 1949 and the beginning of 1950. At that time, the two governments signed the *Sino-Soviet Treaty of Friendship, Alliance, and Mutual Assistance*, and from then on, the intimate union of our two great socialist countries began. The October Revolution was a great victory for the Soviet people and for the proletariat, the working masses, and all the oppressed people of the world. Forty years ago, this victory, achieved by the Soviet people under the leadership of the great Lenin and the great Communist Party of the Soviet Union, ushered in a new era of human history. In the course of 40 years of construction, the Soviet

Figure 37.
In November 1957, Mao Zedong met with Chinese students during his visit to the Soviet Union.

Union was exceptionally rapid in its achievements, standing in many respects at the forefront of the nations of the world and setting a remarkable example for the people in their pursuit of progress and happiness. The launch of the first artificial Earth satellite by the Soviet Union was not a simple event, because a new era of further human conquest of the natural world has since begun.

Knowledge about CPC History

On February 14, 1950, Premier and Foreign Minister of the PRC Zhou Enlai and Foreign Minister of the Soviet Union Andrey Vyshinsky signed the *Sino-Soviet Treaty of Friendship, Alliance and Mutual Assistance* at the Kremlin in Moscow, which agreed on comprehensive cooperation between the two sides in political, economic, military, cultural, and other fields and established the alliance between China and the Soviet Union.

Later, Mao Zedong also stressed that the October Revolution enabled the Chinese people to find the road to prosperity and strength. The Chinese people's revolution and construction received the sympathy and generous help of the Soviet people, and the two countries formed a brotherly alliance.

At 10:00 a.m. (Moscow time) on November 6, the October Revolution celebration was held. Khrushchev, the First Secretary of the Central Committee of the Soviet Communist Party, delivered a report entitled "The 40th Anniversary of the Great October Socialist Revolution." At the meeting held at 4:00 p.m., Mao Zedong delivered a speech. He introduced the situation of China and talked about the great achievements of China's various construction undertakings in the past eight years and the rectification movement carried out by the Chinese people under the leadership of the Communist Party. After that, representatives of various countries made reports one after another.

After the celebration of the October Revolution, the delegation of the CPC participated in the conference of representatives of the Communist Party and the Workers' Party of 12 socialist countries and the conference of representatives of the Communist Party and the Workers' Party of 68 socialist countries held in Moscow in the middle of November. On November 21, Mao Zedong led the Chinese delegation back to Beijing.

All kinds of revolutions have taken place in history, but no previous revolution can be compared with the October Revolution. It was the dream of the world's working people and progressive mankind for thousands of years to build a society where no one exploited people. For the first time ever, the October Revolution turned this dream into reality on one-sixth of the world's land. Therefore, the October Revolution is worth celebrating and commemorating in socialist countries.

1958 The People's Heroes Are Immortal

Keyword: the completion of the Monument to the People's Heroes

On Tiananmen Square in Beijing stands the towering Monument to the People's Heroes. When we walk around the square, we always look up to it. What is the significance of the Monument to the People's Heroes, and how was it built? There are many stories behind this that are worth recalling.

In order to commemorate the people's heroes who died in all the revolutionary struggles in China since 1840, a resolution was made at the First Plenary Session of the Chinese People's Political Consultative Conference on September 30, 1949, to build a "Monument to the People's Heroes" in the capital Beijing. But the committee members disagreed on where it should be built. Some said it should be built on Dongdan Square in Beijing, while others said it should be built on Babao Mountain in the western suburbs of Beijing. Zhou Enlai finally decided to build the monument in Tiananmen Square, according to the opinion of the majority of members. After the agreement was reached, in the afternoon of September 30, 1949, Mao Zedong, together with all the CPPCC members, held a groundbreaking ceremony in Tiananmen Square, at which Mao read the inscription and broke the ground with the shovels on the north side of the former Zhonghua Gate on the south side of Tiananmen Square together

**Figure 38.
Monument to the People's Heroes**

Knowledge about CPC History

In October 1958, the first rocket launch test base in New China was built in Jiuquan City, Gansu Province. The site is flat, sparsely populated, dry, and rainless and can be used for launch tests for more than 300 days a year. Therefore, it is an ideal place to launch spacecraft. Jiuquan Satellite Launch Center is the earliest and largest integrated missile and satellite launch center in China.

with the members. The monument became the first historic building built by the Republic in Tiananmen Square. Its foundation is one day earlier than the founding ceremony of our Republic!

On May 1, 1958, the Monument to the People's Heroes was officially completed. It stands on the north-south axis, about 463 meters south of Tian'anmen Gate and 440 meters north of Zhengyangmen Gate, with a total height of 37.94 meters. On the pedestal are ten huge Chinese white jade relief sculptures on the themes of "Destroying Opium at Humen," "Jintian Uprising," "Wuchang Uprising," "May 4 Movement," "May 30 Movement," "Nanchang Uprising," "Guerrilla War against Japan," "Crossing the Yangtze River in Victory," "Supporting the Front Line" and "Welcoming the People's Liberation Army," which vividly and generally represent the extraordinary history of China's people's revolution over the past century. The heart of the monument is the eight characters inscribed by Mao Zedong: The people's heroes are immortal! Zhou Enlai wrote the inscription drafted by Mao Zedong. The full text is as follows: "The people's heroes who died in the People's Liberation War and the people's revolution in the past three years are immortal! The people's heroes who died in the People's Liberation War and the people's revolution in the past thirty years are immortal! From 1840 onward, the people's heroes who have died in the struggles against internal and external enemies for national independence and people's freedom and happiness are immortal!"

As time goes by, the Monument to the People's Heroes has been completed for more than 60 years. More than 60 years can make a child grow into an old man, and it can also make a country move from subsistence to a well-off society. More than 60 years is enough to change a lot. What remains unchanged is the shining names and the yearning in our hearts.

1959 An Inspiring Discovery

Keyword: the discovery of Daqing Oilfield

In 1959, Daqing Oilfield in Heilongjiang was discovered. For a moment, the whole country was jubilant. Because this not only broke the prediction of foreign experts on China's "poor-oil," but also broke the oil blockade imposed by Western countries on China, changed the backwardness of China's oil industry, and promoted the process of China's modernization.

Like other industries, China's oil industry started in ruins. In addition to its weak foundation, China was initially branded as an "oil-poor country"—American experts could not find oil in China, and Japanese experts could not find oil in the Northeast for more than a decade. Is China really a poor-oil country? This not only troubled the masses but also the central leaders at that time. In 1953, New China began to implement the 1st Five-Year Plan. To develop industry and revitalize the economy, how can we do without oil? To this end, Mao Zedong especially found Li Siguang, the most famous geologist in China at that time, to discuss with him. Mao Zedong said: "We are materialists, and we should proceed from the actual situation. If we are really short of natural oil, we need to consider developing artificial oil or

Figure 39.
Wang Jinxi used his body to mix cement to control the blowout.

extracting oil from oil shale." Hearing this, Li Siguang was full of thought and could no longer sit still. He said: "Chairman, I think China's oil prospect is very good." Then he described the geological environment of China, pointing out that continental strata were widely distributed in China, and from the perspective of its sedimentary environment, it had a good oil generation environment.

Knowledge about CPC History

On March 10, 1959, the local Xizang government and the reactionary group at the top, in collusion with imperialists and foreign interlopers, launched an armed rebellion in Lhasa in a vain attempt to achieve the "Tibet Independence." The PLA garrison in Xizang, with the active assistance of the local patriotic monks and laymen, quickly quelled the rebellion and safeguarded the reunification of the motherland and the unity of all ethnic groups.

After years of research, Li Siguang drew a beautiful blueprint for oil exploration in New China. He first pointed out that there was a good oil-generating environment in the region of Songliao Plain–North China Plain–Jianghan Plain–Beibu Gulf. As a famous Chinese scientist and the Minister of Geology of the PRC, Li Siguang's views provided an extremely important basis for China's oil exploration. In 1956, China began a strategic shift in oil exploration, originally limited to a corner in the northwest to the east, and started hunting for oil in the Songliao Plain and North China Plain.

The oil workers and scientific and technological teams, represented by "Iron Man" Wang Jinxi, marched into the icy northeast of China in a vast way. After several years of hard work, on September 25, 1959, the Chinese petroleum exploration team found industrial oil flow in the continental sediments of Songliao Basin in northeast China. It was the tenth anniversary of National Day, so the oilfield was named after "Daqing" (which means "Great Celebration"). The discovery of the Daqing Oilfield broke the argument that China was a "poor-oil country." Before the founding of New China, there were only three small oilfields in China, namely Laojunmiao in Gansu, Dushanzi in Xinjiang, and Yanchang in Shaanxi, and two gas fields, namely Shengdengshan and Shiyougou in Sichuan, with an annual output of only 100,000 tons of crude oil, which was basically imported from foreign countries. The development of the Daqing Oilfield greatly increased China's crude oil production. After Daqing Oilfield, China successively discovered several large oilfields. The era when the Chinese people could only rely on "foreign oil" was gone forever.

1960 Making Great Achievements through Self-Reliance

Keyword: the Soviet Union withdrawing its experts from China

Since 1949, China has maintained close cooperative relations with the Soviet Union, the "big brother" of the socialist countries. However, with the changes in the international situation and the deepening differences of views between the two parties, bilateral relations gradually deteriorated. After the border conflict between China and India, the leaders of the Soviet Union, regardless of its merits, publicly accused China. This was, of course, severely refuted by the Chinese side. Not long after that, the relationship between the two countries broke down completely.

On July 16, 1960, the Soviet government suddenly sent a note to the Chinese government, unilaterally decided to recall all Soviet experts working in China, and abrogated the agreements on economic and technological cooperation between the two countries. On July 25, without waiting for the Chinese reply, the Soviet side informed the Chinese government that it would withdraw all 1,390 experts in China, terminate the dispatch of more than 900 experts, tear up 343 expert contracts and contract supplements, and cancel 257 science

Figure 40.
Factories closed down due to the withdrawal of Soviet experts.

Knowledge about CPC History

From December 24, 1960, to January 13, 1961, the CPC Central Committee held a working conference in Beijing. The meeting discussed the 1961 national economic plan and made the *Summary of Discussions on Rural Rectification and Several Policy Issues*. At the meeting, Mao Zedong proposed to promote the trend of investigation and research and said that 1961 should be a year of seeking truth from facts.

and technology cooperation projects within one month from July 28. At that time, the Soviet Union's experts in China were distributed in all walks of life. Many of them had not yet completed their terms of employment, and their contracts had not yet expired. Although the Chinese government had repeatedly retained them, it had not succeeded. When the Soviet experts left, they took all the drawings, plans, and materials with them. The Soviet Union stopped supplying important equipment badly needed by China's construction and greatly reduced the supply of complete sets of equipment and key components of various equipment. Many scientific research plans in China were suspended, and more than 250 enterprises and institutions were paralyzed or semi-paralyzed.

Faced with such a situation, Mao Zedong calmly warned everyone that from 1917 to 1945, the Soviet Union was self-reliant and built a socialist country, which was a road of Leninism, and we should also follow this road. He asked everyone to make up their minds to engage in cutting-edge technology and thought that it would be great if Khrushchev did not give us support. Because if the Soviet Union gave us support, the debt would be difficult to pay. At that time, the Soviet Union's help to China was not gratuitous. The so-called "aid" was that the Soviet Union supplied Chinese equipment, and we used materials to repay it. By 1960, China had repaid 7.2 billion rubles. Zhou Enlai calculated at that time: if the remaining account was repaid at 500 million rubles per year, it would take 16 years to pay off; if it was repaid at 800 million rubles per year, then it would take ten years to pay off. After discussion, the CPC Central Committee called on all departments, provinces, and cities to tighten their belts and strive to pay off the debts owed to the Soviet Union in five years. Under such circumstances, the people of the whole country responded to the call of the CPC Central Committee and worked hard in their posts. In the following years, not only were the debts owed to the Soviet Union gradually paid off, but also scientific and technological achievements such as the first successful atomic bomb blast and synthetic bovine insulin were achieved.

The year 1960 was a difficult year for China. That year, China did not hold a National Day parade for the first time. However, the facts that followed proved that the industrious and brave Chinese people could overcome many difficulties and win the socialist construction without external help.

1961 "Life-Saving Fields" in Difficult Times

Keyword: "responsibility farmland" piloted in Anhui

At the end of the 1950s, China experienced the "Great Leap Forward" and the movement of people's communes, which led to serious economic difficulties, and the Chinese people fell into the situation of "not enough to eat." In order to mobilize the enthusiasm of farmers for production, Zeng Xisheng, the first secretary of the Anhui Provincial Party Committee of the CPC, proposed at the end of 1960 that farmland should be subcontracted according to the labor force of members, and work points should be recorded according to the actual output. Later, in the process of the pilot and promotion of this method, it was further developed into the modes of assigning production quotas to teams, assigning production quotas to fields, assigning a large amount of farm work to groups, and assigning a small amount of farm work to households. The rewards and compensation would be calculated according to the proportion of the workers in large and small farm work. This changed the previous situation of doing different work and receiving the same work points and realized the labor model of being responsible for oneself, which was the "responsibility farmland" approach.

At that time, Anhui's agricultural production was seriously reduced, food was extremely scarce, and the phenomenon of "famine, flight, hunger, disease, and death" was widespread. In order to focus on leading the people of Anhui through difficulties, Zeng Xisheng resigned as the first secretary of the Shandong Provincial Party Committee and returned to Anhui

Figure 41.
On January 6, 1958, Zhou Enlai had a cordial talk with farmers during his inspection in Feixi County, Anhui Province.

Knowledge about CPC History
In January 1961, the 9th Plenary Session of the 8th CPC Central Committee was held in Beijing. In view of the serious imbalance in the proportion of the national economy and the difficult situation caused by the "Great Leap Forward," the meeting formally adopted the eight-character policy of "adjusting, consolidating, enriching, and improving" the entire national economy.

by train in February 1961. He held a meeting of local and municipal party committee secretaries and proposed the method of "responsibility farmland," which was supported at the meeting of the provincial party committee secretariat. During the Central Working Conference held in Guangzhou, Mao Zedong listened to Zeng Xisheng's report on the methods, benefits, possible problems and solutions of the pilot of the "responsibility farmland." At this time, Mao Zedong learned that there were serious disasters in rural areas across the country, and he was having trouble sleeping and eating about how to resume agricultural production and increase grain output. When he learned that the implementation of "responsibility farmland" could significantly increase grain output, he said to Zeng Xisheng, "Well, just pilot it, and if you fail, you can still learn a lesson from it. If you succeed, then there will be an increase of 1 billion *jin* (2 *jin* = 1 kg) of the grain, and that's a big deal." The "responsibility farmland," which was approved by Anhui farmers, then got the approval of Mao Zedong, was immediately widely developed in rural areas.

In the second half of 1961, Zeng Xisheng personally led the working group to the outskirts of Hefei to carry out the "responsibility farmland" pilot project. In July, Anhui Provincial Party Committee deployed and promoted the "responsibility farmland." By the middle of October, 84.4% of the total production teams in the province had implemented "responsibility fields," and 90.1% by the end of the year. At the beginning of 1962, the CPC Central Committee held a meeting of 7,000 people. During the meeting, the CPC Central Committee decided to reorganize the Anhui Provincial Party Committee. The restructured Anhui Provincial Party Committee immediately started to "correct" the "responsibility farmland." Therefore, the "responsibility farmland" was only implemented for two years.

The implementation of "responsibility farmland" in Anhui was actually an important attempt to explore a path of rural economic reform that was suitable for China's national conditions. Although it lasted only for two years, it quickly reversed the economic situation in Anhui's rural areas and became a "life-saving field" for Anhui farmers. "Responsibility farmland" was also an important reform carried out by the Anhui people with an innovative spirit, which laid a solid ideological and cadre and mass foundation for the rise of rural reform later. Although the method of "responsibility farmland" was once suspended, in the late 1970s, "responsibility farmland" again emerged in the form of the household contract responsibility system, and then spread across the country, thus promoting the development of agricultural production. History has made a fair assessment of the right and wrong of the "responsibility farmland."

1962 Intellectuals Gathered in Yangcheng

Keyword: the convening of the Guangzhou Conference

The Guangzhou Conference of Intellectuals (Guangzhou Conference for short), held from mid-February to early March 1962, was an unforgettable event for the Chinese intellectual community to this day. At the meeting, Zhou Enlai, Chen Yi, Tao Zhu, Nie Rongzhen, and other comrades made a new scientific analysis and estimation of the status and role of intellectuals in socialist construction, which "sounded very friendly" to the delegates and made them "deeply moved and convinced," helping to relieve the intellectuals of their ideological worries and effectively mobilizing them to participate in socialist construction.

The Guangzhou Conference has its unique historical background and favorable conditions. On the whole, in January 1961, the 9th Plenary Session of the 8th CPC Central Committee formally decided to implement the Eight-Character Policy of "adjusting, consolidating, enriching, and improving" for the national economy. At the meeting, Mao Zedong called for a great rise in the wind of investigation and research, emphasizing the need to restore the fine tradition of seeking truth from facts. After the meeting, Mao Zedong, Liu Shaoqi, Zhou Enlai, and other central leaders took the lead in in-depth investigation and research at the grassroots level. All kinds of signs indicated that the national economy began to enter a new

Figure 42.
In January 1962, Hou Renzhi, a famous historical geographer, communicated with students.

track of comprehensive adjustment. Subsequently, a series of rules and regulations in the national economy, science, culture, and other fields were restored and established, laying the foundation for the development of science, education, and culture and the adjustment of intellectual policies. As far as the favorable conditions are concerned, since the first half of 1961, the CPC Central Committee had begun to formulate a series of regulations conducive to solving the problem of intellectuals, such as the "Fourteen Articles of Science" and the "Sixty Articles of Colleges and Universities," to provide specific guidance for the work of intellectuals. Especially at the beginning of 1962, the CPC Central Committee held a 7,000-member conference. The democratic spirit and self-criticism style promoted at the conference, as well as Mao Zedong and other leaders' new understanding and new views on intellectuals, provided a public opinion guarantee for the smooth convening of the Guangzhou Conference.

Knowledge about CPC History

On December 14, 1962, the CPC Central Committee made the *Decision on the Establishment of a Fifteen-Member Special Committee*. The main task of the Commission was to strengthen leadership over the construction of the atomic energy industry and the acceleration of the development and testing of nuclear weapons, as well as nuclear science and technology. The director was served by Zhou Enlai.

The Guangzhou Conference specifically includes the "National Conference on Science and Technology Work" and the "National Symposium on the Creation of Dramas, Operas and Children's Plays." On February 16, 1962, the National Conference on Science and Technology was the first to be held, with more than 300 delegates of scientists attending. When presiding over the opening ceremony, Nie Rongzhen stressed the "Three No Policy" of "no putting labels on others, no punishing others, and no seizing on others' mistakes or shortcomings" and encouraged delegates to express their views and fully contend to summarize the experience and improve work. In response to the questions generally raised by the delegates about the class attribute of intellectuals and their confusion about the formulation of "bourgeois intellectuals," Zhou Enlai subsequently issued a report entitled "On the Question of Intellectuals," which clearly pointed out that "whether before or after liberation, we have always put intellectuals in the revolutionary alliance, and regarded them as members of the masses." Chen Yi also made an important report to "take off the hat and crown" intellectuals, proposing to take off the hat of the bourgeoisie for intellectuals, and crown them as the proletariat and the working people, and affirmed that intellectuals were "one of the three major parts of the working people and a foot of the country."

The reports of leaders such as Zhou Enlai and Chen Yi responded to the urgent calls of the intellectual community and greatly inspired them to join the cause of socialist construction, which became an indelible memory in the minds of intellectuals of that generation. The correct understanding formed at the Guangzhou Conference was the deep reason for the smooth recovery and development of China's science, education, and cultural undertakings after serious setbacks. It was also a valuable reference for the CPC to deal with various complex relationships in the work of the united front.

1963 Lei Feng's Spirit Will Shine Forever

Keyword: learning from Comrade Lei Feng

On March 5, 1963, Mao Zedong wrote an inscription: "Learn from Comrade Lei Feng." The movement to learn from Lei Feng was immediately launched nationwide.

In 1940, Lei Feng was born into a poor peasant family in Wangcheng County, Hunan Province. At the age of 7, he became an orphan and survived with the help of villagers. In 1949, Lei Feng, with the help of the local government, joined the Children's League and went to primary school. In 1956, after graduating from primary school, he began to work as a correspondent in the township government and a civil servant in the CPC Wangcheng County Committee. He worked actively and was rated as a model by the county party committee. In 1957, Lei Feng joined the Communist Youth League of China. Since then, he had successively worked as a tractor operator and a bulldozer operator at Tuanshan Lake Farm and the Chemical General Plant of Liaoning Anshan Iron and Steel Company. Because of his outstanding work, he was awarded the title of "red flag bearer," "model worker," "advanced

Figure 43.
In March 1963, Mao Zedong wrote an inscription for Lei Feng.

producer," and "socialist construction activist" many times, and attended the Anshan Youth Socialist Construction Activist Congress.

Knowledge about CPC History
On March 1, 1963, the CPC Central Committee issued the *Instruction on the Campaign to Increase Production and Save and to Oppose Embezzlement and Theft, Speculation, Wastefulness, Decentralism, and Bureaucracy*, calling for this campaign to be carried out in a leading and systematic manner in organs and enterprises and institutions above the county level. Since then, the movement against the "five evils" was gradually launched in some cities throughout the country.

In 1960, Lei Feng was drafted into the army and joined the CPC in November of the same year. In the army, he received a higher level of education, improved his awareness, and truly served the people wholeheartedly with his own practical actions. In learning, he knew that his knowledge reserve was not enough, so he studied very hard to learn knowledge; in his post, he was willing to be a "screw" of silent dedication. According to Lei Feng's comrades in arms, he often went to the station near the army station to help the old and young passengers during holidays and breaks. He sent all the money he saved from frugality to the people in the disaster area or his comrades in arms who had difficulties in their families. Lei Feng regarded dedication as his career, and his moving deeds were countless.

On August 15, 1962, Lei Feng was unfortunately killed in the line of duty while carrying out a transport task. His life was very short, but it shines with countless lights. After Lei Feng died, on January 7, 1963, the Ministry of National Defense of the PRC named the class where he stayed "Lei Feng Class." Mao Zedong, Zhou Enlai, Liu Shaoqi, Zhu De, Chen Yun, Deng Xiaoping and other party and state leaders wrote inscriptions for Lei Feng. Mao Zedong wrote: "Learn from Comrade Lei Feng." Zhou Enlai wrote: "Learn from Comrade Lei Feng. He has a clear class stand of love and hatred, a revolutionary spirit that is consistent in words and deeds, a communist-style that is selfless in faced with the masses, and the proletariat's fighting spirit regardless of personal danger." Deng Xiaoping wrote: "Whoever wishes to be a real communist should learn from Comrade Lei Feng's character and style."

Time flies. Lei Feng has been away from us for more than 50 years. During this period, we have experienced many changes in the world, but the spirit of Lei Feng has always been with us, encouraging us, and urging us.

1964 The Oriental Loud Noise Shook the World

Keyword: the successful explosion of China's first atomic bomb

On August 6, 1945, when the World Anti-Fascist War was about to be won, the atomic bomb named "Little Boy" fell from the sky over Hiroshima, and a huge mushroom cloud rose, instantly destroying the city. For the first time, people all over the world saw the power of atomic bombs. Later, the cold nuclear war between the United States and the Soviet Union caused great panic in the world, especially in non-nuclear countries. Would possession of the atomic bomb bring disaster or peace? This aroused people's thoughts.

In 1946, Mao Zedong made a famous conclusion that the atomic bomb was a paper tiger used by the American reactionaries to frighten people. It looked terrible, but in fact, it was not. This was a clear understanding that the use of the atomic bomb was limited due to its excessive power. By the 1950s, the United States had repeatedly threatened its rivals with atomic bombs during the War of Resistance against America and Aid to Korea, and Mao Zedong's ideas had changed. He figured out this question: why do the US authorities make nuclear threats against China at any time? Why does the US dare to do so? It is because China

Figure 44.
China's first atomic bomb exploded successfully in Lop Nur, Xinjiang.

Knowledge about CPC History

On February 10, 1964, the *People's Daily* launched a report on "The Road to Dazhai" and simultaneously published an editorial on "A Good Example of Building Mountainous Areas with Revolutionary Spirit," introducing the deeds of the Dazhai brigade in Xiyang County, Shanxi Province at that time, which struggled hard and developed production on the barren mountain ridge. Since then, a movement of "learning from Dazhai in agriculture" was launched in rural areas across the country.

does not have atomic bombs, hydrogen bombs, and their means of delivery, it does not have a nuclear containment force, it does not have the same means of retaliation, and it does not have the power to counteract them. In 1956, Mao Zedong said at the enlarged meeting of the Political Bureau of the CPC Central Committee that we still needed the atomic bomb. He clarified that in the global context at that time, China couldn't live without atomic bombs if it didn't want to be bullied by others. In this way, China's nuclear industry was officially launched, and the research and development into the atomic bomb began.

On October 16, 1958, the National Defense Science and Technology Commission was established, with Nie Rongzhen as its director. In the same year, China completed the first experimental atomic reactor, and the development of the atomic bomb progressed smoothly. However, in June 1959, the Soviet Union unilaterally tore up the agreement on assistance to China in developing nuclear weapons. In August of the next year, all Soviet experts were evacuated, and important drawings and materials were taken away. The supply of equipment and materials was cut off. At this critical juncture, the CPC Central Committee resolutely decided to start from scratch and prepare to develop the atomic bomb in eight years.

In the spring of 1960, the Central Military Commission ordered General Chen Shiju to lead China's first special engineering units to enter Lop Nur and begin the construction of China's first nuclear test base. At the same time, the CPC Central Committee held many meetings to support the research on nuclear bombs from all sides. In a very difficult environment, many scientific and technological workers overcame difficulties, repeatedly tested and demonstrated. In March 1963, they put forward a theoretical design scheme for developing China's first atomic bomb. At the same time, the Northwest Nuclear Weapon Test Field and R&D Base had been completed, and national defense researchers had moved to the Northwest in succession, starting to enter the general breakthrough stage of developing atomic bombs. By the summer of 1964, China had finally broken through the technical difficulties of the atomic bomb and made great achievements in atomic bomb research.

At that time, under the pressure of the Soviet Union, the US and the United Kingdom to jointly oppose China's development of nuclear bombs, China responded to the attempts of a few major countries with practical actions. On October 16, 1964, China's first atomic bomb exploded successfully. Because the Soviet Union tore up the treaty in June 1959, this atomic bomb, named "596," was like a brand, always urging the Chinese people to work hard. The hard-won atomic bombing also fulfilled the Chinese people's dream of safeguarding world peace. With it, China would have the strength to compete with the world's nuclear powers. China would no longer be bullied by big powers and would be able to make its own contribution to world peace.

1965 Climbing the Peak of Science Bravely

Keyword: the first synthetic crystalline bovine insulin

On September 17, 1965, the Institute of Biochemistry of the Chinese Academy of Sciences and other units, after more than six years of hard work, artificially synthesized a bioactive protein-crystalline bovine insulin for the first time. This was big news in the scientific community, which meant that China became the first country in the world to achieve artificial protein synthesis.

Protein research had always been regarded as the key to solving the mystery of life. Bovine insulin is a kind of protein. Therefore, the synthesis of bovine insulin marked another step forward on the road to solving the mystery of life. However, the success of the artificial synthesis of bovine insulin was not accidental but it had experienced various difficulties.

In 1958, two scientific research groups from China, the United States and Germany, isolated from each other, independently proposed the topic of "insulin synthesis" almost at the same time. At that time, it was less than ten years since the founding of New China, and no one believed that China, with a weak scientific research foundation, could take the lead in completing this seemingly unattainable research task. The world's leading magazine *Nature*

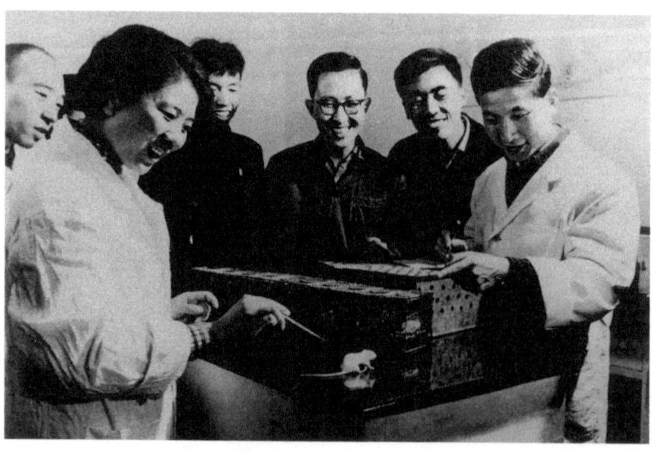

**Figure 45.
The first synthesis of crystalline bovine insulin in China**

> **Knowledge about CPC History**
> On April 12, 1965, the CPC Central Committee issued an instruction on strengthening war preparations. The instruction said that in view of the fact that the United States imperialism was taking steps to expand its aggression in Vietnam, directly invading the Democratic Republic of Vietnam and seriously threatening the security of our country, under the current situation, we should strengthen the preparations for war. The instruction called on the whole party, the whole army and the people of the whole country to prepare for the most serious situation in ideology and work, carry forward the spirit of patriotism and internationalism, and do everything possible to support the Vietnamese people in their struggle to resist the US and save the country.

once published an article saying: "Synthetic insulin is not yet possible in the near future." But the Chinese people took a brave step. At the end of December 1958, the topic of synthetic insulin was officially launched.

Initially, the scientific research on synthetic insulin was carried out in collaboration with the Institute of Biochemistry of the Chinese Academy of Sciences, the Institute of Organic Chemistry of the Chinese Academy of Sciences, and the Organic Teaching and Research Department of the Department of Chemistry of Peking University. However, in 1959, due to the changes in the domestic political environment, the work of insulin synthesis was also impacted. The initial "expert group research" turned into a "corps operation." Many young students without professional knowledge were involved in this project. As a result, several fronts emerged, many ironic jokes were made, and no progress was made in real scientific research.

From 1960 to 1961, the whole of China was in an extremely difficult period, and many projects, large and small, were abandoned. The insulin synthesis project cost a lot of manpower and material resources, brought about considerable losses, but made little progress. Therefore, national leaders once wanted to dismount this project. But in the end, the central leaders decided to stick to the project. In the second half of 1963, the domestic economic situation began to improve significantly, and the fate of synthetic insulin research also turned. In August of that year, under the direction of Nie Rongzhen, the Institute of Biochemistry of the Chinese Academy of Sciences, the Institute of Organic Chemistry of the Chinese Academy of Sciences and Peking University, three competing units, joined hands to carry out research again. At that time, the scientific research team with less than 30 people worked closely together again, and finally on September 17, 1965, a fully synthetic bovine insulin crystal was obtained. When the news was announced, the people of the whole country were elated. China had conquered the world's scientific challenges in less than six years, outperforming developed countries such as the United States and Germany. For China at that time, it was not only a proof of scientific research strength, but also a demonstration of China's international image.

Up to now, taking the lead in realizing the synthesis of bovine insulin is still one of the best proofs that China can make world-class achievements in the scientific field. We believe that there will be more and better scientific research achievements in the future to prove China's scientific research strength.

1966 Model Party Member Jiao Yulu

Keyword: the whole people learning from Jiao Yulu

On the afternoon of February 6, 1966, Qi Yue, a famous announcer of the Central People's Broadcasting Station, who had always been known for his solemn style and calm mind, encountered an unprecedented problem when recording a long communication: because he was deeply moved by the deeds in the communication, he cried several times during the recording, and the machine stopped and opened and stopped again. On the morning of the next day, "The Role Model of County Party Secretaries—Jiao Yulu," a long communication with strong emotional strength, was broadcast on Central People's Radio. This communication about Jiao Yulu's deeds in leading the cadres and masses of the county to fight against the disaster bravely, together with several editorials published later in the *People's Daily*, set off a nationwide upsurge to learn from Jiao Yulu. Jiao Yulu's name suddenly resounded in China's 9.6 million square kilometers of vast land, creating a spiritual monument in the hearts of Chinese people, especially party members and cadres.

In the winter of 1962, Lankao, Henan, suffered from waterlogging, sandstorms, and salinization. Jiao Yulu was assigned to Lankao as the secretary of the county party committee.

Figure 46.
Jiao Yulu

Knowledge about CPC History

In January 1966, the Ulan section of the Lanzhou-Xinjiang Railway from Lanzhou to Urumqi was delivered and put into operation, becoming the longest railway trunk line built after the founding of New China. This railway is the main traffic artery that runs through the east and west of China and plays an important role in developing the economy of the northwest region, strengthening national unity, and consolidating national defense.

After going to work, Jiao Yulu led the county committee team to set up the vow of "fighting hard for three to five years to change the face of Lankao. If we do not achieve the goal, we will not die in peace." Jiao Yulu had been serving the people of Lankao by trekking in the hot sun, rescuing disasters in the flood rapids, delivering food in the snow and wind, and appearing at the moment when the people needed him most. He planted paulownia trees, checked the tuyere, and explored quicksand. He devoted himself to the treatment of "three evils" and wished that one day could be broken into two days. As one of the leading cadres in the Lankao said, "Jiao Yulu spent 475 days in the Lankao by rushing."

In the autumn of 1963, Jiao Yulu's liver disease became more and more serious. When the pain hit him, he initially used the lump on the lid of his teacup and the pen in his hand to press down hard on the painful area. Later, in order not to delay his work, he put one side of the clothes brush against his liver and another side of it against the cane chair while working. After a long time, a hole was forced out of the cane chair. According to Jiao Yulu's daughter, several times when his father's work was just over, he was paralyzed by pain before he stood up. He was nearly 1.8 meters long and could not get up for a long time. His relatives and comrades urged him to see a doctor, and he replied with a smile, "I will see it when I have arranged the work that should be arranged," "Sickness is a thing that bullies the soft and the hard; if you suppress it, it will not bully you."

In March 1964, Jiao Yulu looked at the land of Lankao, where the treatment of the "three evils" was beginning to show results, and sat down at the table with deep emotion, wanting to write an article entitled "The People of Lankao Have Many Strong Ambitions, and Dare to Make Lankao Change Its Appearance." However, when the article just started, the illness forced him to put down his pen. In less than two months, Jiao Yulu left the land he was so attached to forever. At the end of his life, he only put forward one request: "I hope the Party organization will transport me back to Lankao and bury me in the sandpiles. I have not controlled the sand dunes while I am alive, and I will watch you control them after I die!"

Comrade Jiao Yulu, with his own practical actions, created a glorious image of a Communist Party member who had worked hard for the people. Whether it is his public servant feelings of "having all the people in his heart, but not himself," or his spirit rising to the challenge and hard work that "dares to make Lankao change its appearance" that emphasizes "revolutionaries should display gallantry in the face of difficulties," or his moral sentiment of "no specialization at any time" and "ten bans on cadres," they will transcend time and space, and will be forever engraved in the hearts of the people of the country.

1967 "Mushroom Cloud" Rushing into the Sky

Keyword: the successful explosion of China's first hydrogen bomb

A strong flash pierced the sky, a sudden loud noise was deafening, a red fireball lit up the sky, and a spectacular "mushroom cloud" rose in the sky ... At 8:20 a.m. on June 17, 1967, China's first hydrogen bomb exploded successfully. In a flash, a golden artificial red sun rose over the Gobi in Lop Nur, and people living in the area of Xinjiang Urumqi, Hami and Turpan exclaimed that there were two suns in the sky.

After the successful explosion of China's first atomic bomb in October 1964, Mao Zedong twice gave important instructions: "The atomic bomb should be available, and the development of hydrogen bomb should be fast!" Once the instruction came out, scientific researchers represented by Yu Min, Cheng Kaijia and He Zuoxiu accelerated the construction of the physical model of the hydrogen bomb and the breakthrough of key technologies, and overcame one technical difficulty after another in the development process. Although hydrogen bombs and the atomic bombs are both nuclear weapons, the former is fusion, and

Figure 47.
China's first hydrogen bomb exploded successfully in 1967.

the latter is fission. Their principles are quite different, and their power and lethality cannot be compared. In addition, the nuclear powers at that time thoroughly blocked information on hydrogen bomb research. China's hydrogen bomb manufacturing started from a blank sheet of paper, and each step was "crossing the river by feeling the stones."

Knowledge about CPC History

In January 1967, the Chinese "Heping II" solid combustion meteorological rocket was successfully test-fired. So far, the tasks included in the *Outline of the Ten-Year Development Plan for Jet and Rocket Technology* formulated in 1958 had been basically completed. China had the capability of medium- and close-range missile strikes and rocket launches, and a qualitative leap was made in aerospace power.

In order to find the technical path to break through the hydrogen bomb, Yu Min led the scientific research team to work at the Shanghai East China Computing Institute for more than 100 days and nights, often kneeling on the ground to analyze the piles of computing tapes, and finally formed a set of hydrogen bomb physical designs that was basically complete in principle, materials and configuration; in order to carry out the hydrogen bomb principle test by tower explosion, Cheng Kaijia and his colleagues in the Nuclear Test Technology Research Institute repeatedly calculated and simulated, "I don't know how many days and nights we have worked, nor how many times we have worked repeatedly and ineffectively," and finally achieved the success of the first hydrogen bomb principle test. In order to realize the development of hydrogen bombs from scratch in a short period of time, Chinese scientific researchers had become anonymous, rooted in the northwest desert, eating steamed bread mixed with sand and drinking bitter alkaline water. In the Gobi Desert, the sand and rocks were flying, and the cold wind was biting their bones on winter nights. Even so, they always enjoyed themselves. "Being a leaf of no importance, I would like to dedicate my life to grand schemes." The profound patriotic feelings, selfless dedication and firm ideals and beliefs of Chinese scientists are valuable spiritual wealth to inspire Chinese people to move forward bravely without fear of difficulties.

The success of China's first full equivalent hydrogen bomb air explosion test marked that China's nuclear technology had entered a new stage of development and innovation, further breaking the nuclear monopoly of the United States, the Soviet Union, the United Kingdom, and other countries, and once again causing shock to the world. The *Sunday Times* of the United Kingdom published a comment that read: "No country has made such rapid progress." Serge Bell, the science editor of the French news agency Agence France Presse, also published an article that read: "The amazing achievements of the Chinese people in detonating thermonuclear bombs have once again surprised experts around the world. What is surprising is the amazing speed at which the Chinese people have achieved this achievement." This "mushroom cloud" straight into the sky carries China's speed, ambition, and strength!

1968 Graben Became a Thoroughfare

Keyword: the complete and opening to traffic of Nanjing Yangtze River Bridge

The Yangtze River, China's mother river, has been known as the "golden waterway" since ancient times, making an indelible contribution to inland navigation in China but also causing inconvenience to the economic and cultural exchanges between residents on both sides of the rivers. The Yangtze River in Nanjing is like a belly band, with deep water and swift waves. The average width of the river is more than 1,500 meters, and the narrowest part is also 1,100 meters. The water depth is mostly 15–30 meters, the deepest part is more than 70 meters, and the flow rate is 3 meters per second. Such a dangerous terrain has formed a "natural graben along the Yangtze River." After the founding of New China, the Party and state leaders attached great importance to transportation construction, and the construction of the Nanjing Yangtze River Bridge was also included in the construction plan of New China.

On December 29, 1968, the Nanjing Yangtze River Bridge was completed and opened to traffic. It is located on the Yangtze River in the northwest of Nanjing, connecting the urban area and Pukou District. It is the first double-layer railway highway bridge designed and built by China on the Yangtze River. When the Nanjing Yangtze River Bridge was completed, it was recorded in the *Guinness Book of World Records* as the "longest highway railway bridge." Its upper road bridge is 4,589 meters long, and the roadway is 15 meters wide, which can

Figure 48.
Nanjing Yangtze River Bridge

accommodate four large cars in parallel, with more than 2 meters wide sidewalks on both sides; The lower railway bridge is 6,772 meters long and 14 meters wide. It is paved with double tracks. Two trains can run in opposite directions at the same time. The main bridge on the river is 1,577 meters long, and the rest of it are approach bridges. On the rails of the main bridge, the highway approach bridge adopts the form of a double-hole and double-arch bridge with Chinese characteristics. The railings on both sides of the main highway bridge are embedded with 200 cast iron reliefs, and there are 150 pairs of white magnolia-shaped street lights beside the sidewalk, and the whole bridge is like a rainbow over the river.

Knowledge about CPC History

On December 22, 1968, the *People's Daily* conveyed Mao Zedong's instruction: "It is necessary for intellectual youth to go to the countryside and receive re-education from the poor peasants." There was an upsurge of young intellectuals going to the countryside and mountainous areas. During the "Great Cultural Revolution," 16 million young intellectuals went to the countryside and mountainous areas.

The main bridge of Nanjing Yangtze River Bridge has 9 piers and 10 holes. Each pier is 80 meters high. The bottom area of each pier is more than 400 square meters, larger than a basketball court. The highest pier is 85 meters high from the foundation to the top. The distance between piers is 128 meters for the first hole on the north bank and 160 meters for the other nine holes. A 10,000-ton ship can pass under the bridge. There are four bridgeheads more than 70 meters high at both ends of the main bridge.

The Nanjing Yangtze River Bridge was built after the breakdown of Sino-Soviet relations. After the Soviet experts' withdrawal, the task of constructing the Nanjing Yangtze River Bridge fell to Chinese engineers. Therefore, this bridge was also called the "backbone bridge." When it was built, Mao Zedong's inscription of "independence and self-reliance" pointed out its symbolic significance.

Nanjing Yangtze River Bridge has been the symbol of China's national image for a long time. Whenever international friends visited China, state leaders often accompanied them to inspect the Nanjing Yangtze River Bridge. Zhou Enlai asked to use the magnolia-shaped lamp in Tiananmen Square as the street lamp of the bridge. In the past, the Nanjing Yangtze River Bridge often appeared on the pages of primary school textbooks. These showed how important and glorious the Nanjing Yangtze River Bridge was to the national construction in those years. Therefore, although the bridge is not on the tourist map of Nanjing today, it still attracts millions of tourists every year.

Over the past 50 years since the Nanjing Yangtze River Bridge was built, millions of passenger and cargo trains and more than 300 million vehicles of all kinds have passed over its dragon-like body, creating untold direct economic benefits. When it comes to the prospect of the bridge, engineers proudly said, "The quality of the bridge will not be a problem if it is used for another 70 years."

1969 Fighting for the Territorial Integrity of Our Motherland

Keyword: self-defense counterattack of Zhenbao Island

In Hulin City, Heilongjiang Province, China, there is an island with an area of only 0.74 square kilometers. This island was not originally an island but was separated from mainland China only in 1915 due to the long-term washout of the river, becoming a small island in the river. At the beginning of the 20th century, Chinese fisherman Zhang Gai built houses, planted vegetables, and fished on the island, so it was named "Zhang Gai Island" at that time. Since 1928, Chinese resident Chen Yuanjin and his son had lived on the island. Before 1945, Zhenbao Island was under the jurisdiction of the Gongsi Village of Hulin County and later under the jurisdiction of Hutou District. This area had been patrolled by Chinese border guards. Because people thought its shape looked like a gold ingot, they named it "Zhenbao Island."

Figure 49. Soviet tanks invaded the Chinese river on the west side of Zhenbao Island.

This small island on the border between China and the Soviet Union was in a calm and peaceful atmosphere when Sino-Soviet relations were friendly. However, since 1960, the Soviet Union had been planning and creating incidents on the Sino-Soviet border since the Sino-Soviet relations began to crack in the 1950s and 1960s. After 1967, the Soviet border guards began to invade the Chinese territory of Zhenbao Island, obstructing the Chinese border guards from patrolling the island, causing bloodshed many times, killing and wounding many Chinese border guards, and catching Chinese fishermen. As for the provocative acts of the Soviet army, the Chinese border defense forces strictly implemented the instructions of the Chinese government and the Central Military Commission and adopted a restrained and tolerant attitude. However, the Soviet government ignored the Chinese government's solemn protests and warnings, and the Soviet border defense forces' provocative acts were still unrestrained. In March 1969, a world-shaking conflict finally broke out.

Knowledge about CPC History
In August 1969, the CPC Central Committee decided to establish a national civil air defense leading group and provincial, municipal, and autonomous regional civil air defense leading groups to strengthen civil air defense work. Under the guidance of air defense leading groups at all levels, mass activities of digging air-raid shelters and air-raid trenches were carried out.

In the early morning of March 2, 1969, a certain unit of the Chinese army went to Zhenbao Island to stand by. If the Soviet side interfered with our patrol, it would give support to our border defense forces as appropriate. At 8:40 p.m., Sun Yuguo, the head of the border guard station, led the patrol team to patrol the island. When the Soviet army found out, it immediately sent 70 soldiers to the island in two ways, one way directly to Sun Yuguo's patrol team and the other way to encircle our patrol team from behind. At 9:00 p.m., the Soviet army suddenly opened fire, and several of our soldiers were shot and fell to the ground. The Chinese border patrol, out of self-defense, began to counterattack the Soviet army but was heavily shot by the Soviet army in the jungle. Yu Qingyang, a Chinese border guard, jumped up and shot at the Soviet army in the jungle to attract fire. The Soviet troops fired at him and hit him in the head. Soon after he fell down, he stood up tenaciously and continued to fire at the Soviet troops with his submachine gun until he died bravely. In this way, after more than an hour of fierce fighting, the Chinese border guards repulsed the Soviet border guards who had invaded Zhenbao Island. Later, the Soviet army carried out the second and third attacks on Zhenbao Island on March 15 and 17, 1969, respectively, which were repelled by our army.

This conflict was later called the self-defense counterattack of Zhenbao Island. The Chinese army won even though its weapons and equipment fell far behind those of the Soviet army, defending its own territorial security. The Soviet Union was shocked and had to make a new evaluation of China's conventional forces.

1970 "Dongfanghong" from Space

Keyword: the successful launch of China's first artificial Earth satellite

Since ancient times, human beings have had the dream of flying into space. The ancients made many seemingly clumsy attempts, such as wearing wings made of feathers to fly like birds or sitting in hot air balloons to fly to a certain height. However, the real sense of man's entry into space was the launch of the first artificial Earth satellite by the Soviet Union on October 4, 1957. Since then, mankind has announced the arrival of the space age. It was also from this moment that the enthusiasm of all countries to develop and launch satellites grew, including China, which aspired to become a technological power.

On October 13, 1957, the Chinese Academy of Sciences held a symposium. Famous scientists Zhao Jiuzhang and Qian Xuesen proposed that China should develop artificial satellites. During the 3rd National People's Congress held in 1964, Zhao Jiuzhang, who had studied for a long time and was confident, wrote a letter to Zhou Enlai, proposing to continue the development of artificial satellites. This proposal was supported by leaders such as Nie Rongzhen, Zhang Aiping, Zhang Jinfu, and scientists, such as Zhu Kezhen and Qian Xuesen. In 1965, the Chinese Academy of Sciences established the Satellite Design Institute. Under the leadership of the scientist Qian Ji, the researchers demonstrated the overall plan for China's

Figure 50. Dongfanghong-1 satellite operating in space

first artificial satellite. It was hoped that, on the basis of ensuring the successful launch of satellites, other indicators would be one step ahead of those of other countries, that was, they could send a continuous signal without interruption. But what signal should be chosen? Scientific researchers thought of the famous dance epic "Dongfanghong" ("The East Is Red") at that time, which was a recognition signal with Chinese characteristics. The receiving and broadcasting system of "Dongfanghong" music was unique to China's first satellite. In 1966, the relevant departments agreed that China's first man-made satellite was named "Dongfanghong-1."

Knowledge about CPC History

In November 1970, Zhou Enlai chaired the meeting of the Political Bureau of the CPC Central Committee and approved in principle the report on the construction of the Gezhouba Water Control Project, a component of the Three Gorges Water Control Project. On December 30 of the same year, the Gezhouba Water Control Project broke ground and took 18 years to complete. By the end of 1988, the entire Gezhouba Water Control Project was completed.

In December 1967, the overall goal of China's first satellite was to be able to go up, grasp, see, and hear. "Dongfanghong-1" went through the development stages of appearance, prototype, sample, and authentic sample, and a vast number of scientific researchers worked hard to overcome one difficulty after another. On April 1, 1970, two "Dongfanghong-1" satellites and one "Long March 1" carrier rocket arrived at the Northwest Jiuquan Satellite Launch Center. At 9:35 p.m. on April 24, the exciting moment finally arrived. The "Long March 1" carrier rocket carrying the "Dongfanghong-1" satellite was launched. Ten minutes later, the satellite successfully entered orbit. At 10:00 p.m., the carrier rocket stages 1, 2, and 3 worked normally, the satellite and the rocket separated normally, and the satellite entered orbit accurately. Zhou Enlai was very happy when he got the news and announced the news that China had successfully launched its first artificial satellite at the meeting of the three countries and the four parties that were being held the next day.

"Dongfanghong-1" opened a new era of space technology in China. Since then, China's satellite industry has developed vigorously. Remote sensing satellites have been successfully launched and recovered many times; the synchronous communication satellite was successfully launched and fixed; the polar-orbiting meteorological satellite was successfully launched. This series of achievements demonstrates that China's satellite technology has reached the world's advanced level in many important fields and that China has embarked on a path of satellite development in line with China's national conditions and has Chinese characteristics.

1971 The Five-Star Red Flag Rose at the United Nations

Keyword: China resuming its seat in the United Nations

On October 25, 1971, the 26th United Nations General Assembly adopted a resolution to restore the legitimate seat of the PRC. When the news came, the whole of China celebrated. Looking back on the process of China's restoration of its legitimate seat in the United Nations, it can be said that China experienced many twists and turns.

As early as September 1950, the Soviet Union, India and other countries proposed to the United Nations to restore China's legitimate seat. But under the manipulation of the United States, the fifth United Nations General Assembly vetoed these proposals and decided to form a seven-member special committee to consider the issue of China's representation. Until a resolution was made, representatives of the "Republic of China" were still allowed to occupy seats in the United Nations. During the ten years from 1951 to 1960, the United States refused to allow the General Assembly of the United Nations to discuss the issue of China's representation, using the excuse of the so-called "China's aggression against Korea."

Figure 51.
The Chinese delegation beamed at the UN General Assembly.

Knowledge about CPC History
From April to June 1945, delegates from more than 50 countries met in San Francisco and signed the *Charter of the United Nations*, and Dong Biwu, the representative of the CPC, signed the Charter. China, the United Kingdom, France, the United States, and the Soviet Union were permanent members of the United Nations Security Council and founding members of the United Nations.

In 1961, the General Committee of the 16th United Nations General Assembly adopted the topic of discussing China's seat in the United Nations. This was undoubtedly the first wake-up call to the heavy obstacles put up by the United States to prevent China from regaining its rightful seat. The United States then proposed that the restoration of China's representation must be approved by a two-thirds majority of the General Assembly of the United Nations, with a view to further delaying the resolution of the issue of China's representation.

At the 25th United Nations General Assembly, the proposal "On Restoring China's Legal Rights" put forward by 18 countries, including Albania, was supported by 51 countries and opposed by 47 countries. This was the first time in 20 years that more than half of the countries supported the restoration of China's legal seat, and although it was not adopted because it was less than two-thirds, it foreshadowed the end of the United States policy of isolating China, and China's restoration of its legal seat in the United Nations was not far off.

On September 21, 1971, the 26th United Nations General Assembly opened. The 23 countries, including Albania and Algeria, put forward to the General Assembly a proposal to restore all the legitimate rights of the PRC in the United Nations and immediately expel the representatives of the Chiang Kai-shek clique from all the organs of the United Nations. The General Assembly held a heated debate on the issue of restoring China's seat. At the 1976 plenary meeting on the 25th, the proposal was voted on. The General Assembly first rejected, by 59 votes to 55, the proposal of 22 countries, including the United States and Japan, that a two-thirds majority of the General Assembly of the United Nations be required for the restoration of China's representation and then rejected, by 61 votes to 51, the proposal of US Representative Bush to delete the phrase "to expel the representatives of the Chiang Kai-shek clique immediately from the seats they illegally occupy in the United Nations and in all its organs." Subsequently, the General Assembly adopted the proposal to "restore all the legitimate rights of the PRC in the United Nations and immediately expel the representatives of the Chiang Kai-shek clique from all organs of the United Nations" by 76 votes in favor, 35 votes against and 17 abstentions.

The restoration of China's legitimate seat in the United Nations was a major breakthrough in China's diplomatic work, the result of the joint efforts of all peace-loving and justice-upholding countries in the world, and of profound significance. As an American newspaper said at that time, the United Nations had entered a new era since China's five-star red flag was first raised at the United Nations headquarters.

1972 Handshake across the Pacific

Keyword: US President Nixon visiting China

At 11:30 a.m. on February 21, 1972, President Nixon's special plane landed at Beijing Airport. Nixon had not yet stepped down the gangway of the plane when he extended his hands to Zhou Enlai, who was coming to meet him. Zhou Enlai immediately welcomed them, and they clasped their hands tightly. In Nixon's words at that time, "I shook hands with the Chinese people across the Pacific Ocean." Later, the week of Nixon's visit to China was a week that changed the world. In the world pattern at that time, the "two big ships" of China and the United States began to make a big turn. As a result, China and the United States gradually broke the ice and began to establish mutually respectful international relations.

The idea of Nixon visiting China had been around for a long time. In the 1960s, Nixon entered the White House and became the President of the United States. He advocated improving China-US relations, carrying out "balance of power diplomacy," strengthening the strength of the United States against the Soviet Union, and adjusting its policy toward

Figure 52.
On February 21, 1972, Mao Zedong met with Nixon.

Asia. As a result, the United States repeatedly made a gesture of seeking to "improve relations with the CPC," including taking the initiative to establish a channel for exchanging messages with China through Pakistan and Romania. On the Chinese side, in the early 1970s, Mao Zedong and Zhou Enlai, proceeding from the need for the diplomatic strategy to adjust the relationship between China, the United States, and the Soviet Union, sent a message that they were willing to contact the United States and strive to break the stalemate between China and the United States by entrusting American journalist Snow to deliver a message and inviting the American table-tennis teams to visit China.

Knowledge about CPC History

On September 25 to 29, 1972, Japanese Prime Minister Kakuei Tanaka was invited to visit China. Zhou Enlai and Kakuei Tanaka held talks on the normalization of diplomatic relations between China and Japan. Mao Zedong met with Kakuei Tanaka. On the 29th, representatives of China and Japan signed the *China-Japan Joint Statement* in Beijing, which normalized the diplomatic relations between China and Japan.

In 1971, the United States proposed to hold a high level dialogue with China. The Chinese government believed that to fundamentally improve China-US relations, the United States must withdraw all armed forces from Taiwan and the Taiwan Strait. The only way to resolve this critical issue was through direct talks between the two countries at a high level. Therefore, the Chinese government reiterated its willingness to publicly welcome Dr. Kissinger, the US Special Envoy, the US Secretary of State, or even the US President himself to Beijing for direct talks. Nixon agreed with this and arranged for Kissinger to visit China first to hold a preparatory meeting. China agreed with this proposal. On July 9, 1971, Kissinger arrived in China. China and the United States discussed the issues about the international situation and China-US relations, reached an agreement on Nixon's visit to China, and issued a statement on July 15. The announcement pointed out that President Nixon expressed his wish to visit the PRC, and Premier Zhou Enlai, on behalf of the Government of the PRC, invited President Nixon to visit China at an appropriate time before May 1972. President Nixon accepted the invitation with pleasure.

After that, there was a scene in which Zhou Enlai greeted US President Nixon. Later, Mao Zedong met with President Nixon, and China and the United States held talks, focusing on issues of Indochina and Taiwan, China. On February 28, 1972, after repeated consultations, the United States and China finally issued the *Joint Communiqué* in Shanghai (also known as *Shanghai Communiqué*). On January 1, 1979, China and the United States formally established diplomatic relations, starting a new stage in the development of bilateral relations.

1973 China's Speed Caught Up with the World

Keyword: the successful manufacture of China's first million-times integrated circuit electronic computer on a trial basis

On August 26, 1973, surprising news came out from Peking University, Beijing Cable Power Plant, the Ministry of Combustion and Chemical Industry, and other units. The first integrated circuit electronic computer with one million operations per second in China jointly developed by them was successfully trial produced. Up to August 1973, in more than half a year, after more than 3,000 hours of trial operation, it had been proved that this computer had stable performance and good quality. The main indicators of the host computer, such as problem-solving ability, external equipment and management, language compilation, and symbol assembly, had all met the design requirements. This was a major achievement in the history of contemporary Chinese science and technology development and a milestone in the history of Chinese computer development.

The level of computers directly reflects a country's scientific and technological competitiveness. In the 1950s and 1960s, our country mainly relied on paper and pen when conducting mathematical operations. Chen Jingrun, a famous mathematician, studied the

Figure 53.
China's first million-times integrated circuit electronic computer

Knowledge about CPC History

On March 10, 1973, according to Mao Zedong's instructions, the CPC Central Committee decided to restore Deng Xiaoping's organizational life and the post of Vice Premier of the State Council. On April 12, Deng Xiaoping attended the reception by Zhou Enlai to welcome Prince Sihanouk, the head of state of Cambodia, back to Beijing from the liberated areas of Cambodia and made a public appearance in the state affairs activities.

Goldbach Conjecture in 1966 and successfully proved "1+2." At that time, the news caused a sensation in the world. He filled several sacks with the drafts of his calculations with pen and paper. What a hard calculation! However, if Chen Jingrun could have a large computer to perform tedious data processing at that time, his mathematical achievements would be far more than "1+2."

It was precisely because of the recognition of the importance of computers that in the 1950s, Professor Hua Luogeng, a famous mathematician in China, and Professor Qian Sanqiang, the founder of China's atomic energy industry, recruited talents from relevant fields at home and abroad to join the ranks of the development of China's computer industry. In 1956, Zhou Enlai listed computer development as the focus of national scientific and technological development. In 1958, with the help of Soviet experts, China developed the first computer in only two years, with a running speed of 1,500 times per second and a memory capacity of 1,024 bytes.

However, China was not satisfied with being able to make computers since it had higher goals and pursuits. Because of this, in 1973, China's first integrated circuit electronic computer with one million operations per second came out. This computer had a word length of 48 bits, an internal storage capacity of 130,000 words, and a total of 22 external devices of nine types, including tape drives, disk drives, typewriters, hole-making machines, and output and input machines. During the trial operation, the operator could accurately calculate the 200-order algebraic equations in only ten seconds. If the manual calculation was used, at least 100 people were required to calculate for one year. The operator also performed dozens of calculations on this computer for complex engineering design, weather prediction, seismic data processing, and other problems, all of which achieved good results. Some of these problems, which were difficult for small and medium-sized computers to complete, could be calculated more quickly with this computer. The success of its trial production marked another big step forward in China's computer technology.

Such success was rare and inspiring at that time. After that, China's computer industry developed vigorously and made many surprising and amazing breakthroughs.

1974 New Thinking of China's Diplomacy

Keyword: strategic thinking in dividing "Three Worlds"

On February 22, 1974, Mao Zedong met with Zambian President Kaunda. During the meeting, Mao Zedong mentioned for the first time the idea of the "Three Worlds" division. He pointed out that the United States and the Soviet Union were the first world countries; the centrists, Japan, Europe, and Canada, were the second world countries; China was the third world country. Why was this distinction made? Mao Zedong believed that the United States and the Soviet Union were rich with many atomic bombs. The second world, namely, Europe, Japan, Australia, and Canada, were not so rich but richer than the third world. The third world had a large population. All the countries in Asia, except Japan, were the third world. The whole of Africa was the third world, and Latin America was also the third world. Mao Zedong did not make these remarks on the spur of the moment, but were the result of long-term observation and reflection.

As early as the 1950s, there was growing recognition of the need for a specialized term to describe the new types of countries that were emerging in the world landscape, which differed significantly from the developed world. At that time, the division was that the capitalist countries led by the United States were the first world, the socialist camp led

Figure 54.
On April 10, 1974, Deng Xiaoping addressed the Sixth Special Session of the United Nations General Assembly.

by the Soviet Union was the second world, and outside the two camps was a group of new countries that had just won independence. Obviously, such a division was not comprehensive. By the 1970s, major changes had taken place in the international situation. The competition between the United States and the Soviet Union was developing in favor of the Soviet Union, and the United States was weakened, so it began to adjust its foreign policy. On the one hand, it opened the door to improve China-US relations; on the other hand, it sought to get away from Indochina in order to concentrate on ensuring its position in Europe. Mao Zedong keenly observed the international situation and put forward the theory of the "Three Worlds" division.

Knowledge about CPC History

Mao Zedong's theory on the division of "Three Worlds" sprouted from his "middle zone theory" in the 1940s. In August 1946, Mao Zedong put forward in a talk with the American journalist Anna Louis Strong that the United States and the Soviet Union were separated by the middle zone composed of many capitalist countries and colonial and semi-colonial countries in Europe, Asia, and Africa. Before the United States attacked the Soviet Union, it must first bring these middle zone countries into its sphere of influence.

The theory of the "Three Worlds" division strengthened the ties between China and other underdeveloped third world countries, indicating that the two superpowers were the main sources of the world's unrest and turmoil at that time and hoped to get support and help from the second world countries. On April 6, 1974, Deng Xiaoping led a Chinese delegation to New York, the United States, to attend the sixth special session of the General Assembly of the United Nations. This was the first time that a leader of the PRC attended a United Nations conference, and it attracted worldwide attention. It was proposed by Mao Zedong that Deng Xiaoping should be the head of the delegation. On April 10, Deng Xiaoping delivered a report at the conference, comprehensively elaborating Mao Zedong's theory on the division of the "Three Worlds" and explaining China's foreign policy. He pointed out that China was a socialist country as well as a developing country, and China belonged to the third world. China had similar suffering experiences to most third world countries and faced common problems and tasks. China regarded it as its sacred international obligation to resolutely fight with other third world countries against imperialism, hegemonism, and colonialism.

As the guiding ideology for China to formulate and adjust its foreign policy at that time, the theory of "Three Worlds" conformed to the objective needs of historical development, won the recognition of many countries, and added vitality to China's diplomacy.

1975 Open-Mindedness and Tolerance Created an Often-Told Story

Keyword: amnesty of war criminals

On March 17, 1975, the Second Session of the Standing Committee of the 4th National People's Congress was held in Beijing. At this meeting, it was decided to grant amnesty and civil rights to all prisoners of war.

Under the leadership of the CPC, the Chinese people won the New Democratic Revolution and established New China after an indomitable struggle. Criminals who fought against the CPC and the people in the war had become prisoners of the people. What should be done about these war criminals? The CPC Central Committee initially established a policy of "giving way out" to educate and reform war criminals so that they could become new people who reflected on their sins and embraced peace.

In order to implement this policy, the CPC Central Committee also carefully arranged organizations and departments responsible for the management of war criminals to provide them with a good environment for learning and reforming through labor. Before

Figure 55.
The pardoned people went to Beijing.

the National Day in 1959, according to Mao Zedong's opinion, the CPC Central Committee proposed to the Standing Committee of the National People's Congress a special amnesty for war criminals, which was quickly responded to. On September 17, 1959, President Liu Shaoqi issued the *Decree of the Chairman of the People's Republic of China on Amnesty*, and a number of reformed war criminals left the prison. This action aroused strong repercussions both nationally and internationally, demonstrating the enlightened policy adopted by the CPC in reforming war criminals. Later, the CPC Central Committee decided to release a group of war criminals every year. However, after the outbreak of the "Great Cultural Revolution," the amnesty work came to a standstill.

Knowledge about CPC History

In October 1975, the Chinese Academy of Agriculture and Forestry Sciences held a hybrid rice appraisal meeting in Changsha, which was attended by agricultural scientists from 21 provinces, cities and autonomous regions, to identify indica hybrid rice that had been studied and tested in 1964. Subsequently, indica hybrid rice was gradually popularized and planted in large areas in China, resulting in huge yield gains.

On March 17, 1975, the Second Session of the Standing Committee of the 4th National People's Congress was held in Beijing. After discussion, the meeting unanimously agreed on Zhou Enlai's proposal on amnesty for all prisoners of war and Hua Guofeng's statement and adopted the *Decision of the Standing Committee of the National People's Congress on Amnesty and Release of All Prisoned War Criminals*. For the amnestied war criminals, those who were capable would be assigned appropriate jobs; those who were sick would be treated like our cadres and enjoy publicly funded medical treatment; those who were incapacitated would be supported; those who were willing to return to Taiwan could do so, with adequate travel expenses and convenience provided. Two days later, the Supreme People's Court issued a release notice, and 293 war criminals were released. These war criminals shed tears of excitement when they received the notice. At that time, when a reporter went to interview them and asked about their life in prison, a prisoner of war said with emotion, "We were given preferential treatment in food and housing, and the Communists did not kill or humiliate us. Although we were prisoners of war, we lived in the same management house as ordinary civilian houses and ate the same food as the Communist cadres."

The amnesty of war criminals showed the openness and tolerance of the CPC, interpreted the humanitarian spirit of the CPC, and made the world understand what was called "good for bad." Because of this, the CPC won the respect of the world.

1976 Tangshan Was in Trouble, and All Sides Helped

Keyword: Tangshan earthquake

History will always remember this moment: on July 28, 1976, at 3:42 a.m. Beijing time. Less than half a minute left the world in eternal pain.

Tangshan shrouded in darkness, was quiet. Suddenly, a dazzling blue light pierced the night sky. Then, the sky rotated, and the earth shook. Streets, railways, and buildings were dislocated, deformed, and collapsed with strong shaking ... Within 23 seconds, a famous industrial city in North China with a population of one million was razed to the ground and turned into ruins.

The earthquake, with a magnitude of 7.8 on the Richter scale, caused a huge disaster to the people of Tangshan: more than 240,000 people died, more than 160,000 people were seriously injured, tens of thousands of families were broken, and 97% of the ground buildings were destroyed. At that time, it was reported in the West that "Tangshan will be erased from the map of China."

Figure 56.
The PLA ran to Tangshan downtown for disaster relief because the road subsidence blocked the vehicles of the rescue forces.

Knowledge about CPC History

In July 1976, the Yunnan–Xizang Highway was completed and opened to traffic, becoming the fourth highway leading to Xizang after the Sichuan–Xizang Highway, the Qinghai–Xizang Highway, and the Xinjiang–Xizang Highway. Due to the complex geological conditions of the road section and the difficulties in construction, there were several stoppages during the construction. The opening of the Yunnan–Xizang Highway was of far-reaching significance for further improving the traffic conditions between Yunnan and Xizang and stimulating the development of areas along the line.

After the earthquake, due to the destruction of communication equipment and line interruption, conventional communication means couldn't be used. At the critical moment, the aircraft of the Chinese PLA stationed in Tangshan Air Force took off to Beijing in an emergency; Li Yulin of Kailuan Mine and others also drove an ambulance to Beijing. After arriving in Beijing, Li Yulin and others reported to the leaders of the Political Bureau of the CPC Central Committee about the Tangshan earthquake. When they talked about the tragic scene of the earthquake, the party and state leaders couldn't help crying.

After listening to the report of Li Yulin and others, as well as information from other sources, the Political Bureau of the CPC Central Committee studied the Tangshan earthquake relief plan in time and made specific arrangements. In order to quickly organize forces for earthquake relief, the Political Bureau of the CPC Central Committee decided to form a central headquarters for earthquake relief and set up a front headquarters in Tangshan. On the day of the earthquake, rescuers rushed to Tangshan to send messages of condolences, letters of sympathy, and relief supplies to Tangshan in large quantities from all sides of the country.

On August 4, Hua Guofeng, entrusted by Mao Zedong, led the CPC Central Committee's condolences delegation to Tangshan to visit the people of Tangshan and convey the condolences and concerns of Mao Zedong and the CPC Central Committee. Thanks to the strong support of the people all over the country, the people of Tangshan were constantly striving for self-improvement and tenacity, and the relief and post-disaster reconstruction work was progressing smoothly. After more than 20 days of efforts, rescuers rescued a large number of victims, settled hundreds of thousands of people affected by the disaster, and initially resumed production and transportation.

After the earthquake, the people of Tangshan carried forward the earthquake resistance spirit of "selflessness in public, sharing weal and woe, perseverance, and courage," and gained new life in the destruction. After more than 40 years of construction and development, a brand-new Tangshan stood erect in the world. Today's Tangshan has not only healed the wounds of the earthquake but also kept up with the pace of the times.

Numerous Students Finally Realized Their Dreams

Keyword: resuming the College Entrance Examination System

In the eyes of most people, the term "college entrance examination" means too much. It is almost a baton of fate. Countless students spend their time just to gain victory in this battle without gunpowder smoke. However, this system was once abolished. After ten years of civil strife during the "Great Cultural Revolution," China experienced a serious talent gap.

On July 23, 1977, on the third day of his reinstatement, Deng Xiaoping summoned the leaders of universities to listen to the report. In view of the shortage of scientific and technological personnel, Deng Xiaoping advocated that key universities recruit students from fresh high school graduates.

From August 4 to 8, Deng Xiaoping presided over a symposium on scientific and educational work, inviting 33 scientists and educators to discuss and listen to their opinions on scientific and educational work face to face. The participants felt the trust of the CPC Central Committee and Deng Xiaoping deeply, and poured out their hearts one after another. Everyone unanimously requested that the current enrollment system of colleges and universities be reformed, and the entrance examination be resumed immediately. Deng Xiaoping asked, "Is it too late to change this year?" People said that it was not too late to change that year, and

Figure 57.
Scene of the 1977 college entrance examination

at best the registration time could be postponed. Deng Xiaoping immediately said that since there was still time that year, they would resolutely change! That year, they would make up their minds to resume the direct recruitment of students from high school graduates and resume the entrance examination for colleges and universities.

Knowledge about CPC History

The restoration of the college entrance examination system in 1977 put China's talent cultivation back on track for healthy development. In 1979, Deng Xiaoping clearly proposed that China should establish a degree system. In February 1980, the 13th Session of the Standing Committee of the 5th National People's Congress adopted the *Regulations of the People's Republic of China on Academic Degrees*, which was implemented on January 1, 1981, marking the formal establishment of China's academic degree system.

On August 13, 1977, the Ministry of Education, in accordance with Deng Xiaoping's instructions, held the second national conference on college enrollment. After 44 days of intense discussion, the *Opinions on the Enrollment of Higher Education Institutions in 1977* was finally issued. On October 12, the State Council approved this opinion, and formally decided to change the practice that colleges and universities did not take the examination for enrollment during the "Great Cultural Revolution" that year, and to resume the college entrance examination by adopting the method of voluntary enrollment, unified examination and selective admission. After the door of the college entrance examination, which had been closed for ten years, was reopened, it was immediately welcomed by all walks of life. That year became a carnival year for Chinese students. The earth of China was surging with students who wanted to take the examination.

From November 28 to December 25, more than 5.7 million young intellectuals poured into the examination rooms and participated in the college entrance examination that year, of whom 273,000 were admitted to university.

The restoration of the college entrance examination system opened the door to universities for a large number of young intellectuals who were delayed by the "Great Cultural Revolution" and provided opportunities to obtain higher education through examinations, their own efforts, and fair competition. As a result, young people in society had set off a new upsurge of learning scientific and cultural knowledge. A large number of professionals needed for national modernization had begun to be trained in a planned way and had become the backbone of China's reform and development today.

The college entrance examination not only changed the fate of individuals but also changed the fate of the country and the nation. In 2020, the number of applicants for the national college entrance examination was 10.71 million, and the number of students enrolled was 8.67 million. This means that China's higher education has grown luxuriantly after more than 40 years of development.

1978 A Profound Turn

Keyword: Third Plenary Session of the 11th CPC Central Committee

After the downfall of the "Gang of Four" in October 1976, the Party and the country faced a major choice as to where to go. On the one hand, the broad masses of cadres strongly demanded that the mistakes of the "Great Cultural Revolution" be corrected, that the chaos caused by the ten years of civil strife be completely reversed, and that the Party and the country rise again from danger; on the other hand, this desire to conform to the requirements of the development of the times met with serious obstacles, and the work of the Party and the state was wandering in the process of progress. At the same time, the world economy was developing rapidly, scientific and technological progress was changing with each passing day, national construction needed to flourish, and the discussion on the criterion for testing truth was surging. The development of the situation at home and abroad required our Party to make political decisions and strategic choices as soon as possible on the major policies that affect the future and destiny of the Party and the country.

Before the Third Plenary Session of the 11th CPC Central Committee, a 36-day central working conference was held. At this meeting, many revolutionaries and leading cadres of the older generation criticized the problems in the Party's leadership work in the past two years after the end of the "Great Cultural Revolution." They put forward reasonable suggestions on shifting the focus of the Party's work to economic construction, restoring and carrying

Figure 58.
Venue of the Third Plenary Session of the 11th CPC Central Committee

forward the Party's fine traditions. Deng Xiaoping delivered an important report entitled "Emancipate the Mind, Seek Truth from Facts, and Unite to Look Ahead" at the closing ceremony of the meeting. This central working conference made full preparations for the upcoming Third Plenary Session of the 11th CPC Central Committee.

Knowledge about CPC History

On May 10, 1978, the article "Practice is the Only Criterion for Testing Truth" was published in *Theoretical Dynamics*, an internal publication of the Central Party School. On May 11, *Guangming Daily* published it on the first page as a special commentator's article. Xinhua News Agency reprinted the full text on the same day, and the *People's Daily* and *PLA Daily* reprinted it the next day. On the 13th, it was reprinted by several provincial newspapers. This article aroused strong repercussions throughout the country, and an extensive discussion on the criterion for testing truth was launched.

From December 18 to 22, 1978, the Third Plenary Session of the 11th CPC Central Committee was held in Beijing. There were 169 CPC Central Committee members and 112 alternate CPC Central Committee members present at the meeting. Under the leadership of Deng Xiaoping and the support of other revolutionaries of the older generation, the Third Plenary Session of the 11th CPC Central Committee began to comprehensively and seriously correct the "Leftist" errors during and before the "Great Cultural Revolution" resolutely criticized the wrong policy of "two whatevers," fully affirmed the need to grasp the scientific system of Mao Zedong Thought completely and accurately, highly evaluated the discussion on the criterion for testing truth, and determined to emancipate the mind, set our wits to work, seek truth from facts, and unite to look ahead, resolutely stopped using the slogan of "taking class struggle as the key link," reviewed and solved a number of major unjust, false and wrong cases in the history of our Party and the merits and demerits of some important leaders, and made a historic decision to shift the focus of the Party and the country's work to economic construction and implement reform and opening-up.

The Third Plenary Session of the 11th CPC Central Committee marked the re-establishment of the ideological, political, and organizational lines of Marxism, the great awakening of the CPC in the new era, and the strong determination of the CPC to follow the trend of the times and the aspirations of the people and forge ahead with the new road of building socialism. Since then, under the spring breeze of the Third Plenary Session of the 11th CPC Central Committee, everything in the land of China had recovered and flourished, and everything had been put into full swing. Solving the problems left over by history had been carried out step by step. The construction of socialist democracy and the legal system had been on the right track. The leadership institution and system of the Party and the state had been improved step by step, and various national undertakings had been developing vigorously. Since then, China ushered in the spring of ideological liberation, economic development, political prosperity, vigorous education, literary and artistic prosperity, and scientific progress. The Party and the country had embarked on the great journey of socialist modernization with hope and vitality.

The Third Plenary Session of the 11th CPC Central Committee realized a great turning point of far-reaching significance in the history of the Party since the founding of New China, and opened a new historical period of reform and opening-up in China.

1979 The Policy of Peaceful Reunification

Keyword: "Message to Compatriots in Taiwan"

In Jinmen, the waves raised by the wind kept beating the shore, and a gray-haired old man stood on a crutch staring at the other side of the sea. Sunrise and sunset, the old man had maintained this habit for many years, and almost everyone who visited this beach knew that, rain or shine, there would be a man watching across the sea, but day by day, he had gone from a robust pace to a staggering gait.

At sunset, the old man took a bottle out of his pocket with a trembling hand and carefully threw it into the sea. It had been 30 years since this was the thirtieth drifting bottle. He didn't know whether they had reached the other side of the sea, whether anyone had picked it up, or whether they had forwarded it to his relatives in the distance. The old man silently watched the drifting bottle being swept away by the waves until it disappeared in the distance.

The old man did not know that there was also a letter sent from the other side of the sea, a letter promising to let him go home. The letter reads:

> Dear Compatriots in Taiwan:
>
> Today is New Year's Day in 1979. We hereby extend our cordial and sincere greetings to you on behalf of the people of all nationalities on the mainland of

人民日报

RENMIN RIBAO

停止炮击大、小金门等岛屿

中华人民共和国全国人大常委会

告台湾同胞书

(一九七九年一月一日)

Figure 59.
"Message to Taiwan Compatriots" published in *People's Daily*

> our motherland. As an old saying goes, "When festival times come around people think all the more of their loved ones." On this happy occasion, as we celebrate New Year's Day, our thoughts turn all the more to our kith and kin, our old folks, our brothers and sisters in Taiwan. We know you have the motherland and your kinsfolk on the mainland in mind too. This mutual feeling of many years standing grows with each passing day.
>
> From the day when Taiwan was unfortunately separated from the motherland in 1949, we have not been able to communicate with or visit each other, our motherland has not been able to achieve reunification, relatives have been unable to get together, and our nation, country and people have suffered greatly as a result. All Chinese compatriots and people of Chinese descent throughout the world look forward to an early end to this regrettable state of affairs ...

Knowledge about CPC History

From January 29 to February 5, 1979, Deng Xiaoping was invited to the United States for an official visit. This was the first time that Chinese leaders had visited the United States since the founding of New China. Deng Xiaoping said in his report in Washington that it was China's internal affair to solve the problem of Taiwan's return to the motherland. CPC would no longer use the term "liberate Taiwan." As long as Taiwan would return to the motherland, the reality and current system there would be respected.

This letter was the "Message to Compatriots in Taiwan" issued by the Standing Committee of the National People's Congress on New Year's Day in 1979. Its issue indicated that cross-strait relations would enter a new stage, and the cross-strait relations had opened a new historical chapter.

"Message to Compatriots in Taiwan" solemnly declared the major policy of striving for the peaceful reunification of the motherland and expressed the sincerest call of the motherland to Taiwan compatriots. It clearly stated that achieving China's reunification was the aspiration of the people and the general trend of the times; the realities must be taken into account to accomplish the great cause of the reunification of the motherland, and the current situation in Taiwan and the views of people from all walks of life in Taiwan should be respected, and reasonable policies and measures should be adopted to avoid losses to the people of Taiwan. At the same time, it clearly stated that the hope for solving the Taiwan issue lied in the Taiwanese and the Taiwan authorities. In order to change the state of isolation between the two sides of the Taiwan Straits, the "Message to Compatriots in Taiwan" clearly proposed to end the military confrontation across the Taiwan Straits through negotiation, remove the barriers that block the exchanges between compatriots on both sides of the Straits, promote free exchange, realize navigation, postal and trade links, and carry out economic and cultural exchanges.

On December 15, 2008, direct shipping, air transport, and direct mail services across the Straits were launched, announcing the advent of the era of "three links" between the two sides of the Straits. The lonely old man who looked across the sea should never be seen on the beach of Jinmen.

1980

The Grand Plan of the Special Construction Zone

Keyword: establishing Special Economic Zones

"In 1979, it was spring. An old man drew a circle near the South China Sea, where the city rose up like a myth, and the mountain of gold was gathered miraculously ..." With the beautiful melody of "The Story of Spring," people familiar with this period of history can't help thinking of the unforgettable word "special economic zones" in China's reform and opening-up history.

In 1977, China had just ended a decade of havoc, and everything here was waiting to prosper. In November, Deng Xiaoping went out for his first inspection after his comeback, and his first stop was Guangdong. In Guangdong, Deng Xiaoping's eyes were on Shenzhen, a small coastal county just across the river from Hong Kong. In that year, local farmers' daily income was only 1 yuan, while Hong Kong farmers' daily income was more than 60 Hong Kong

Figure 60.
Shenzhen Special Zone under construction in 1980

dollars. "How can we make the masses prosperous as soon as possible?" "How can China keep up with the pace of world development as soon as possible?" These problems caused Deng Xiaoping to think deeply ...

Knowledge about CPC History

From August 18 to 23, 1980, the enlarged meeting of the Political Bureau of the CPC Central Committee was held in Beijing, where Deng Xiaoping made a speech entitled "Reform of the Party and State Leadership System," forming a more complete basic idea of political system reform. In fact, this speech became a programmatic document for the reform of China's political system, especially the reform of the Party and state leadership system.

The Third Plenary Session of the 11th CPC Central Committee was held, which pushed China into a new era of reform and opening-up. In April 1979, at the Central Working Conference, the leading comrades of the Guangdong Provincial Party Committee put forward a new idea: taking advantage of the favorable conditions adjacent to Hong Kong and Macao, implementing special policies and flexible measures to accelerate the opening-up and economic development. Xi Zhongxun, then secretary of the CPC Guangdong Provincial Committee, reported to Deng Xiaoping about this idea. Deng Xiaoping was very happy and agreed with this assumption. Subsequently, the CPC Central Committee sent Gu Mu to lead leading comrades of relevant ministries and commissions of the State Council to Guangdong and Fujian for field visits.

The CPC Guangdong Provincial Committee and Fujian Provincial Committee reported to the CPC Central Committee respectively that they asked to designate some places in the two provinces to "take the lead" in the reform and opening-up, and to take advantage of the favorable conditions of neighboring Hong Kong and Macao to implement special policies to attract foreign capital and expand exports.

After repeated deliberation and research, on July 15, the CPC Central Committee and the State Council officially issued a document approving the reports of Guangdong and Fujian provincial committees, deciding to establish special export zones in Shenzhen, Zhuhai, Shantou, and Xiamen, and later renamed them "special economic zones" with more connotations.

On August 26, 1980, the 15th Session of the Standing Committee of the 5th National People's Congress approved the *Regulations of Guangdong Special Economic Zones* proposed by the State Council, announcing to the world that socialist China had established special economic zones. The *New York Times* of the United States exclaimed at that time: "The Iron Curtain has been opened, and the pointer to China's great change is being launched."

The birth and development of special economic zones showed that China had opened a window to the outside world and stepped toward the world. Without the "drill" of special economic zones, China's economic construction achievements wouldn't have reached the speed and height of today. As a breakthrough and experimental field of reform, as a window and base for opening-up, special economic zones have made a significant contribution to China's reform and opening-up history and will continue to strive to be the vanguard of China's economic construction in the future.

1981

Women's Volleyball Team's Performance Promotes the National Prestige

Keyword: Chinese women's volleyball team winning the World Championship for the first time

On November 16, 1981, the eyes of the whole world were focused on Osaka Stadium in Japan. That night, the final of the Third World Cup Women's Volleyball was held here, and the Chinese and Japanese teams had a leading match. It was also here that the Chinese women's volleyball team won the world championship for the first time and won the top of the world, opening a glorious era for the Chinese women's volleyball team.

The game between China and Japan that night was the climax of this competition, and the Chinese and Japanese teams were the favorites to win the championship. Before the start of the match, the Chinese team won 6 out of 6, and the Japanese team won 5 out of 6. After carefully studying and observing the match between China and the US the previous afternoon, the Japanese team seemed more confident, and they clamored to defeat the Chinese team. The Chinese team was calm and collected. They carefully analyzed the situation, were not arrogant or impetuous, and were determined to win. This was a fierce contest to compare ideas, will, style, tactics, and courage. Both sides were going all out.

Figure 61.
The Chinese women's volleyball team won five consecutive championships.

Knowledge about CPC History

In June 1981, the Sixth Plenary Session of the 11th CPC Central Committee was held in Beijing. The Plenary Session deliberated and adopted the *Resolution on Certain Questions in the History of Our Party since the Founding of the People's Republic of China*, made a correct judgment on the major historical events of the Party since the founding of the PRC, especially the "Great Cultural Revolution," and summarized and evaluated the merits and demerits of Mao Zedong and the basic content and guiding significance of Mao Zedong Thought.

The Japanese team, who had all the advantages of time, location, and people, and racked their brains to the match, seemed to be just a stone's throw away from the championship. However, the Chinese women's volleyball girls on the cusp of the storm were calm and imperturbable. They consolidated step by step and were getting stronger and stronger. They played tenaciously, stopped beautifully, hung lightly, and easily won the first two games.

With the last goal in the second game falling, the Chinese women's volleyball girls jumped excitedly, hugged each other, and began to celebrate the victory within reach. However, it was this strong sense of happiness that made the girls on the court lose their goals, and the war situation turned worse. They then lost two games in a row and fell behind 14:15 in the last game.

When the time came to decide the outcome, the head coach of the Chinese team, Yuan Weimin, decisively called for a pause. He stared at the girls of the Chinese women's volleyball team without saying a word, let the silence stimulate everyone, and then roared: "Let's not smear our faces, don't forget that we are Chinese!"

After listening to the coach's words, the players suddenly came to their senses. Relying on the heavy dunk of "Iron Hammer" Lang Ping and the block of "Tiananmen City Wall" Zhou Xiaolan, the Chinese team scored two consecutive points, 3:2, and won a difficult victory!

While the girls cried to welcome the victory, the Chinese people who waited in front of the radio and TV were even more enthusiastic. Many people gathered in Tiananmen Square and shouted all night: "Long live China, long live the women's volleyball team!"

It was a historic breakthrough for China in the world's three major ball games of football, basketball, and volleyball, winning the title of world champion for the first time and earning the honor for the motherland. The next day, the *People's Daily* published an article, "Learn Women's Volleyball Team, Revitalize China," praising the spirit of the women's volleyball team vigorously, and the patriotic craze swept the country. Later, the Chinese women's volleyball team won the championship in the 9th Women's Volleyball World Championships. In 1984, the Chinese women's volleyball team won the gold medal in the Los Angeles Olympic Games. In addition, in the 1985 World Cup and the 1986 World Championships, the Chinese women's volleyball team achieved an unprecedented five consecutive championships. As a result, the spirit of the women's volleyball team became a banner to encourage people from all walks of life to work hard for the motherland.

1982 No. 1 Document Opened a New Horizon

Keyword: establishing the Household Contract Responsibility System

In 1978, eighteen farmers in Xiaogang Village, Fengyang County, Anhui Province, took great risks to press a red fingerprint on the "life and death contract" of farm output quotas fixed by households, which opened the prelude to China's rural reform and pioneered the household contract responsibility system. At that time, they never thought that their bold action of "getting ready to risk everything" would make Xiaogang Village achieve a bumper harvest of food in less than a year and had a great demonstration effect. The "life and death contract" written on the paper torn from the children's exercise books, even with a few wrong characters, was thus recorded in history.

After the Third Plenary Session of the 11th CPC Central Committee, the household contract responsibility system was first implemented in Anhui, Sichuan, Guangdong, and other provinces. However, since there was no specific policy defining the household contract responsibility system at that time, many local governments inevitably had concerns and were conservative in promoting the reform and implementation of agricultural policies. On New Year's Day of 1982, the CPC Central Committee issued the No. 1 Document on the "three rural issues"—*National Rural Work Conference Minutes*, which clearly affirmed that fixing

Figure 62.
Xiaogang Village today

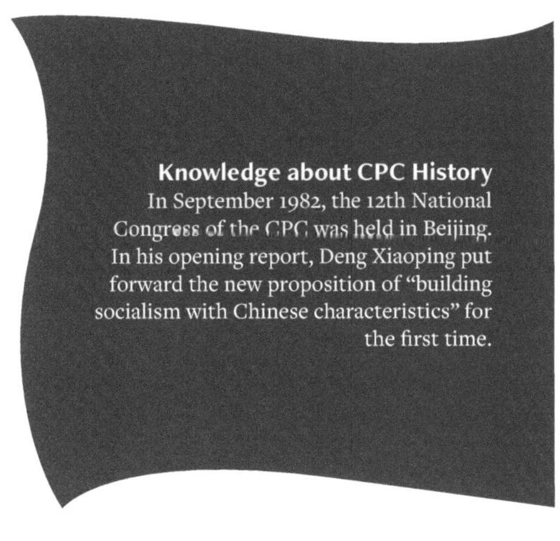

farm output quotas for each household and group, and household-based and group-based contract system and so on "were all socialist collective economic production responsibility systems," putting the relationship between fixing of farm output quotas for each household and socialism in one fell swoop, responding to the disputes in past policies and theories, and giving rural grassroots cadres and farmers a "reassurance." The family contract responsibility system was able to take root in the countryside in a justifiable manner.

Different from the small-scale peasant economy, the household contract responsibility system refers to a form of agricultural production responsibility system in which farmers contract land and other means of production and production tasks to collective organizations on a household basis. On the basis of respecting the interests of farmers, this system corrected the long-standing shortcomings of highly centralized land management and excessively monotonous management mode, enabling farmers to gain autonomy in labor and management in the collective economy. The production achievements were directly linked with interests, greatly mobilizing farmers' enthusiasm for production, giving better play to the potential of labor and land in China, and rapidly liberating the long-suppressed rural productivity, thus opening-up a new situation for China's rural economic system reform.

By September 1982, the production teams in rural areas nationwide that implemented the system of farm output quotas to individual households and farm output quotas fixed by household had accounted for 74% of the total. The 12th National Congress of the CPC fully affirmed this, emphasizing that "the various forms of production responsibility system established in rural areas have further liberated the productive forces, which must be adhered to for a long time, and can only be gradually improved on the basis of summing up the practical experience of the masses. We must not change lightly against the will of the masses, let alone go back."

Since then, the household contract responsibility system had increasingly shown its strong vitality, which had played a significant role in promoting China's agricultural development and improving the economic situation of farmers. From 1980 to 1984, China's grain output increased for five consecutive years, with an average growth rate of 5.4%. In 1982, China's total agricultural output value increased by 11.2% compared with 1981. Rural areas throughout China took on a new look. Farmers' enthusiasm for work was gradually stimulated, and the problem of food and clothing for farmers was preliminarily solved.

As a basic economic system in China's rural areas since the reform and opening-up, the establishment and promotion of the household contract responsibility system not only formed a system guarantee for China's agricultural development but also provided a solid agricultural foundation for promoting the reform and opening-up.

1983 "Three Orientations" Educated New Generation

Keyword: Deng Xiaoping proposing "Three Orientations"

In the early morning, the early autumn sun shone on Jingshan School, and in a corner of the playground, students in school uniforms neatly recited, "Education should be oriented to modernization, the world, and the future." The loud and clear voice, accompanied by the rising five-star red flag, went straight into the sky and broke through the sky. They wanted the whole of China to hear the voice that represented the direction of China's education development in the new era.

In 1983, it was at the stage of trying to carry out reforms in various undertakings across the country. Jingshan School, which had been the vanguard of the national primary and secondary education reform, also encountered unprecedented problems in the education sector. As He Hongchen, the main founder of Jingshan School, recalled, at that time, Jingshan School entered a new stage of a comprehensive reform of primary and secondary education, but how should the overall reform of primary and secondary schools in China be changed, and in what direction should it be designed? The problem that plagued the educational reform of China's primary and secondary schools was also puzzling them. At this important juncture, which concerned the success or failure of educational reform, the teachers of Jingshan

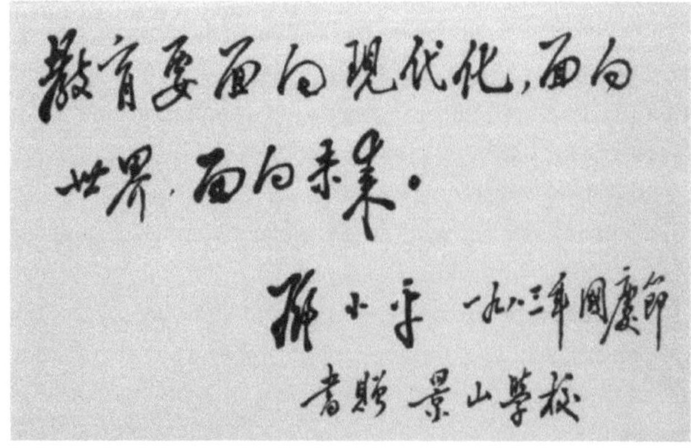

Figure 63.
Deng Xiaoping's inscription

Knowledge about CPC History

The "Four Qualifications" of the New Generation with "Four Qualifications" refer to the qualifications of socialist citizens "with high ideals and moral integrity and were cultured and disciplined." On May 26, 1980, Deng Xiaoping wrote an inscription to *China Youth Daily* and *Counsellor* magazine: "I hope that children all over the country will aspire to be people with ideals, morality, knowledge, and physical strength." This was the sprout of the "Four Qualifications" proposition.

School naturally thought of Deng Xiaoping, the chief designer of China's reform and opening-up. They decided to ask Deng Xiaoping to inscribe for the school or say a few words to point out the direction of educational reform for all teachers in the new era.

On September 7, 1983, the hopeful Jingshan School wrote a letter to Deng Xiaoping in the name of all the teachers and students. On October 1, Deng Xiaoping wrote an inscription for Jingshan School: "Education should be oriented to modernization, the world, and the future." The "Three Orientations" embodied his comprehensive review and strategic thinking on educational reform and development. On May 27, 1985, the *Decision of the Central Committee of the Communist Party of China on the Reform of the Education System* once again mentioned that education must be oriented to modernization, to the world and to the future. As a result, China's educational reform and development had strategic guidelines and development directions.

More than 30 years later, Jingshan School, located in Dengshi Street, Dongcheng District, Beijing, has developed rapidly. Under the guidance of Deng Xiaoping's thought of "Three Orientations," the school formulated a comprehensive overall reform plan of "laying the foundation for all-round development and developing personality education." In terms of educational theory, length of schooling, curriculum arrangement, teaching material content, teaching methods, teaching means, examination system, extracurricular activities, ideological and labor education, developing education of personality and specialty, education of supernormal intellectual ability and school leadership management system, it provided a rich experience for the reform and development of primary and secondary education in China.

Jingshan School is only one of the primary and secondary schools in China; the achievements of Jingshan School are also the epitome of the achievements of national educational reform and development.

Like a ship sailing through the wind and waves, Deng Xiaoping's inscription led China's education to a promising future. Later, people extended the connotation of "Three Orientations" to science, technology, and other social life fields as the guidelines and slogans for reform and opening-up work in this field and industry.

The Tight Pace of Construction of the Special Zone

Keyword: Deng Xiaoping inspecting the Special Economic Zones

One day 37 years ago, Deng Xiaoping took a special train to the south. He wanted to go to the special zones. The excited people of Shenzhen had prepared excellent rice paper, hoping the elderly could leave something for Shenzhen. However, until Deng Xiaoping left Shenzhen, the rice paper was still blank ... However, Deng Xiaoping did not disappoint the Shenzhen people. After inspecting the Shenzhen and Zhuhai Special Economic Zones, Deng Xiaoping wrote an inscription for Shenzhen on the Lunar New Year's Eve: "Shenzhen's development and experience have proved that our policy of establishing special economic zones is correct." The signing date was the date when he left Shenzhen—January 26.

History still remembers that moment at 10:05 a.m. on January 24, 1984, the special train from Beijing slowly pulled into Guangzhou Station. Lin Ruo, Secretary of the CPC Guangdong Provincial Committee, Liang Lingguang, Governor of Guangdong Province, and Wang Meng, Political Commissar of the Guangzhou Military Region, had been waiting here for a long time

Figure 64.
On February 1, 1984, Deng Xiaoping wrote an inscription for the Shenzhen Special Economic Zone: "Shenzhen's development and experience have proved that our policy of establishing the Special Economic Zones is correct."

and boarded the special train. As soon as Deng Xiaoping saw them, he said: "It is my idea to set up special zones. I will see if it can succeed."

Knowledge about CPC History

On October 1, 1984, a military parade and mass parade were held in the capital to celebrate the 35th anniversary of the founding of the PRC. Deng Xiaoping reviewed the troops and delivered a speech, highly valuing the universally recognized achievements since the founding of New China, especially since the Third Plenary Session of the 11th CPC Central Committee.

At that time, the development of the special zones was under great pressure: Is the name of the special zones "socialist" or "capitalist"? Was the special zone a "new foreign concession area"? In the face of all these doubts, it was necessary to make a fair judgment on the reform and opening-up of the Special Zone in the past three years. At that moment, Deng Xiaoping came. After inspecting Shenzhen and Zhuhai, Deng Xiaoping strongly affirmed the achievements of these two special economic zones and clearly pointed out that "the special economic zones do not only refer to Shenzhen, Xiamen, Zhuhai, and Shantou, but also Guangdong and Fujian provinces. Special Zone policy can not only be implemented in those few places; the central government hopes that both provinces should implement special policies and flexible measures. You should give full play to this advantage, figure out the rules and make a figure."

On February 24, Deng Xiaoping said in a talk in Beijing that we should have a clear guiding ideology for establishing special zones and implementing the policy of opening-up, that was, not to close, but to release. He also said that the special zones were a window of technology, management, knowledge, and foreign policy. From the special zones, people could also introduce technology, acquire knowledge, and learn management skills. Management was also knowledge. If the special coastal zones were well developed, the income could be higher, which could enable some places to get rich first because equalitarianism was undesirable.

In May of the same year, the CPC Central Committee decided to continue to expand opening-up, adding 14 coastal open cities. In January of the next year, three more coastal economic open zones were established: the Yangtze River Delta, the Pearl River Delta, and the South Fujian Delta forming a coastal open zone.

Since then, the rumors about the development of the special economic zones and the noise against the reform and opening-up disappeared instantly.

1985 Respecting Teachers, Valuing Education, and Spreading Virtues

Keyword: setting up Teachers' Day

In 1984, Wang Zikun left Nankai University, where he had taught for 32 years, and was transferred to the post of President of Beijing Normal University. During this period, he had been thinking about why teachers did not have their own festivals. After thinking about it, he couldn't help disclosing his idea to a familiar reporter of the *Beijing Evening News*, and it was soon published in the newspaper. A few days later, Wang Zikun held a meeting with Tao Dayong, Zhong Jingwen, Qi Gong, Huang Ji, Zhu Xianzhi, Zhao Qinghuan, and other famous scholars of Beijing Normal University to discuss and jointly advocate the establishment of a "Teachers' Day."

In fact, Wang Zikun jointly proposed to set up Teachers' Day because of his gratitude to teachers. Born in a poor family, he was able to go out of the remote village of Ji'an, Jiangxi Province, to study at Wuhan University when his family could not fulfill his dream of studying. Later, he worked at Nankai University and was sent to Moscow University for further study. Every step forward was inseparable from the care and support of teachers. He still

Figure 65.
Scene of celebrating the first Teachers' Day in 1985

remembered that when he couldn't pay the tuition fees and worried about his meal expenses every month, it was the teacher who saved him the expense, so that he had the opportunity to study and could study with peace of mind. Because of this, even after becoming a famous professor, becoming president of a famous university, and being elected as an academician of the Chinese Academy of Sciences, Wang Zikun always remembered his teachers' kindness. Whenever he returned to his hometown, he would visit his teachers at different times. He wrote letters to his middle school teachers every year until they died. He said: "The teacher is the guide for each of us. I hope the whole of society will respect this profession."

Knowledge about CPC History
On May 15, 1985, the CPC Central Committee and the State Council held the National Education Work Conference in Beijing. The meeting discussed the *Decision of the CPC Central Committee on Education System Reform (Draft)* and studied the steps and measures to implement the education system reform. On May 27, the CPC Central Committee promulgated the *Decision on the Reform of the Education System.*

The appeal of Wang Zikun and others received a positive response from the relevant departments. On January 21, 1985, the 9th Meeting of the Standing Committee of the 6th National People's Congress adopted a resolution to designate September 10 as Teachers' Day. In this way, all freshmen would recognize that teachers should be respected from the beginning of their enrollment, and society would have a good atmosphere of respecting teachers and valuing education. What Wang Zikun would never forget was the scene of the first Teachers' Day. It was September 10, 1985, when Li Xiannian, the then President of the State, wrote a letter to teachers across the country to congratulate them on Teachers' Day; the Publicity Department of the CPC Central Committee, the State Education Commission, the Beijing Municipal People's Government, the Central Committee of the Communist Youth League, the National Education Trade Union and other units held a grand meeting in the Great Hall of the People to celebrate the first Teachers' Day of New China. At the meeting, four students each raised a character to form "Long Live the Teacher." That scene made Wang Zikun excited and unforgettable.

Starting from the second Teachers' Day, all provinces and cities across the country celebrated Teachers' Day grandly. Party and state leaders participated in various commendation activities for Teachers' Day or went to various schools to express condolences to teachers in person. As a result, the teaching profession began to be valued and became an enviable profession; teachers' social status was improved, and they became a respected group; the seeds of respecting teachers and valuing education were also quietly sown in the minds of generations of students, promoting the improvement of the Chinese nation's civilization.

1986 Catching Up with High-Tech

Keyword: 863 Plan

From the ancient civilization five thousand years ago to the information society today, from the hardships of drilling wood to make a fire to the magic of voice-controlled chandeliers, from the huge body of a giant computer to the portable and small laptop, from the letters sent by geese from thousands of miles to the Internet that makes people be with each other though far apart ... What has made such big changes in the society we live in? What makes our life change with each passing day and develop at a tremendous speed? Yes, that's science and technology.

With the advent of the new technological revolution, the world situation had undergone profound changes since the 1980s. Economic competition became the main form of competition between countries, and the essence of economic competition was the competition of science and technology, especially the competition of high technology and talent. As a result, countries around the world significantly increased investment in science and technology and regarded the development of science and technology, especially high-tech, as an important element of national strategy.

Figure 66.
The sign of the National High Technology Research and Development Plan (863 Plan)

On March 3, 1986, a report entitled "Proposals on Tracking Strategic High-Tech Developments in the World" was submitted to the CPC Central Committee. Later, the high-tech research and development plan based on this report was called the "863 Plan." This report was jointly proposed by four famous Chinese scientists, Wang Ganchang, Chen Fangyun, Yang Jiachi, and Wang Daheng. In view of the urgent reality of the rapid development of high-tech in the world, the report suggested to the CPC Central Committee that in the face of the challenges of the new technological revolution in the world, China should not fall behind but move forward bravely. The report emphasized that China should start from then on and track the development process of new technologies with the funds and manpower within its reach, rather than wait until the economic strength would be quite good in ten or fifteen years, or China would miss the opportunity and end up in a situation of passive backwardness.

Knowledge about CPC History

On August 3, 1986, the Shenyang Municipal People's Government held a press conference to announce the bankruptcy treatment measures of Shenyang Explosion Proof Equipment Factory. Up to that time, Shenyang Explosion Proof Equipment Factory had lost money for ten consecutive years, and its liabilities exceeded two-thirds of its total assets. This was the first state-owned enterprise to officially declare bankruptcy after the founding of New China.

Deng Xiaoping attached great importance to this report. He personally instructed that the matter should be decided as soon as possible without delay. Since the plan and Deng Xiaoping's instructions were put forward at the same time in March 1986, the plan jointly launched by politicians and scientists soon became known as the "863 Plan." In March 1987, the 863 Plan was officially implemented. From then onwards, China's high-tech research entered a new stage of development. Tens of thousands of scientists worked together in various fields to tackle key problems, and soon achieved fruitful results.

In 1991, Deng Xiaoping wrote the 863 Plan motto: "Develop high-tech and realize industrialization." Once again, it encouraged scientists to tackle key problems in order to realize the 863 Plan and also pointed out the direction for China's high-tech development. The first batch of 863 Plan included 15 theme projects in seven fields, with a total funding of 10 billion yuan. The seven fields were: biotechnology, aerospace technology, information technology, laser technology, automation technology, energy technology, and new materials.

The implementation of the 863 Plan laid a solid foundation for China to occupy a place in the world's high-tech field. It can be said that without the formulation and implementation of the "863 Plan," there would be no high-tech in China today.

1987 The Basic Line Showed the Direction

Keyword: the 13th National Congress of the CPC establishing the basic line of the Party

In Mao Zedong's view, the Party's basic line is like a "beacon that lights our work." If we deviate from the correct guidance of the basic line when implementing specific work lines and policies, the Party will "lose its direction, swing from side to side," and risk hitting the rocks in the boundless sea at any time. In Deng Xiaoping's view, whether the Party's line is correct is "related to the future of the country and the success or failure of the socialist cause." The CPC has always attached great importance to the Party's basic line.

The Third Plenary Session of the 11th CPC Central Committee held in 1978, was a great turning point with far-reaching significance in the history of the Party since the founding of New China. The plenary session resumed the ideological line of emancipating the mind and seeking truth from facts, decided to shift the focus of the Party's work to economic development, and established the basic policy of reform and opening-up. Then Deng Xiaoping delivered an important speech entitled "Adherence to the Four Cardinal Principles" at the work when theory was discussed, emphasizing that adherence to the Four Cardinal Principles was the fundamental prerequisite for realizing modernization. With the steady development of reform practice and the proposal and improvement of the theory of the primary stage of socialism, in 1987, the 13th National Congress of the CPC formally put forward and

Figure 67.
The poster of "Adhere to the Basic Line of the Party for a Hundred Years" at Shenzhen Deng Xiaoping Portrait Square

established the Party's basic line in the primary stage of socialism: "To lead and unite the people of all ethnic groups in China, focus on economic development, adhere to the Four Cardinal Principles, adhere to reform and opening-up, self-reliance, and work hard to build China into a prosperous, strong, democratic, and civilized socialist modern country." The CPC put forward this line based on summing up the experience and lessons of more than 30 years of leading the socialist revolution and construction, grasping the main contradictions and basic characteristics of China at that time, and putting forward the general task of the new period. It was a scientific line that accurately grasped China's basic national conditions and conformed to the laws of social development. Its proposal provided a solid basis for the CPC to lead all the people in socialist construction.

Knowledge about CPC History

On September 26, 1987, the CPC Central Committee and the State Council issued the *Notice on the Establishment of Hainan Province and its Preparatory Work*. The Notice said that, in view of the importance and necessity of Hainan's development, the State Council proposed to delimit the Hainan Administrative Region from Guangdong Province and establish Hainan Province.

"There must be a process for understanding the laws of building socialism." The formation and proposition of any correct line of the Party would not be achieved overnight. The general line for the transition period lasted five years from its conception at the Second Plenary Session of the 7th CPC Central Committee in March 1949 to its establishment at the Fourth Plenary Session of the 7th CPC Central Committee in February 1954. The basic line of the Party in the primary stage of socialism lasted nine years from its founding at the Third Plenary Session of the 11th CPC Central Committee in 1978 to its establishment at the 13th National Congress of the CPC in 1987. In order to establish a correct line to guide China's socialist construction for a long time, the CPC has gone through a tortuous and long exploration process. This process was, as Deng Xiaoping said, "Successful experience is valuable wealth, while wrong experience and failed experience are also valuable wealth." In this process, the CPC gradually improved its governing ability, deepened its understanding of the laws of socialist construction, solved the problems of the times engendered by the complex situation one by one, and gradually developed into a stronger, more mature, and more reliable party.

"Practice is the only criterion for testing truth, and practice is the only criterion for testing the correctness of the line, principles, and policies." The historical practice and development achievements of China's reform and opening-up for more than 40 years show that the Party's basic line established in 1987 is completely correct and must be "managed for a hundred years without wavering." No matter what difficulties and challenges we may encounter in the future, we must unswervingly implement the Party's basic line and adhere to the path of socialism with Chinese characteristics.

1988 The Military Style Shone in China

Keyword: restoration of military ranks

The military rank is a symbol to distinguish the ranks of soldiers and indicate their status. It represents the military achievements of soldiers and is also an honor given by the country to soldiers. In 1955, the PLA began to implement the system of military ranks in an all-round way. However, for various reasons, this system was abolished in 1965 and was not restored until 1988.

On March 12, 1980, Deng Xiaoping proposed that the military should still establish a military ranks system. In that year, with the implementation of the policy of opening to the outside world, the PLA's foreign exchanges also increased. After going abroad, it was found that all foreign troops had military ranks, but our army did not. The uniform of our officers and soldiers was all the same, namely, it was "one red star on the head, and the revolutionary red flags on both sides," which made it difficult to communicate with foreign troops on an equal footing, which was awkward and inconvenient. In addition, there was another problem at that time, that was, many generals with outstanding military achievements during the war were no longer alive or were old, and were not within the scope of awarding of the

Figure 68.
Ten Grand Marshals

Knowledge about CPC History

On July 1, 1988, the Second Session of the Standing Committee of the 7th National People's Congress adopted the *Regulations on the Military Ranks of Officers of the Chinese People's Liberation Army*, which adjusted the military ranks system established in 1955. In this adjustment, the ranks of marshal, senior captain, and senior general were abolished. They were replaced by lieutenant and general, classified into three levels of upper, middle, and lower ranks. In comparison, field grade officers still had four levels, namely, senior, upper, middle, and lower ranks. Military ranks were set to three grades with ten ranks.

rank of marshal. In contrast, military generals' achievements in peacetime could not be compared with those in wartime. Therefore, many people did not support the establishment of high titles, that was, marshals and generals. Deng Xiaoping finally decided to set the highest military rank to general.

According to Deng Xiaoping's instructions, at the beginning of 1982, the executive meeting of the Central Military Commission formally made a decision to restore the military ranks system, and in May 1983, a leading group for restoring the military ranks system was established. The leading group had an office composed of more than 20 cadres drafted from all major units of the army. On May 31, 1984, the Second Session of the 6th National People's Congress adopted the *Military Service Law of the People's Republic of China*, which stipulated that "the Chinese PLA implements the military ranks system." In June 1985, the Central Military Commission held an enlarged meeting, which clearly proposed to "implement a new military ranks system."

On September 14, 1988, the Central Military Commission held a grand ceremony for conferring the rank of General in Huairentang, Zhongnanhai. Seventeen senior officers were awarded the rank of general. They were Hong Xuezhi, Liu Huaqing, Qin Jiwei, Chi Haotian, Yang Baibing, Xu Xin, Guo Linxiang, Wang Chenghan, Zhao Nanqi, Li Desheng, Zhang Zhen, You Taizhong, Liu Zhenhua, Xiang Shouzhi, Wan Haifeng, Li Yaowen, and Wang Hai. In the following days, the awarding ceremony of all major units of the army was held in succession to the sound of military music. One thousand four hundred fifty-two soldiers were awarded the rank of general, 180,000 were awarded the rank of field grade officers, and 405,000 were awarded the rank of lieutenant.

Among the officers newly awarded the rank of general, Hong Xuezhi was the only general who was awarded the rank of general twice. Five female officers were awarded the rank of major general, and 20 experts and professors were awarded the rank of professional and technical major general. Since then, the soldiers of the republic appeared in front of the world with a new look.

On October 1, 1988, on the occasion of the 39th anniversary of the founding of the PRC, officers and men of the three armed forces changed into new uniforms with military ranks. The gallant soldiers appeared more radiant, and people's respect for them arose spontaneously.

1989 The Sino-Soviet Meeting Eliminated Past Disagreements

Keyword: normalization of Sino-Soviet relations

Since the late 1950s, the Sino-Soviet border had been full of dark clouds and tense swords. As time went by, the old man of history came to the late 1980s. In 1989, when the two giants stood in front of the world again with a new attitude, the whole world gave a cheer.

On May 16, 1989, Deng Xiaoping met with visiting Soviet leader Mikhail Gorbachev in the Great Hall of the People. This was a historic meeting, and it marked the fact that after a long period of confrontation, Sino-Soviet relations finally moved toward reconciliation and normalization. From then on, people could calmly review and reflect on the long and bumpy history of China and the Soviet Union from alliance to confrontation to normalization.

On September 27, 1979, the first round of Sino-Soviet negotiations on state relations was held in Moscow. During the negotiations, the two sides had great differences, and by the end of November, the negotiations had not achieved any results. Nevertheless, after years of tense confrontation, the fact that representatives of the two countries could sit together and conduct high level dialogue on improving bilateral relations was of extraordinary significance in itself.

In March 1982, Soviet leader Leonid Brezhnev made a speech in Tashkent, recognizing that China was a socialist country; emphasized China's sovereignty over Taiwan; he was willing to improve relations with China and suggested that the two sides consult on this issue.

Figure 69.
On May 16, 1989, Deng Xiaoping met with Gorbachev in the Great Hall of the People.

In August, Yu Hongliang, Director General of the Soviet and Eastern Europe Department of the Ministry of Foreign Affairs of China, went to Moscow in the name of inspecting the work of the embassy, and proposed to the Soviet side that they hold a political consultation with special envoys at the level of deputy foreign minister. In October, the consultations began in Beijing. This consultation was actually a continuation of the negotiations in 1979. It not only marked the end of the state of confrontation and the lack of dialogue between the two countries at that time, but also indicated that bilateral relations would shift from long-term confrontation to relaxation.

Knowledge about CPC History

The cold war period refers to the period from 1947 to 1991 when the two camps of the Western capitalist countries led by the United States and the socialist countries led by the Soviet Union were in a state of confrontation in economic, political, military, diplomatic, cultural, ideological, and other aspects, except for direct fighting.

Since 1982, three leaders of the Central Committee of the Communist Party of the Soviet Union had died one after another. China sent special envoys to the Soviet Union to attend funerals, and the level had been raised again and again, maintaining high level dialogue between the two sides. Attending funerals became a special channel of diplomatic contact. In March 1985, Gorbachev took the post of the highest leader of the Soviet Party and state and began to pursue foreign and domestic policies that were different from those in the past. In July 1986, he delivered a speech in Vladivostok, saying that the Soviet Union was willing to discuss the establishment of good neighborly relations with China at any time and at any level, and agreed to divide the Amur River (Heilongjiang River) border according to the main waterway. At the same time, he announced that the Soviet Union would withdraw troops from Afghanistan in stages, and was discussing the issues of withdrawal with Mongolia.

In December 1988, Qian Qichen, then Chinese Foreign Minister, visited the Soviet Union. In February 1989, the then Soviet Foreign Minister Shevardnadze visited China. So far, preparations for the Sino-Soviet leaders' meeting had been basically completed. On May 16, 1989, the meeting between Deng Xiaoping and Gorbachev, which was of great historical significance, was finally held in Beijing.

After the Sino-Soviet leaders' meeting, the *Sino-Soviet Joint Communiqué* was issued on May 18. The main contents included: the normalization of Sino-Soviet relations conformed to the interests and aspirations of the two peoples and was conducive to maintaining world peace and stability; the normalization of Sino-Soviet relations was not aimed at a third country and did not harm its interests; China and the Soviet Union would develop mutual relations on the basis of the Five Principles of Peaceful Coexistence; China and the Soviet Union were willing to settle all disputes between the two countries through peaceful negotiations; the two sides stood for a just and reasonable solution to the Sino-Soviet border problems left over from history on the basis of the current treaties on the Sino-Soviet border.

The normalization of Sino-Soviet relations was not only in the interests of the two peoples but also conducive to world peace and development. It was of extraordinary significance.

1990 New Vitality Added to the Economy

Keyword: the establishing of Shanghai Stock Exchange

The year 2020 was the 30th anniversary of the establishment of the Shanghai Stock Exchange. China's capital market had gone through an extraordinary journey in 30 years. Over the past 30 years, China's stock market has set many amazing records. More importantly, stocks has entered thousands of households, become a part of life, and connected individuals with enterprises and even national interests.

On December 19, 1990, a gong sounded in the Peacock Hall of the Pujiang Hotel, No. 15 Huangpu Road on the north side of the Bund in Shanghai, signaling not only the birth of the Shanghai Stock Exchange but also the ability of the capital market to serve socialist China. A generation of securities market figures, with their missions and ideals in mind, used their wisdom and strength to outline a new chapter of China's securities market and kick off the construction of a capital power in China.

In the early 1980s, debates over whether to identify as "socialist" or "capitalist" still pervaded that era. For many people deeply affected by the "Great Cultural Revolution," the establishment of a joint-stock company, the issuance of company shares, and the

Figure 70.
Shanghai Stock Exchange

establishment of a stock exchange were simply a fantasy and even risky moves that would make political mistakes.

> **Knowledge about CPC History**
> On April 18, 1990, then Premier Li Peng announced in Shanghai that the CPC Central Committee and the State Council had agreed to accelerate the development of the Pudong area in Shanghai and to implement the policy of economic and technological development zones and certain special economic zones in Pudong. Developing and opening Pudong was another major deployment made by the central government to deepen reform and expand opening-up.

In 1986, the People's Bank of China organized a special one-month study trip to Nomura Securities in Japan for the governors of 13 branches nationwide, headed by Cai Esheng (then a cadre of the Department of Financial Management of the People's Bank of China), with all expenses borne by Nomura Securities. Through this study, the personnel who went to study brought back a lot of important experience and materials, which laid the ground for very important preparations for the establishment of the Shanghai Stock Exchange in the future. In the same year, the State Commission for Restructuring the Economic System also set out to explore the pilot shareholding reform of enterprises. Shanghai was one of the pilot cities. Wang Daohan, the former mayor of Shanghai, participated in the seminars on shareholding reform three times, and Jiang Zemin, who was later in charge of Shanghai, was even more aggressive. With his personal advice and care, two stocks, Feile Audio and Yanzhong Industry, came into being.

What really made the international community realize that China's reform was unstoppable was the world-famous "reciprocity." In November 1986, John J. Phelan Jr., chairman of the New York Stock Exchange, visited China. When meeting Deng Xiaoping, he presented the emblem of the New York Stock Exchange to Deng Xiaoping, and Deng Xiaoping presented some "Feile Audio" stock in return.

However, the sudden political turmoil at the turn of spring and summer in 1989 made foreign public opinion generally doubt whether China's reform and opening-up policy would continue to be implemented and whether the door to opening-up would be closed. As a result, the attraction of investment ceased, a large amount of foreign capital withdrew, and even the construction project of Oriental Pearl TV Tower, a landmark building in Shanghai, was facing a shutdown. Under such a difficult background, how could we make international public opinion realize that China's reform and opening-up policy would not waver? Therefore, the establishment of the Shanghai Stock Exchange, which shouldered this political mission, was put on the agenda.

Economic construction needed a lot of funds. Thus, while opening to the outside world to attract foreign capital, it was also urgent to open the domestic capital market. The Shanghai Stock Exchange came into being at the right time. It is the first stock exchange opened since the founding of the PRC, marking the initial formation of China's securities market.

1991 Holding Up the Hope of the Future

Keyword: Hope Project

In May 1991, at Zhangwan Primary School in Jinzhai County, Anhui Province, the first-grade students came to the classroom to learn as usual, but today they sat in the classroom with very complicated feelings. This might be the last time they came to the classroom that they were so attached to, because, one by one, the seats in the classroom were emptying out, and they themselves might be next. They looked at the teacher puzzled as if they were asking: "Why can't we attend school?" This scene was just taken by Xie Hailong, a photographer for *China Youth Daily*. The girl with big eyes in the picture held her pencil, looked straight ahead, and was eager for knowledge. Soon, this group of black-and-white photos entitled *I Desire to Go to School* were reprinted by the major national media. The whole country began to pay attention to the out-of-school children, and the Hope Project came into the public's view.

At the end of the 1980s, more than 1 million primary school students in China dropped out of school each year because their families were poor and could not afford to pay for books and miscellaneous fees. However, we shouldn't let the children suffer even if life was

Figure 71.
I Desire to Go to School

hard, and we shouldn't save money on education even if people lived in poverty. Therefore, on October 30, 1989, the China Youth Development Foundation, with Xu Yongguang as its Secretary General, announced to the world that it would implement the Hope Project aimed at assisting out-of-school children in poverty-stricken areas.

Knowledge about CPC History

In March 1991, Shanghai *Liberation Daily* published articles signed by Huang Fuping, "New Ideas for Reform and Opening-Up" and "More Consciousness for Expanding Opening-Up." The former article pointed out that the key to studying new situations and exploring new ideas was to further emancipate the mind. The latter pointed out that the opening-up of Shanghai in the 1990s needed to take a big step forward, and that it required us to have a series of new ideas, dare to take risks, and do things that have never been done before.

Although many people in society knew well about basic education in poverty-stricken areas and tried to change the fate of out-of-school children, the "Hope Project," at the beginning of its establishment, did not develop smoothly. For the newly established China Youth Development Foundation, 100,000 yuan of registered capital and 10,000 yuan of working funds were not enough for the basic office costs. According to the minimum subsidy standard established at the beginning of the foundation, it was 20 yuan per semester for each out-of-school child. Even if only 50,000 children were subsidized each year in China, 2 million yuan needed to be raised yearly.

The appearance of the photo *I Desire to Go to School* brought dawn to the Hope Project facing difficulties. Helping children in poverty-stricken areas enter school became the focus of public attention. Consequently, people began to donate money, materials, and love, and the whole of China was flooded with love; overseas Chinese also extended their hands of friendship and love. The Hope Project started in this way.

As of 2019, the Hope Project had raised 16.1 billion yuan of donations, subsidized 61,702 million students from economically disadvantaged families, and built 20,359 hope primary schools. The Hope Project had expanded its funding targets to the children of migrant workers in cities, middle school students from economically disadvantaged families in poor rural areas, students from secondary vocational and technical schools, and college students. The mobilization and service mode of the Hope Project had also developed from a single financial support to a diversified pattern of "financial support + work-study program + public welfare practice" as well as psychological assistance and social work services. The Hope Project has become the earliest, largest, most widely involved, and most effective social public welfare undertaking launched in China over the past 40 years of reform and opening-up.

We have every reason to believe that with the care of all sectors of society, the fire of hope of the Hope Project will burn forever, warming more hearts eager for knowledge.

1992 Development Is the Absolute Principle

Keyword: Deng Xiaoping's Southern tour speeches

In the early spring of 1992, Shekou Wharf in Shenzhen welcomed a hale and hearty old man. He was Deng Xiaoping, the chief architect of China's reform and opening-up. In the south of the motherland, he wrote a huge poem about China's reform. From that moment on, the music of reform was played throughout the country, and a rolling spring tide rose in the world.

The reform and opening-up started at the end of 1978 and had gone through 13 years by 1992. Since the reform and opening-up, great achievements had been made, but it had not been smooth. The drastic changes in Eastern Europe and the Soviet Union in the late 1980s and early 1990s cast a shadow on the prospects of socialism. Would reform continue? Would reform change to the opposite of socialism? Not only did ordinary people feel confused, but even some people at high levels were also confused. On the road to reform and opening-up, we came to a key point: should we advance or retreat?

At a time when destiny was at stake, the footsteps of history were particularly heavy. Shortly after the collapse of the Soviet Union, 88-year-old Comrade Deng Xiaoping, began his trip to the South as an ordinary Communist. In the meantime, he firmly said that we should not panic and think that Marxism would disappear, be useless and fail, which was not true!

Figure 72.
Shenzhen Shekou Wharf

Knowledge about CPC History

From October 12 to 18, 1992, the 14th National Congress of the CPC was held in Beijing. Jiang Zemin, on behalf of the 13th CPC Central Committee, delivered a report entitled "Accelerating the Pace of Reform, Opening-Up and Modernization, and Striving for Greater Victory in the Cause of Socialism with Chinese Characteristics." The Congress made it clear that the goal of China's economic restructuring was to establish a socialist market economy.

In order to clarify the problems concerning the reform goals and the reform path that were puzzling the people of the whole country, Deng Xiaoping clearly put forward the standard of "three benefits" in his southern tour speeches. According to this standard, Deng Xiaoping pointed out that the essence of socialism was to liberate and develop productive forces, eliminate exploitation, eliminate polarization, and finally achieve common prosperity. After the essential problem was solved, Deng Xiaoping also made the most comprehensive and clear statement on such major issues as the relationship between the plan and the market since the reform and opening-up and made clear the reform goal of establishing a socialist market economic system. He also reminded us that China should be alert to the "Right," but mainly to prevent the "Left," which was the guiding principle in a long historical period.

On this trip to the South, Deng Xiaoping inspected and talked, and with his insight into history, he solved the mysteries that had enveloped people after the great changes in the international situation. In October 1992, the 14th National Congress of the CPC was held, and the theory of building socialism with Chinese characteristics was solemnly written into the Party Constitution. Five years later, at the 15th National Congress of the CPC, this theory was named "Deng Xiaoping Theory" and written into the Party Constitution, becoming the guiding ideology of the Party alongside Marxism, Leninism, and Mao Zedong Thought. Since then, the process of China's reform and opening-up had been irreversible.

It can only be a dead end not to develop the economy. "Development is the absolute principle" was Deng Xiaoping's strong voice of the times in the South. At this important juncture of reform and opening-up, he integrated his own life with reform and opening-up and once again pointed out the development path for China with his unique spirit of forging ahead, pioneering, and innovation, which strongly boosted the ship of China's reform.

1993 Cross-Strait Talks Broke the Ice

Keyword: Wang-Koo Talks

On April 29, 1993, at the meeting place on the fourth floor of the NOL Building in Singapore, two elderly people solemnly signed their names on the documents. After exchanging documents with each other, the two wise old men looked at each other and smiled, simultaneously extending their hands and holding them tightly together. This meeting was the highest-level meeting held publicly by high level people on both sides of the Straits in the name of non-governmental communication since 1949. Since then, the history of cross-strait relations had turned a new page.

Over the years, the Taiwan issue had been a matter of great concern to the Chinese people on both sides of the Straits. The shallow Taiwan Strait not only geographically separates the two sides of the Taiwan Strait but also bears the deep nostalgia of Chinese people who share the same roots and cultures on both sides of the Taiwan Strait. Since Taiwan's unfortunate separation from the mainland in 1949, there had been no communication between the two sides. The fact that relatives couldn't be reunited and the motherland couldn't be reunified became a pain in the hearts of all Chinese people. To end the isolation between the two sides of the Taiwan Straits at an early date and achieve peaceful reunification was the strongest desire of every Chinese person.

Figure 73.
Wang Daohan (left) shook hands with Koo Chenfu (right) before Wang-Koo talks on April 27, 1993.

However, due to various reasons, despite the efforts made by both sides of the Straits, the contact between the two sides had not made substantive progress over the years. The leaders on both sides of the Taiwan Straits who were striving for a peaceful settlement of the Taiwan issue and the peaceful reunification of the motherland began to realize that people-to-people exchanges should be strengthened in dealing with cross-Straits issues, so both sides began to adjust their policies.

Knowledge about CPC History

The Association for Relations Across the Taiwan Straits was established in Beijing on December 16, 1991. According to the Articles of Association, it is a social organization legal person with the purpose of promoting cross-Strait exchanges, developing cross-Strait relations, and achieving the peaceful reunification of the motherland. The highest authority of the Association is the Council. The first chairman of the ARATS was Wang Daohan.

On November 21, 1990, the Straits Exchange Foundation (hereinafter referred to as the Straits Foundation), with Mr. Koo Chenfu as its chairman, was established in Taiwan and began to solve the problems in cross-Strait exchanges. In response, on December 16, 1991, the Association for Relations Across the Taiwan Straits (hereinafter referred to as the ARATS), with Wang Daohan as its chairman and a social organization as a legal person, was established in Beijing.

The establishment of two non-governmental organizations ushered in a new era for cross-Strait relations. From April 27 to 29, 1993, the world-famous "Wang-Koo Talks" was held in Singapore. After repeated consultations, seeking common ground while reserving differences, Koo Chenfu and Wang Daohan, on behalf of the Straits Foundation and the ARATS, respectively, formally signed four agreements, including the *Agreement on Verification of the Use of Cross-Straits Notarial Instruments*, the *Agreement on Cross-Straits Registered Letter Query Compensation*, the *Common Agreement on the Wang-Koo Talks*, and the *Agreement on the Contact and Participation System of the Two Associations*, thereby realizing a historic breakthrough after more than 40 years of the separation and isolation of compatriots across the Taiwan Straits. Although the talks were limited to the scope of folk, economic, transactional and functional issues, their significance and impact on cross-Strait relations aroused the great attention of Taiwan leaders and the general concern of the international community.

The handshake between Wang Daohan and Koo Chenfu was like lighting a lamp in a long dark tunnel, which made the people on both sides of the Taiwan Straits see the hope of breaking the ice. The Wang-Koo Talks played a positive role in promoting cross-Strait exchanges and enhancing mutual trust and cooperation. In particular, the emphasis on adhering to the "1992 Consensus" during the talks has become an important cornerstone for cross-Strait exchanges since then.

1994 A High Gorge Arose from a Flat Lake

Keyword: commencement of the Three Gorges Project

The construction of the Three Gorges Project was a dream of the Chinese people for a hundred years. As early as 1919, Sun Yat-sen proposed to improve the waterway in the upper reaches of the Yangtze River. In the *Plans for National Reconstruction*, he pointed out that the Yangtze River "flows from Yichang to the gorge" and that "the water should be subject to weirs with sluice gates so that the boats could follow the current and use its water power." This was the first proposal for the Three Gorges Project. According to this assumption, in the mid-1940s, the National Government signed a contract with the US Bureau of Reclamation to build hydropower stations with US funds and invited the chief engineer of the Bureau and the world-famous water conservancy expert Savage to visit China. After three field visits to the Three Gorges area, Savage wrote the "Preliminary Report on the Yangtze Gorge Plan"; he believed that the Three Gorges Project was feasible and arranged to carry out preliminary work. Later, due to the outbreak of civil war, the matter ended without any outcome. Since then, a dream of a high gorge rising out of a flat lake had been planted in the hearts of Chinese people, leaving behind the complex of building the Three Gorges Project.

Since the founding of the PRC, frequent floods in the upper reaches of the Yangtze River had repeatedly threatened the safety of cities in the middle reaches of the Yangtze River, such as Wuhan, and caused great harm to the development of the national economy. As a

Figure 74.
Three Gorges Dam

> **Knowledge about CPC History**
> In August 1994, the CPC Central Committee issued the *Implementation Outline of Patriotism Education* and issued a notice pointing out that patriotism had always been a banner to mobilize and encourage the Chinese people to work together, a huge force to promote the progress of China's social history and a common spiritual pillar for the people of all ethnic groups.

result, the construction of the Three Gorges Project was put on the agenda again. When Mao Zedong inspected the Three Gorges at the beginning of 1953, he believed that the Three Gorges Project needed to be built and could be built, but the final decision of the determination to construct it and the exact time to start could not be made until all important preparations were basically completed. Under the auspices of Zhou Enlai, relevant parties started the exploration, design, and demonstration of the Three Gorges Project and invited Soviet water conservancy experts to participate. Taking into account the national strength, technology, and domestic and international situations at that time, Mao Zedong finally decided to suspend the construction of the Three Gorges Project.

After reform and opening-up, the Three Gorges Project was put on the agenda again. In 1983, the Ministry of Water Resources and Electric Power submitted a feasibility study report of the project and began to make preliminary preparations. The State Council approved the feasibility study report in 1984. From 1986 to 1988, the State Council convened hundreds of experts and scholars to conduct a comprehensive re-demonstration of the Three Gorges Project on 14 special topics. The conclusion was that the Three Gorges Project was technically feasible and economically reasonable, and it was better to build it sooner than later.

In 1992, the National People's Congress passed the *Resolution to Construct the Three Gorges Project* and decided to adopt the construction method of "one-time development, one-time completion, staged water storage, and continuous resettlement" to build the Three Gorges Project.

According to the resolution, the Three Gorges Project would be completed in three phases, starting from 1994 to 2009, with a total time span of 17 years. After completion, the Three Gorges Dam Project had a total length of 3,335 meters, a dam height of 185 meters, a designed normal water storage level of 175 meters in the dry season (145 meters in the wet season), and a total storage capacity of 39.3 billion cubic meters, including 22.15 billion cubic meters of flood control storage capacity, an average annual power generation of 100 billion kilowatt hours, and an annual one-way traffic capacity of 50 million tons, integrating the functions of flood control, power generation, and shipping.

The Three Gorges Project is the largest hydropower station in the world and the largest engineering construction project in the history of New China. It not only great economic benefits to China but also made beneficial contributions to the development of water conservancy and hydropower technology and related science and technology in the world.

1995 Kong Fansen, a Public Servant

Keyword: learning from Kong Fansen

In the CCTV broadcast hall, a Tibetan girl holding a photo cried, "Uncle, come back soon!" The sound of crying broke through the hall and spread everywhere in the country. Countless Chinese people shed sad tears. That year, people remembered the owner of the photo, a cadre sent to aid Xizang who ended his life as the 50 years old Kong Fansen.

In 1979, Kong Fansen responded to the call of the state and volunteered to participate in the work to aid Xizang, and came to Gangba County. During three years of working in Gangba, he traveled all over the villages and pastoral areas of the county, visited the poor, harvested and farmed with the local people, did agricultural work and built water conservancy projects, and established deep feelings with the people of Gangba County. In 1981, Kong Fansen was ordered to return to his familiar hometown Liaocheng, Shandong, but he always worried about the poor life of the people in Xizang.

Figure 75.
Kong Fansen heals herdsmen.

Knowledge about CPC History

On November 29, 1995, the "drawing lots from the golden urn" ceremony identifying the reincarnation of the 10th Panchen Lama was held in front of the Sakyamuni statue in the Jokhang Temple in Lhasa in accordance with the Tibetan Buddhist ritual and historical customization. Gyantsen Norpo, a 6-year-old boy from Lhari County, Nagchu Prefecture, Xizang, won the bid. Later, the People's Government of the Xizang Autonomous Region reported to the State Council for approval, and the State Council approved the succession of the 11th Panchen Lama Erdeni to Gyantsen Norpo.

In 1988, Kong Fansen came to Xizang again after bidding farewell to his elderly mother, his weak and sickly wife, and his three underage children. This time, he served as the deputy mayor of Lhasa Municipal People's Government in charge of culture, education, health, and civil affairs. Only four months after he took office, he went to all public schools and more than half of village primary schools in eight counties and districts of the city to work hard for the development of minority education. The medical and health conditions in remote areas of Xizang were poor. Every time he went to the countryside, he took a medicine box with him and spent several hundred yuan buying commonly used medicines for farmers and herdsmen in urgent need. Although one medicine box couldn't solve all the problems, it was often a timely help to the patients receiving treatment.

In 1992, an earthquake occurred in Lhasa City. Kong Fansen raised three orphans who lost their parents because of the earthquake and often used his own wages to help the poor people in Xizang. As a result, his salary often ran out in less than half a month, and he even secretly sold blood. In one year, he sold 900 ml of blood successively and spent more than 900 yuan of the nutrition fee he received on living subsidies for the three orphans.

Kong Fansen, the model of the Communist Party members in the new era, was a good cadre who was uncorrupted. In July 1994, Kong Fansen led Ali's comrades to Beijing for a project. For several days, he and his comrades ate noodles at street stalls. The comrades accompanying him felt that it was unsightly for a prefectural party secretary to eat at a stall, but Kong Fansen solemnly said: "Ali is too poor. Think about the people who are not rich there. How can we eat a lot of meat and fish? As cadres of the people, we should always think of the people!"

After the death of comrade Kong Fansen, the comrades in the Ali prefectural Party committee found that in addition to a pocket radio, there were several simple clothes to change, and there were only 8 yuan and 60 cents left. Who would believe that this was all the property of a prefectural Party secretary?

Kong Fansen gave his money, blood, health, and finally life to the people in Xizang. He realized what he wrote in his poem: "I gave my heart to Xizang and the cause of the Party." His love for the people is as pure, deep, and broad as the blue sky on the plateau!

1996 Sacred Land Forever Defended

Keyword: reaffirm the sovereignty of the Diaoyu Islands

On an uninhabited island in the East China Sea at 25 degrees north latitude, a group of unexpected visitors broke the tranquility of the area. On August 18, 1996, a Japanese right-wing organization, regardless of the feelings of the Chinese and Japanese people, forcibly landed on the Diaoyu Islands and erected the Japanese flag and a war monument on the island without authorization. This series of actions made the Diaoyu Islands issue, which had been paid close attention to, come to public attention again.

The Diaoyu Islands, also known as Diaoyu Valley and Diaoyu Mountain, were included in China's territory as early as the Ming Dynasty. Like Taiwan, the Diaoyu Islands are a sacred and indivisible part of China's territory. After the Sino-Japanese War of 1895, Japan forced the Qing government to sign the Treaty of Shimonoseki, which humiliated the country and forcibly occupied Taiwan and the Diaoyu Islands. Since then, the ownership of the Diaoyu Islands had become one of the major issues affecting China-Japan relations.

On May 15, 1972, when the United States handed over the jurisdiction of Ryukyu to Japan, it also handed over the administrative jurisdiction of the Diaoyu Islands to Japan. This act of the United States was immediately strongly opposed by the Chinese people. On the land of China, a vigorous campaign for defending the Diaoyu Islands sprang up. China declared its sovereignty over the Diaoyu Islands to Japan and the world. However, in 1978, some Japanese

**Figure 76.
The Diaoyu Islands**

parliamentarians who were hostile to China did not stop and proposed that China recognize Japan's sovereignty over the Diaoyu Islands. The Japanese government also complied with its request and dispatched patrol boats and aircraft to monitor Chinese fishermen fishing in the waters of the Diaoyu Islands. In May 1978, the Japanese government also built a helicopter airport on the island and sent a survey mission and a survey ship there. This act was strongly condemned by the Chinese government and the people. However, the Japanese did not withdraw their evil claws from the Diaoyu Islands. In 1990, with the acquiescence of the government, some right-wingers in Japan built lighthouses on the Diaoyu Islands and even dispatched 12 ships and two helicopters to prevent Taiwan fishing boats from approaching the Diaoyu Islands. In this way, they tried to make the international community recognize that the Diaoyu Islands belonged to Japan.

Knowledge about CPC History

On January 28, 1996, the State Council and the Central Military Commission announced that the PLA troops stationed in the Hong Kong Special Administrative Region had been established. The troops stationed in the Hong Kong Special Administrative Region were composed of the army, navy, and air force of the Chinese PLA and were under the leadership of the Central Military Commission of the PRC.

However, in the face of historical facts, these practices of Japan appeared powerless. In October 1996, the famous Japanese historian Kiyoshi Inoue reiterated in the preface of the reprint of his book *The Senkaku Islands: A Historical Analysis of the Diaoyu Islands* that the Diaoyu Islands and their affiliated islands were the inherent territories of China. A large amount of historical data shows that, at least since the 16th century, the Diaoyu Islands and its affiliated islands have been Chinese territory, not "ownerless land." Especially from the relevant literature of Japan shows this point more accurately. As early as 1785, Japan published the *Sangoku Tsūran Zusetsu* (*An Illustrated Description of Three Countries*) and its accompanying drawings, which indicated in different colors that the Diaoyu Islands and its affiliated islands were Chinese territories.

Since 1996, the Chinese government has repeatedly reaffirmed its sovereignty over the Diaoyu Islands and its affiliated islands. More than 70 years have passed since the victory of the War of Resistance against Japanese Aggression. The increasingly powerful Chinese people will never allow any country to abuse our territory again. The Diaoyu Islands and its affiliated islands are an inseparable part of China's territory, and the tragedy of national territory being divided must never be repeated. We have every reason to believe that history will give a fair verdict on the Diaoyu Islands issue.

1997 A Journey Home in Wind and Rain

Keyword: Hong Kong's return to the motherland

At 4:10 p.m., on June 30, 1997, Hong Kong was shrouded in a thin rain and fog.

At the Governor's House on Albert Road, halfway up Central, Chris Patten, the 28th British Governor of Hong Kong, was saying his final farewell. The last governor stood alone on the high platform, letting the rain wet his hair and stiff suit, and said nothing. To the melody of "Sunset Sounds," the governor's flag slowly fell.

Two hours later, Prince Charles and Prime Minister Blair appeared at the "Sunset Ceremony," the British farewell ceremony, in the "Tamar Barracks" of Victoria Harbor. In the bleak wind and rain, to the sound of "God Save the Queen," the Union Flag slowly lowered.

History will never forget that in June 1840, the explosion of the Opium War broke the Qing government's dream of being the center of the world. The corrupt and incompetent Qing government, under the threat of the British invaders' strong ships and powerful guns, signed three humiliating treaties, namely, the Treaty of Nanking, the Beijing Convention, and the Convention between Great Britain and China Respecting an Extension of Hong Kong Territory. From then on, the Union Flag hanging over the other side of the Xiang River stung every Chinese. After the Qing government was overthrown, all subsequent Chinese

Figure 77.
Hong Kong, the beautiful pearl of the orient

governments did not recognize the Treaty of Nanking, the Beijing Convention, and the Convention between Great Britain and China Respecting an Extension of Hong Kong Territory. The previous Chinese government also made efforts to recover lost territory. However, weak countries had no diplomacy. China, which was in warfare of warlords and political turmoil, failed in all diplomatic efforts.

Knowledge about CPC History

"One country, two systems" means "there are two systems in one country." Its basic meaning is: under the premise of one China, the main body of the country adheres to the socialist system; Hong Kong, Macao, and Taiwan are inseparable parts of China. As special administrative regions, they maintain the original capitalist system and way of life.

After the reform and opening-up, with the improvement of the international situation and the prosperity of the country, the Chinese were finally able to straighten their backs and raise the issue of Hong Kong's sovereignty to the British. On September 24, 1982, the Fujian Hall of the Great Hall of the People gathered the eyes of people from all over the world. A large number of journalists came to the meeting place early, and the adjusted cameras were all aimed in the same direction. They were all waiting for the appearance of a woman, Mrs. Thatcher, the then British Prime Minister. The purpose of her visit to China was to discuss with Chinese leaders the issue of Hong Kong's return to China. Although Mrs. Thatcher, known as the "Iron Lady," did not want to make concessions on the Hong Kong issue, the Chinese government's firm attitude toward the Hong Kong issue forced her to make concessions. Deng Xiaoping clearly pointed out that China would take back Hong Kong in 1997. The firmness of his attitude was beyond Mrs. Thatcher's expectations. After several rounds of negotiations, on September 26, 1984, China and the UK initialed the *Joint Statement* and three annexes, declaring Hong Kong's official return to the motherland in 1997.

At 00:00 a.m. on July 1, 1997, with the rise of the five-star red flag in Hong Kong, the Chinese nation finally realized what it had expected for a century and a half under the eyes of the world. From this moment on, China resumed the exercise of sovereignty over Hong Kong, and Britain's 156-year colonial rule in Hong Kong came to an end. After a century of vicissitudes, Hong Kong's return to the motherland completed an important step toward the complete reunification of the motherland. It was a successful practice of the great concept of "one country, two systems." Since then, Hong Kong's development has entered a new era.

1998 I Use My Life to Build a Long Dike

Keyword: flood fighting and disaster relief

In 1998, a catastrophic flood, which was rare in a century, ravaged the country. From the Songhua River to the Yangtze River and then to the Pearl River, several major river basins across the country were in danger, and hundreds of millions of residents were under the threat of flooding. The floods were devastating, and this revealed the true heroes. The people's soldiers came forward at the most dangerous moment. In Jingzhou and Jiujiang, they created a miracle that people fought against natural disasters.

That year, the rainstorms in the south of the Yangtze River came very early, with very high frequency and long duration. The Yangtze River was full, like a soup pot overflowing with boiling water at any time; the Yangtze River was "crazy," just like a trapped animal trying to break free. Jingjiang, located in the lower reaches of the Yangtze River with a very twisty shape, was the most dangerous part of the Yangtze River. Its situation was directly related to the outcome of the Yangtze River flood fighting struggle. Therefore, the people's soldiers wrote a magnificent poem on the Jingjiang dike, and Li Xiangqun was the most beautiful sentence in this poem.

Figure 78.
PLA officers and soldiers participating in the flood fighting

Knowledge about CPC History

On May 4, 1998, the centennial celebration of Peking University was held in the Great Hall of the People. Jiang Zemin pointed out in the celebration speech that the whole Party and society should attach great importance to the important role of knowledge innovation and talent development in economic development and social progress. Our universities should become a powerful, vibrant force for rejuvenating the country through science and education.

At about 4:00 a.m. on August 10, young soldier Li Xiangqun followed the troops to the Hubei Jingjiang Yangtze River dike to carry out the task of fighting against danger. During the inspection, he found a hole in the dike and immediately sent out an emergency signal while holding sandbags to block the hole. The sand rushed out of the hole like a spring, which made him look like a clay figure. But he could not care so much then. He tried his best to press the sandbag with his body until his comrades came. Three days later, there were three holes in the nearby Taipingkou Happiness Gate, and Li Xiangqun, who was performing the task, jumped into the river without hesitation. A minute later, he emerged from ten meters downstream and reported to the company commander: "The current is too fast to control my body!" Then he picked up a sandbag and plunged into the water. Led by Li Xiangqun, his comrades rushed to jump into the water with sandbags in their arms and soon subdued the piping.

With the efforts of Li Xiangqun and his comrades in arms, Jingjiang River kept riding out five flood peaks, and the water level began to fall back gradually. However, on the 16th, the situation changed again. The flood arrived again, and the Jingjiang River was extremely dangerous. For successive days, Li Xiangqun took part in eight relief operations while ill. He fainted on the dike four times due to excessive fatigue. But on the 21st, when he heard that the flood was surging and the dike was in urgent need, he immediately carried two sandbags onto the dike. At this time, he fainted again on the dike and was rushed to the hospital by his comrades in arms. Although the medical staff tried their best to rescue him, Li Xiangqun, a flood fighter, sacrificed his young life at the age of 20.

Li Xiangqun is just one of the thousands of people's soldiers on the flood fighting front, and his story is just one of the thousands of stories that happened on the flood fighting front. In that year, Chinese soldiers used their lives to build a solid dike for the motherland and the people. Chinese soldiers proved to the world that as long as the motherland and the people needed them, they would be able to unite and build a ten-thousand-mile dike to protect their lives.

The great spirit of love that gives up life for the righteousness of the people's soldiers is another hymn of self-improvement sung by the Chinese people. Jiang Zemin summed up the flood fighting spirit that shocked the world like this: the spirit of a nation united as one, jointly facing challenges with united strength, not afraid of difficulties, tenacious struggle, indomitable struggle and perseverance, and daring to win.

1999 The Long Road Home for a Wanderer

Keyword: Macao's return to the motherland

"You know that Macau isn't my name truly, I've been away from you for too long my mommy. But what they captured is just my body, you have been taking care of my soul continually." When this song, "Song of the Seven Sons," is played, Chinese people will always be filled with emotion. The lyrics of this song are adapted from the patriotic poem "The Song of the Seven Sons · Macao" written by the famous poet Wen Yiduo in 1925. In his poem, Wen Yiduo compared the seven "lost lands," including Hong Kong, Macao, and Taiwan, that were looted by foreign powers to seven children far away from their mothers.

Since ancient times, Macao has been a defense line at the southern gate of China. After the middle of the 16th century, Portugal, in the name of the trade, forcibly occupied Macao for a long time. On December 1, 1887, Portugal and the Qing government signed the Draft Treaty of the Sino-Portuguese Conference and the Sino-Portuguese Treaty of Amity and Commerce, formally occupying Macao through diplomatic instruments. After the founding of New China, the Party and the country needed to concentrate on dealing with major and urgent tasks, restore and develop the national economy, and break the blockade of international anti-China forces. In consideration of the situation, the Chinese government adopted the policy of "long-term planning and full utilization" for Hong Kong and Macao, that was, to

Figure 79.
The handover ceremony of the Chinese-Portuguese Macao regime

Knowledge about CPC History

On October 1, 1999, a celebration for all walks of life in the capital to commemorate the 50th anniversary of the founding of the PRC was held in Tiananmen Square. Comrade Jiang Zemin reviewed 42 ground teams composed of the PLA army, navy and air forces, and the People's Armed Police Force and Militia Reserve Forces. 500,000 soldiers and civilians participated in the grand military parade and mass march.

maintain the current situation of Hong Kong and Macao for a long time while making full use of their special status to serve China's socialist construction and diplomatic strategy. When conditions were ripe, the Hong Kong and Macao issues would be resolved peacefully through negotiation. Facts have proved that this policy of the Chinese government was farsighted.

On December 19, 1984, China and Britain signed a joint statement on the return of Hong Kong in Beijing. Ten days after the agreement was reached, Deng Xiaoping pointed out in his interview with the delegation from Hong Kong and Macao compatriots to observe the National Day celebration that "the Macao issue should be resolved at the same time in the same way as Hong Kong." Soon, China and Portugal formally held talks on the Macao issue. However, the road to negotiation was not smooth. In the first round of negotiations, Portugal proposed to discuss only the negotiation agenda, trying to prolong the negotiation time, citing insufficient preparation. It was not until the third round of talks that the Portuguese representatives finally discussed the documents submitted by China in the first two rounds of talks. In the first three rounds of negotiations, the two countries had no objection to the sovereignty of Macao, but the two sides always debated the specific time of Macao's return. Even before the fourth round of talks between China and Portugal was about to start, the Macao Portuguese authorities extended the franchise contract for the gambling industry signed with Macao entertainment companies to 2001, in violation of the previous commitment of Portuguese representatives to return Macao in the 20th century. In response, the spokesman of the Ministry of Foreign Affairs of China solemnly stated on December 31, 1986: "To recover Macao before 2000 is an unshakable firm position and strong desire of the Chinese government and the 1 billion Chinese people, including Macao compatriots. Any proposal that goes beyond returning to Macao after 2000 is unacceptable." After heated debate, the two sides finally reached a consensus and formally signed a joint statement on the Macao issue on April 13 of the next year.

At 00:00 a.m. on December 20, 1999, the PLA military band played the national anthem of the PRC, and the national flag of the PRC and the regional flag of the Macao Special Administrative Region of the PRC were raised. Macao's return to the motherland marked the official start of Macao's practice of "one country, two systems." The "Song of the Seven Sons," which was full of pathos and thoughts back then, is now sung again, and people are already full of pride and joy.

2000 "Beidou" Lifted off on Its Journey

Keyword: the successful launch of "Beidou" navigation test satellite

"5, 4, 3, 2, 1, ignition! Take off!" At 0:20 a.m. on December 21, 2000, the second "Beidou" navigation test satellite developed by China took the "Long March 3A" rocket to its launch at the Xichang Satellite Launch Center and accurately entered its predetermined orbit. Together with the first "Beidou" navigation test satellite launched on October 31 of the same year, it formed the "Beidou" navigation satellite test system. This not only meant that China had made a major breakthrough in the field of satellite navigation technology but also marked the fact that China had realized the development of satellite navigation systems from scratch, becoming the third country in the world to have an autonomous satellite navigation system after the United States and Russia, breaking the passive situation of relying on foreign navigation and positioning technologies for a long time, and greatly promoting the construction of China's space information infrastructure, as well as making important contributions to national defense and national economic development.

"Move the small stool and lean on the window so as to teach to learn about the Big Dipper in the sky." Since ancient times, the Big Dipper has been endowed with the function

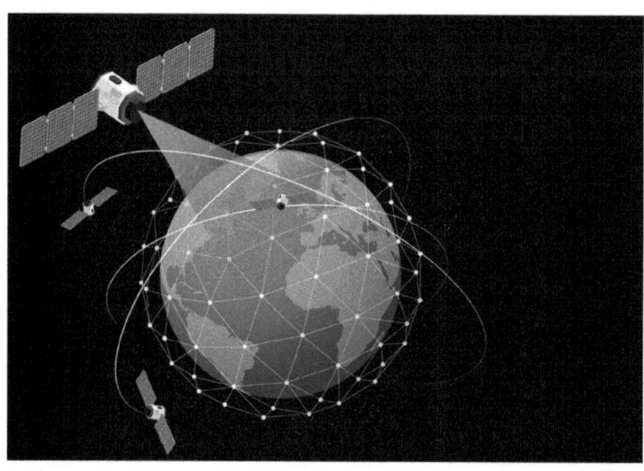

Figure 80.
Global networking of "Beidou" system (cartoon)

Knowledge about CPC History

On February 25, 2000, Jiang Zemin put forward the important idea of "Three Represents" during his working tour in Guangdong. He stressed that as long as our Party was always the faithful representative of the development requirements of China's advanced social productive forces, the direction of China's advanced culture, and the fundamental interests of the broadest number of Chinese people, our Party would always be invincible and would always receive the heartfelt support of the people of all nationalities and lead them forward.

of Sinan (compass in ancient China) to indicate a direction, distinguish the four seasons, and mark the time. The Chinese people have always been familiar with the Big Dipper. Now, looking up at the starry sky, the Big Dipper, on which people used to rely for guidance, has been redefined by Chinese aerospace personnel with modern science and technology. As Yang Changfeng, the chief designer of the "Beidou" satellite navigation system project, emphasized, "Beidou was created by the Party and the state through the mobilization of thousands of teams, by the unity of hundreds of thousands of people across the project, and by the firm support of the masses." From the pioneers of "Two Bombs, One Satellite," who began to make arduous exploration in the field of satellite navigation in the 1970s, to the experts and scholars represented by Academician Chen Fangyun in the 1980s who proposed the design scheme of "two-body position fixing," to the official launch of the Beidou 1 Project in the 1990s, the first chief designer of the project, Academician Sun Jiadong, led the team to creatively put forward the "step by step" strategy of "test before construction, domestic before surrounding, regional before global"; "Beidou" personnel had been pioneering all the way, and finally overcome many difficulties such as foreign technology blockade against China and immature domestic technology, and successfully established the world's first regional active satellite positioning system based on the "two-body position fixing" principle. The light of Beidou shone in the sky.

Twenty years later, the 55th "Beidou" satellite was successfully launched into space, marking the completion of the global networking of the "Beidou" system and its move toward the era stage of serving the world and benefiting mankind. On July 31, 2020, Xi Jinping announced forcefully at the completion and opening ceremony of the "Beidou-3" global satellite navigation system: "The Beidou-3 Global Navigation Satellite System is officially opened!" Looking back on the 20-year history of the launch of "Beidou," from "one satellite" to "all satellites in the sky," it is a magnificent and dedicated construction history of "Chinese Constellation"; from "impossible" to "great achievement"; it is a history of independent, innovative and surpassing technology peaks, from a "late start" to "fast surpassing pace," it is a history of China's space struggle "to smooth the rough road." The "Beidou" satellite navigation system embodies the continuous efforts of countless aerospace personnel and is full of the spirit of self-reliance and self-improvement of the Chinese nation. It refreshes the "Chinese speed" of scientific and technological power, demonstrates the "Chinese precision" of independent innovation, and demonstrates the "Chinese spirit" of openness and inclusiveness.

2001 Accession to WTO Opened a New Era

Keyword: China's accession to the World Trade Organization

On the afternoon of November 10, 2001, in Doha, the capital of Qatar, the beautiful "sports city," the Fourth Ministerial Conference of the World Trade Organization (WTO) deliberated and adopted the decision on China's accession to the WTO by consensus. With China's formal accession to the WTO, the long road to the WTO had finally come to a successful end. When the news reached China, people were elated. On December 11, 2001, China formally joined the World Trade Organization, becoming its 143rd member.

The dream of 15 years of waiting finally became a reality. From July 10, 1986, when China submitted its application for re-entry, it had taken 15 years to negotiate China's accession to the WTO. When Zhu Rongji, the then Premier of the State Council, talked about China's long WTO accession negotiations, he could not help sighing: "We have talked for 15 years ... black-haired people have become gray-haired people." Fifteen years may only be a short time for the whole universe, but it is a long journey for a country and a person. In these 15 years, Shen Jueren, Tong Zhiguang, Gu Yongjiang, and Long Yongtu successively served as the head of China's WTO Entry delegation. On September 11, 2001, Long Yongtu, then Vice Minister and Chief Negotiator of the Ministry of Foreign Trade and Economic Cooperation of China, laughed at the 18th meeting of the WTO China Working Group in Geneva and said, "In order to propel China joins the WTO, I have been to the headquarters of the WTO no less than

Figure 81.
World Trade Organization headquarters in Geneva, Switzerland

50 times. Benefiting from the airline's preferential plan, the free tickets we got from the airline are enough for us to fly to the moon." When it came to China's accession to the WTO, he sighed: "Now the long march-like journey has finally seen its end. I hope this is the last time I come to this beautiful lakeside city of Geneva for the negotiations on China's accession to the WTO." As Long Yongtu predicted, in the first year of the new century, China finally opened the door to the WTO.

Knowledge about CPC History

On February 19, 2001, the CPC Central Committee and the State Council held the State Science and Technology Award Conference in Beijing, and Jiang Zemin presented Wu Wenjun and Yuan Longping with the 2000 State Preeminent Science and Technology Award. The State Preeminent Science and Technology Award is the highest honor awarded by the CPC Central Committee and the State Council in the name of the country to scientists who have made outstanding contributions to the development of science and technology.

The WTO, whose predecessor was the General Agreement on Tariffs and Trade signed in 1947, is a permanent international organization independent of the United Nations. It was officially put into operation on January 1, 1995, and is mainly responsible for managing the world economic and trade order. Its headquarters is located at the beautiful Lake Lemon in Geneva, Switzerland.

Opening the door of the WTO to China not only meant that China could obtain a more stable international economic and trade environment, enjoy the convenience of trade and investment liberalization of other countries and regions, and participate in international competition under more equal conditions, but also could promote technological progress, industrial upgrading, and economic restructuring, and inject new vitality and vigor into the global development of China's economy.

Although the opening of the door of WTO also brought severe challenges to China's vulnerable industries, it still couldn't change the significance of China's accession to the WTO for its future development. As some scholars have said, "China's modernization process, whether calculated from the visit of the Macartney Mission in 1793 or the humiliation of the Opium War in 1840, ended with China's accession to the WTO, and has a new start."

2002 South-to-North Water Diversion for the People's Livelihood

Keyword: commencement of the South-to-North Water Diversion Project

On December 27, 2002, the main venue of the Great Hall of the People was solemnly and simply arranged. At 10:00 a.m., a happy movement was played in the auditorium, and the commencement ceremony of the world-famous South-to-North Water Diversion Project officially began. At the construction site of the South-to-North Water Diversion Project in Jiangsu Province and Shandong Province, the commencement ceremony was held simultaneously, and the whole country was excited to celebrate the arrival of this historic moment.

As we all know, water is the source of life and an important resource for human survival. If there is no water, there will be no choppy oceans, endless rivers, calm and charming lakes, snow-capped mountains, underground flowing undercurrents, gushing springs, silent rain, and flying snow on our lovely earth. Without water, human beings will not survive.

In China, although the total amount of water resources is rich, the per capita water quantity is very small. More importantly, the distribution of water resources in China is uneven. The runoff of the Yangtze River basin and the rivers to the south of it accounted

Figure 82.
Route diagram of South-to-North Water Diversion middle route trunk line project

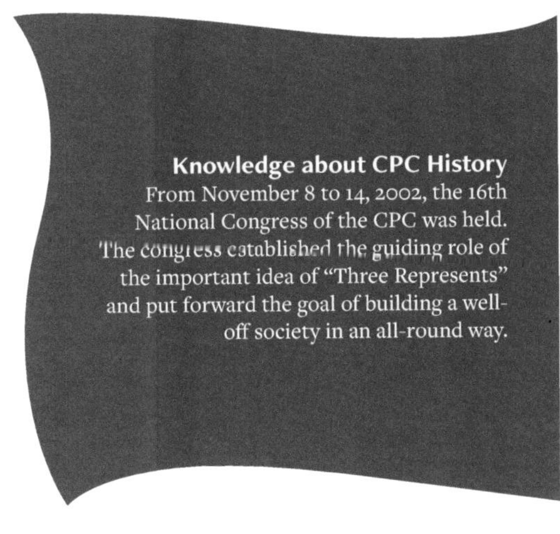

for 81% of the total runoff of the seven major rivers in China. The water resources per capita and per mu were both higher than the national average. It was a region with relatively rich water resources. However, the water resources in the Huang-Huai-Hai River basin only accounted for 7.2% of the national average, and the per capita water resources were only 21% of the national average and only 1/16 of the world average. The north was poor in water resources, while the south was rich in water resources, which not only affected the economic development of the north but also directly affected the daily life of the people. In this case, the South-to-North Water Diversion Project came into being.

After the founding of the PRC, the Party's central leadership of all generations attached great importance to and cared about the South-to-North Water Diversion Project. Under the leadership of the CPC Central Committee and the State Council, a vast number of scientific and technological workers carried out a large number of field investigations and surveys. Based on the analysis and comparison of more than 50 schemes, three water transfer routes, namely the east route, the middle route, and the west route, had been formed.

The western line project passes through the Qinghai–Xizang Plateau, the roof of the world, and can connect the whole of northwest and north China. Due to the limited water volume in the upper and middle reaches of the Yangtze River, it can only replenish water for the northwest and parts of north China in the upper and middle reaches of the Yellow River; the middle route project drew water from the middle reaches of the Yangtze River and its tributary, the Hanjiang River, which can supply water to most areas of the Huang-Huai-Hai Plain on its own; the east line project drew water from Yangzhou in the lower reaches of the Yangtze River, and used the Beijing–Hangzhou Grand Canal and its parallel rivers to lift water to the north step by step. Through the connection between the three water transfer routes and the four major rivers of the Yangtze River, the Yellow River, the Huai River, and the Haihe River, the overall layout with the "four horizontal and three vertical" as the main body was formed, so as to realize the rational allocation pattern of China's water resources from south to north and from west to east.

The South-to-North Water Diversion Project is a strategic project with the largest amount of investment and the most extensive coverage since the founding of New China, and it is a great undertaking that will affect future generations of the Chinese nation. Some people say that the South-to-North Water Diversion is a myth because it allowed the motherland to have valuable water resources from south to north; some people say that the South-to-North Water Diversion is a miracle because it once again proved the wisdom of human beings.

2003 Unite to Fight against SARS

Keyword: fighting against SARS

In 2003, when the flames of war were spreading over the Mesopotamian plain, another war without gunpowder was quietly unfolding on the other side of the Asian continent. This war was to fight against SARS. In today's China, people who do not even know the 26 English letters are familiar with the connotation of the word "SARS."

People who have experienced SARS can't help feeling that if the first patient had been effectively controlled at that time if it had been isolated from the beginning as it was later, if… However, in the face of the crisis, any assumption that subverts reality became meaningless. Perhaps, this disaster was doomed to be an inevitable accident; perhaps this spring of 2003 was destined to be an extraordinary spring.

On December 22, 2002, a critically ill patient was transferred from Heyuan, Guangdong Province, to the First Affiliated Hospital of Guangzhou Medical College. The patient's symptoms were very strange: continuous high fever, cough, shadows occupying the whole lung, and any antibiotic used to treat pneumonia had no effect. Two days later, news came from Heyuan that eight medical staff in the local hospital where the patient was admitted

Figure 83.
Beijing Xiaotangshan Hospital, a famous SARS hospital at home and abroad

had contracted the disease with the same symptoms as the patient. For a moment, Zhong Nanshan, an academician of the Chinese Academy of Engineering, was shocked, and the medical community was shocked. This strange disease was finally called "Severe Acute Respiratory Syndrome." It was an infectious disease that was a hundred times more terrible than ordinary pneumonia with a mortality rate of nearly 11%. It not only seriously threatened the health and life safety of the people but also affected China's economic development, social stability, and international exchanges.

Knowledge about CPC History

On October 11 to 14, 2003, the Third Plenary Session of the 16th CPC Central Committee was held, which adopted the *Decision on Several Issues Concerning the Improvement of the Socialist Market Economy System* and put forward the idea of putting people first and establishing a comprehensive, coordinated and sustainable development outlook as well as the "five balanced aspects" concept.

In the first half of 2003, the CPC Central Committee and the State Council took a series of decisive measures against the SARS epidemic that occurred in most provinces, autonomous regions, and cities across the country, and the whole country mobilized urgently to wage an arduous struggle against this sudden disease. In this war, where there was no smoke or gunpowder and no enemy could be seen, everyone was on the front line. The phrase "unite as one" began to appear frequently in major media. No other words could accurately describe the then state of mind of the Chinese nation more than this. Ye Xin, Deng Lianxian, Li Xiaohong ... People remembered with tears the medical workers who died to save the patients, as well as the thousands of brave and fearless angels in white who fought on the front line.

After several months of effort, on June 24, 2003, the World Health Organization (WHO) announced in Geneva that the SARS epidemic in Beijing had eased significantly and had met the relevant WHO standards. Therefore, the travel warning for Beijing was lifted, and Beijing was excluded from the list of SARS-affected areas. It marked the initial victory of the Chinese people in the fight against SARS.

The luck of surviving after the disaster is certainly gratifying. However, for a rational person or a nation coming out of this costly disaster, we need more time to reflect on pain of nature and precipitate the understanding of life.

2004 West–East Gas Transmission for Development

Keyword: West–East Gas Transmission

In autumn, along the Qinhuai River, the sound of oars, the lights, and the rippling blue waves showed a picture of the ancient capital of Jinling (today's Nanjing). Mr. Lu, a citizen who lives in Nanjing, repeatedly praised such a beautiful scene: "Since the West–East Gas Transmission Project was put into operation, the air and environment in Nanjing have been obviously better!"

The entry of natural gas into thousands of households not only saved the common people from the trouble of burning coal, firewood, and changing gas tanks but also was of great significance for improving environmental quality. By 2020, in the process of fulfilling the mission of protecting clear water and blue sky, the West–East Gas Transmission Project had replaced a total of 610 million tons of standard coal and reduced greenhouse gas emissions by 720 million tons and 420 million tons of dust, directly benefiting nearly 500 million people.

With white clouds blossoming in the blue sky, populus euphratica shows its tenacious vitality in the endless sea of sand, which is a unique and beautiful picture in Xinjiang in the

Figure 84.
West–East Gas Transmission Project under construction

Knowledge about CPC History
The China Western Development is a policy adopted by the Chinese government to coordinate regional development, with the aim of "using the surplus economic development capacity of the eastern coastal areas to improve the economic and social development of the western region and consolidate national defense." In January 2000, the State Council established a leading group for the development of the western region, headed by Zhu Rongji, then Premier of the State Council.

northwest of China. In that peculiar land, there is not only beautiful scenery and hardworking people but also very rich resources. The special topography of "three mountains with two basins" of the Altai Mountains, Tian Mountains, Kunlun Mountains, Junggar Basin, and Tarim Basin, forms the overall geomorphological layout of Xinjiang. The mountainous area makes Xinjiang rich in mineral resources; the two major basins are rich in oil and natural gas resources, which are the great treasure Xinjiang brought to the motherland. According to the survey, the natural gas reserves in the Tarim Basin in Xinjiang have reached more than 80,000 billion cubic meters, accounting for about 22% of the total onshore natural gas resources in China. In the Kuqa area in the north of the Tarim Basin, natural gas resources amount to more than 20,000 billion cubic meters, which is the most abundant area in the Tarim Basin and has the development potential to form a world-class gas area. The discovery of natural gas in the Tarim Basin made China a major natural gas country after Russia, Qatar, Saudi Arabia, and other countries.

In order to promote China's energy structure and industrial structure adjustment, drive the economic development of the eastern and western regions together, improve the quality of life of people in the Yangtze River Delta and areas along the West-East gas pipeline, and effectively control air pollution, in February 2000, the CPC Central Committee and the State Council officially approved the launch of the West-East Gas Transmission Project.

The West-East Gas Transmission Project is a landmark project of China Western Development and is another major investment project following the Three Gorges Project. This huge project, with a total length of about 4,000 kilometers, starts in Lunnan, Xinjiang, passing through 66 counties in 10 provinces (districts and cities) of Xinjiang, Gansu, Ningxia, Shaanxi, Shanxi, Henan, Anhui, Jiangsu, Shanghai, and Zhejiang, running through the east and west of China, and connecting the vast desert with the coastal regions of the East China Sea. The pipeline project passes through the Gobi Desert, the Loess Plateau, and the Taihang Mountains, and crosses the Yellow River, Huai River, and the Yangtze River. It is currently the pipeline project with the largest pipe diameter, the thickest pipe wall, the highest pressure rating, and the highest technical difficulty in China, creating a number of leading records for domestic natural gas pipelines and also creating a high speed in the world pipeline construction history.

On December 30, 2004, the West-East Gas Transmission Project was fully completed and officially put into operation, which greatly accelerated the economic development of Xinjiang and the central and western regions along the project and brought huge economic and social benefits. The operation of the West-East Gas Transmission Project once again proved to the world the intelligence, wisdom, and courage of the Chinese people.

2005 China's Shenzhou VI Traveled to Space

Keyword: "Shenzhou VI" traveling to space

A roar broke the clear sky, a cheer intoxicated the hearts of the whole nation, and a leap amazed the eyes of the world. On October 12, 2005, the Chinese people once again opened the mysterious gate of the universe—"Shenzhou VI" spacecraft was launched at Jiuquan Satellite Launch Center. Fei Junlong and Nie Haisheng, two Chinese astronauts, flew into mysterious space.

On October 15, 2003, the "Shenzhou V" test spacecraft was launched, sending astronaut Yang Liwei into space, marking a historic breakthrough in China's manned space program.

"Shenzhou VI" manned spacecraft is one of the "Shenzhou" series of spacecraft in China. It is basically the same shape as "Shenzhou V" and is still a three-compartment structure of propelling module, return capsule and orbital capsule, with a weight of about 8 tons. It was launched by "Long March II" F-type carrier rocket. It is the second Chinese spacecraft to carry astronauts, and the first Chinese manned spacecraft to carry out a "multi-person, multi-day" mission.

Figure 85.
The moment of "Shenzhou VI" manned spacecraft's lift-off

> **Knowledge about CPC History**
> After the 16th National Congress of the CPC, the CPC Central Committee made a major decision to establish three executive leadership academies in Pudong, Jinggangshan, and Yan'an in China to meet the strategic needs of large-scale training of cadres and substantial improvement of their quality in the new era. In March 2005, three executive leadership academies were completed and officially put into use.

At 9:00 a.m. on October 12, 2005, "Shenzhou VI" officially took off. At 3:55 p.m., when the "Shenzhou VI" spaceship flew to the fifth circle, under the control of the ground command and control center, it changed from an elliptical orbit to a circular orbit, and the entire orbit change process took only two minutes. At 2:36 p.m. on the 14th, the astronauts took pictures of the earth through the porthole of the spacecraft with a handheld camera, through which they could see the blue earth. As of 4:00 p.m. on the 14th, the "Shenzhou VI" spacecraft had been in space for 55 hours. Two astronauts witnessed sunrise and sunset 36 times in space, flying about 1.51 million kilometers, and successfully returned to land.

The successful flight of "Shenzhou VI" made a great achievement in China's space history, creating many "firsts": the first multi-person space flight, the first multi-day space flight, the first space experiment, the first spacecraft orbit, the first comprehensive launch of the environmental control and life support system, and the first addition of rocket safety agencies. These all mark China's "Shenzhou" achieving a new leap forward.

During the development of China's aerospace industry, a kind of aerospace spirit of "being able to bear hardships, fight, tackle key problems, and contribute" was formed, and Yang Liwei, Fei Junlong, Nie Haisheng, and others are representatives of this spirit. In order to meet the needs of multi-day space missions, astronauts had to carry out up to seven years of hard training. In addition to 58 professional pieces of training, they also needed to learn basic courses such as astronomy, celestial bodies, aerospace medicine, aerodynamics, foreign languages, etc. It takes a college student four years to learn them, and they had to master them all in two years. There were many exercises that pushed the physical limits of the human body.

When the huge return capsule fell down, the heroes who came back that day shook the five-star red flag in their hands. As Chinese, we felt extremely proud. The successful flight of "Shenzhou VI" proved the rise of the Chinese nation and played a moving movement of human wisdom.

2006 Going to Lhasa by Train

Keyword: the complete and opening to traffic of Qinghai–Xizang Railway

There was a saying in Xizang: "It is more difficult to enter Xizang than to reach the sky." It is said that after the peaceful liberation of Xizang in 1951, the central government used more than 40,000 camels to form a large camel caravan to transport goods to Xizang. Due to the treacherous natural conditions, an average of twelve camel carcasses were left behind for every kilometer traveled.

In order to change this situation, at the beginning of the founding of New China, the construction of the Qinghai–Xizang Railway was put on the agenda of the first generation of central leadership. In 1955, the Northwest Design Branch of the Ministry of Railways sent the first investigation team, which took the first step in investigating the railway to Xizang. However, due to technical constraints and changes in the political situation, the construction of the Qinghai–Xizang Railway experienced several ups and downs since 1956.

Time flies. With the spring breeze of reform and opening-up, China's comprehensive national strength and scientific and technological level were greatly improved. With the attention of the second and third generation of central leadership, and the sweat of thousands of technicians, the historical camera finally stopped at this moment: on the morning of June 29, 2001, the world-famous Qinghai–Xizang Railway officially started construction. The railway starts from Xining, Qinghai Province in the east and ends at Lhasa in the west, with a total length of 1,956 kilometers, of which the 814 kilometers section from Xining to Golmud

Figure 86.
Qinghai–Xizang Railway

Knowledge about CPC History

Since January 1, 2006, China has abolished the agricultural tax, ending the history of farmers' farming tax payments. The agricultural tax that had lasted for more than 2000 years in China finally entered the history museum. The abolition of the agricultural tax marked the beginning of a new era in the fate of China's farmers and the development of China's rural areas and was a milestone in the history of Chinese civilization.

was constructed in 1979 and put into operation in 1984. The Golmud–Lhasa section of the Qinghai–Xizang Railway starts from Golmud City, Qinghai Province, in the north, passes through Naij Tal, Wudaoliang, Tuotuo River, and Yanshiping, crosses the Tanggula Mountains, and then passes through Amdo, Nakchu, Damxung, and Yangbajain of the Xizang Autonomous Region to Lhasa, with a total length of 1,142 kilometers. The Qinghai–Xizang Railway is the highest and longest plateau railway in the world. The highest point of the railway crossing Tanggula Mountains is 5,072 meters above sea level, and it passes through areas over 4,000 meters above sea level for 960 kilometers and continuous permafrost areas over 550 kilometers. The geology of the areas along the line is complex, and disasters such as landslides, mudslides, earthquakes, and lightning strikes are frequent.

On July 1, 2006, the Golmud–Lhasa section of the Qinghai–Xizang Railway was officially completed after five years of hard work by more than 100,000 railway-building teams. This not only solved the three worldwide engineering and technical problems of permafrost, alpine cold and hypoxia, and ecological fragility but also made this steel artery open to traffic one year ahead of schedule, creating a number of the world's highest records in terms of the railway. So far, the whole line of the Qinghai–Xizang Railway was successfully completed and opened to traffic.

The towering Kunlun Mountains show the charm of "dancing silver serpents and advancing waxy elephants," and the winding Tuotuo River expresses the charm of "the endless river rolls its waves hour by hour." Such fascinating scenery could finally be seen from the train. How could it not be exciting and exalting? Not only that, the completion of the Qinghai–Xizang Railway ended the history that there was no access to the Xizang Autonomous Region, which accounts for one-eighth of the country's land area, completely changed the dilemma of "going abroad is easier than entering Xizang" in the past, and strengthened the linkage between other regions of the country and the Qinghai–Xizang region in terms of people flow, logistics, and capital flow.

The 1.3 billion people and 130,000 railway construction workers united to form the Qinghai–Xizang Railway, the Heavenly Way of the Chinese nation. It is the result of mankind's constant understanding and exploration of the Qinghai–Xizang Plateau for thousands of years, and it is also a miracle created by the Chinese nation on the roof of the world. It is like a string of pearls embedded in the snow-covered plateau of the motherland.

2007 Chang'e Grasped the Bright Moon

Keyword: the successful launch of "Chang'e-1"

Since ancient times, Chinese people have had a unique complex about the moon. The moon is always so poetic in the eyes of Chinese people. Whether it is the lofty aspiration of "we have the same ideal to fly, up to the moon in the blue sky" or the beautiful vision of "over the sea grows the moon bright, we gaze on it far, far apart,"* it reflects the imagination and curiosity of the Chinese people about the moon.

On October 24, 2007, the legend of "The Goddess Chang'e's Flight to the Moon," which had been passed on for thousands of years in China, finally became a reality on this beautiful autumn day, and the mysterious moon finally opened the door to the Chinese people. At 6:05 p.m. on the 24th, China's first lunar probe satellite, "Chang'e-1," carrying the blessings of many Chinese people, was successfully launched from the No. 3 tower of Xichang Satellite Launch Center, starting China's first "lunar probe" trip. Chang'e-1, the first lunar probe independently developed and launched by China, was developed by the China Academy of Space Technology. It was mainly used to obtain three-dimensional images of the lunar surface, analyze the distribution characteristics of related material elements on the lunar surface, detect the thickness of lunar soil, and explore the Earth-Moon space environment.

Figure 87.
"Chang'e-1" satellite successfully launched.

* Xu Yuanchong, *Three Hundred Tang Poems* (Beijing: China Intercontinental Press, 2011), 19.

Knowledge about CPC History

The 17th National Congress of the CPC was held in Beijing from October 15–21, 2007. The first plenary session of the 17th CPC Central Committee elected Hu Jintao as the General Secretary of the CPC Central Committee and Hu Jintao, Wu Bangguo, Wen Jiabao, Jia Qinglin, Li Changchun, Xi Jinping, Li Keqiang, and He Guoqiang as the Standing Committee of the Central Political Bureau.

The successful launch of "Chang'e-1" indicated that China had become the fifth country in the world to launch a lunar probe, marking the fact that after the realization of the artificial earth satellite flight and manned space flight, China's space industry had made another important step toward deep space exploration, and was another milestone in the development of China's space industry.

On May 28, 1978, on the eve of the establishment of diplomatic relations between China and the United States, Zbigniew Brzezinski, the National Security Adviser of the President of the United States, visited China and presented a one-gram moon rock to China. Many people regarded this as the earliest origin of China's lunar exploration. But in fact, since 1962, Chinese scientists had begun to conduct tracking and comprehensive research on lunar probes, such as "Luna," "Ranger," "Surveyor," "Lunar Orbiter," and "Apollo," and then concentrated their efforts on urgent and practical satellites. In the early 1990s, some domestic scientists put forward the idea of "The Goddess Chang'e's Flight to the Moon," and proposed to launch an iron symbol of China on the moon with a carrier rocket, and "brand" it on the moon forever to promote national prestige. This assumption, which was based on political considerations and had little scientific research value, aroused great controversy in the scientific community. The report was finally rejected by CPC Central Committee. In 1994, Ouyang Ziyuan, the chief scientist of China's lunar exploration, formally proposed the concept of lunar exploration. He, together with other scientists, submitted a report to the 863 Plan team, noting that "the rich resources on the moon will be the object of contention for all countries to solve the energy crisis. As a major developing country, we must consider our own interests on the moon." The report was highly praised by the team, but when the plan was submitted to other ministries, questions arose. After repeated argumentation on the issues of "whether it is necessary to explore the moon" and "whether it is feasible," the first phase of the scientific objectives and payload configuration of "launching satellites around the moon" led by Ouyang Ziyuan passed the review in 2001, and many scientists' efforts and appeals for many years finally came to fruition. As a result, China's lunar exploration project started, and the central government officially approved the lunar exploration plan in 2003.

In just over three years, Chinese aerospace personnel overcame many technical difficulties and successfully launched the Chang'e-1 satellite into space, proving once again to the world the wisdom of the Chinese people who were constantly striving for self-improvement and once again carving a new height for the Chinese nation in space.

2008 The Beijing Olympic Games Connected Five Continents

Keyword: the Beijing Olympic Games

Looking forward to a hundred years, we finally realized a dream. At that moment, our hearts were formed into five rings.

On August 8, 2008, the Olympic Goddess fixed her beautiful sideburns, and with her unchanging faith, fraternal smile, and friendship spreading all over the world, she gladly walked toward the rising Oriental Dragon. After seven years of waiting, the wishes of 1.3 billion Chinese people were successfully realized at the moment when the Olympic Torch was lit at the Bird's Nest in Beijing. It was a moment for the Chinese people to cheer and for the world to remember.

As time went by, it was still remembered that the eternal moment was fixed at 10:10 p.m. Beijing time on July 13, 2001. That night, Samaranch, then President of the International Olympic Committee, took out an envelope, opened it, and solemnly announced: "The host city of the 2008 Olympic Games is Beijing!" Since then, China became the third Asian country

Figure 88.
Opening ceremony of the Beijing Olympics

Knowledge about CPC History

On May 12, 2008, a massive earthquake measuring 8 on the Richter scale struck Wenchuan, Sichuan Province, killing 69,227 people, leaving 17,923 missing and 374,643 injured. Under the leadership of the CPC Central Committee, the State Council, and the Central Military Commission, China quickly organized the earthquake relief activities, which were the fastest in rescue speed, the widest in mobilization, and the largest in investment in history, and seized a major victory in the struggle against earthquakes and disasters.

to hold the Summer Olympic Games after Japan (1964 Tokyo Olympics) and South Korea (1988 Seoul Olympics).

For this Olympic feast of all mankind, Beijing worked hard for seven years. From Mount Olympia to the Great Wall, the sacred flame reflected the journey of civilization spreading and communication, witnessing the integration of an ancient nation into the world trend. The miraculous Bird's Nest and the crystal-clear Water Cube sprang up; the Olympic Torch with the pattern of auspicious cloud on it passed the Olympic spirit of "faster, higher and stronger" across the country. Every Chinese person acted and shouted "One World, One Dream," and contributed to the "Green Olympics, Technology Olympics, and People's Olympics."

At 8:00 p.m. on August 8, 2008, when the centuries-old wish of the Chinese nation was about to become a reality, and when the Olympic Torch was lit, one voice resounded in the hearts of every Chinese with a sincere patriotic heart: Beijing succeeded! China succeeded! At that moment, Beijing at night was particularly beautiful. At that moment, in Beijing, the night was very colorful. The colorful fireworks lit up the night sky, and suddenly the National Stadium became a sea of joy.

From August 8 to 24, the world witnessed every wonderful moment of the Beijing Olympic Games. In 16 days, 28 major events and 302 minor events were held in the Beijing Olympic Games, resulting in 302 gold medals, with more than 60,000 athletes, coaches, and officials participating. The Olympic Games finally broke 132 Olympic records and 43 world records. The Chinese team won 51 gold medals, ranking first in the gold medal table for the first time.

On the evening of August 24, the main Torch of the Beijing Olympic Games was extinguished slowly, and the Olympic goddess reluctantly said goodbye to Beijing. With 16 days of competition, 16 days of friendship, and 16 days of exchange, the Beijing Olympics infected all the participants and guests with its great charm.

The 2008 Beijing Olympic Games was a carnival of mankind and a full physical examination of China. The strong national power, the open posture, and the tolerant greatness show the world the new image of China. We were pleased to see that the world's vision was changing and China's image was sublimating.

2009 "Tianhe-1" Came to Being

Keyword: the successful develop of China's first petaflop supercomputer

In September 2009, the country's first petaflop supercomputer system, Tianhe-1, was successfully developed, and the peak performance of China's high-performance computers increased to 1,206 trillion times per second. What did this number mean? It meant that one day of Tianhe-1 computing was equivalent to 160 years of computing on a microcomputer with an Intel dual-core CPU and a main frequency of 2.5 GHz. In today's world, high-performance computing has become a strategic technology to promote scientific and technological innovation, economic and social development, and thus enhance national comprehensive competitiveness.

The international computer community generally believed that, in the process of supercomputers' continuous improvement of computing speed, it was an insurmountable bottleneck to upgrade from exaflop to petaflop. As early as the 1990s, the United States put forward the goal of developing petaflop supercomputers of billions, but it was not realized until 2007. As of June 2009, there were only three petaflop computers in the world. Compared with developed countries that had developed supercomputers, China was not only one order of magnitude weaker in computing capacity but also far away from them in the number of installed machines. In order to develop "Tianhe-1," scientific researchers broke through a

Figure 89.
"Tianhe-1" supercomputer

number of key technologies and solved many historical problems.

Knowledge about CPC History
When the PRC was founded, the military parade was listed as an important part of the National Day celebrations. From the founding ceremony in 1949 to the 60th anniversary of the founding of the PRC in 2009, 14 National Day parades were held. From 1949 to 1959, 11 National Day parades were held.

The first was in the field of architecture. Every time a computer's computing capacity increases by order of magnitude, it needs a lot of optimization and innovation in its architecture. In the architecture design of "Tianhe-1," researchers creatively proposed a multi-array, configurable, collaborative, and parallel architecture and adopted mixed language programming technology to greatly improve the system operation speed. The second was in the aspect of dealing with mistakes. "Tianhe-1" was composed of more than 10,000 components. From a scientific perspective, failures were inevitable. In order to improve the fault tolerance performance, the researchers specially designed the monitoring and diagnosis subsystem, which realized the real-time safety monitoring and debugging diagnosis of the whole system, and effectively guaranteed the reliability of the system. The third was in the aspect of safety performance. In order to meet the security requirements of various users, researchers developed the highest B2-level security standard operating system in China and adopted software security isolation technology. Even if multiple users use "Tianhe-1" together, they also had their own independent computing spaces and completely isolated working environments. For users, this was equivalent to renting a safe in the bank, with the key in their own hands. In addition, "Tianhe-1" was a world leader in terms of computing efficiency, cooling, and heat dissipation, energy consumption control, and related areas.

As Zhou Xingming, an academician of the Chinese Academy of Sciences, said, "We can see supercomputers in all fields closely related to public life." If supercomputers were used in the field of biopharmaceutics, scientists could screen out effective drug compounds in a relatively short time, and the research and development cycle of a new drug could be shortened by 3–5 years; the use of supercomputers in the field of aircraft manufacturing could save a lot of finalization experiments, and the production cycle of an aircraft could be shortened by 3–6 months; the use of supercomputers in the field of network services could handle tens of millions or even hundreds of millions of user access requests every second, and provide the information required by users in a timely manner; etc. All cutting-edge scientific and technological issues and many key areas closely related to people's livelihoods needed the support of supercomputers.

The birth of "Tianhe-1" was another major breakthrough in the development of China's high-performance computer technology, another important achievement in the national and military information construction, and marked China's becoming the second country after the United States to develop a petaflop supercomputer system, which had far-reaching strategic significance for improving China's comprehensive national strength.

2010 The Wave of Expo Came from the Sea

Keyword: Shanghai World Expo

When the curtain opened, the two sides of the Huangpu River presented a magnificent picture of human civilization; with colorful fireworks, the East of the World played the music of a future life full of passion.

The 2010 World Expo in Shanghai, China, through 184 colorful days and nights, presented a grand meeting for the people of the world to probe into urban human life, reproduced a condensed history of mankind's continuous progress, and launched a wonderful dialogue of human civilization. China successfully fulfilled its bid commitment of "the world gives China a chance, and China will return a piece of splendor to the world."

In December 1999, at the 126th General Assembly of the Bureau International des Expositions, the Chinese government officially announced its bid to host the 2010 World Expo. On December 3, 2002, Shanghai, China, was awarded the right to host the 2010 World Expo by a vote of the General Assembly of the Bureau des International Exhibitions. Since then, China had embarked on its first trip to the World Expo. Over the past seven years,

Figure 90.
The China Pavilion at the Shanghai World Expo

with the strong support of the CPC Central Committee and the State Council, China mobilized forces from all over the world and worked with the Bureau International des Expositions and exhibitors from all over the world, marking the Shanghai World Expo with the profound impression of "mobilizing resources throughout the country and pooling the wisdom of the world." The Expo Park covered an area of 5.28 square kilometers, 246 participating countries, regions, and international organizations, and more than 70 million Chinese and foreign tourists jointly created a "successful, wonderful, and unforgettable" Expo.

Knowledge about CPC History

From November 12 to 27, 2010, the 16th Asian Games was held in Guangzhou. More than 10,000 athletes from 45 countries and regions in Asia participated in 42 major events and 476 minor events, making it the Asian Games with the largest number of participants and events. This Asian Games, with the vision of "Thrilling Games, Harmonious Asia," fully demonstrated the image of China as a great power and enhanced Guangzhou's international influence.

The Expo Park was magnificent and bustling with visitors. Each ingenious and novel exhibition attracted patient waiting, many amazed eyes, many quiet thoughts, and many understanding smiles. Every advanced facility, every thoughtful service, every busy figure, and every subtle improvement was filled with the sweat and effort of the people of the host country and the sincere desire of the Chinese people to embrace the world. China's all-out investment ignited the enthusiasm of all participating countries and regions, making the World Expo with a long history and a new show of youth and charm. The giant screen film of the Saudi Arabia Pavilion, the seven national treasures of the France Pavilion, the little mermaid in the Denmark Pavilion, the intelligent robot in the Japan Pavilion, the top flamenco dance in the Span Pavilion transcended the barriers of region, and language and transcended the differences in beliefs and customs. People here freely communicated and learned from each other discussed the problems faced by urban development and looked for a path for sustainable development of human society. The Expo Park became a miniature global village, perfectly presenting the Expo theme of "Better City, Better Life," and more vividly interpreting the Expo concept of "understanding, communication, togetherness, and cooperation."

More than a hundred years ago, Liang Qichao gave a magnificent and romantic description of China's hosting of the World Expo. However, in an era when the country was fragmented, poor, and weak, this could only be a distant and ethereal dream. More than a hundred years later, New China achieved sustained and rapid development and embarked on a new path of development that conformed to China's national conditions and the trend of the times. The dazzling brilliance of the Shanghai World Expo reflected the hard work of the Chinese nation in its efforts to achieve national rejuvenation and told the story of a country with an ancient civilization that created a new glory.

2011 The Magnificence of 90 Years

Keyword: the 90th anniversary of the founding of the Party

The year 2011 was of special significance for the CPC. In this year, we celebrated the 90th anniversary of the party. On July 1, 2011, the conference to celebrate the 90th anniversary of the founding of the CPC was held in the Great Hall of the People in Beijing. Hu Jintao delivered an important speech at the conference, pointing out that: “Over the past 90 years, the Chinese Communists and the people of all ethnic groups have gone forward and backward, struggling tenaciously to win major victories in revolution, construction, and reform. Today, a vibrant socialist China is standing tall in the east of the world, and 1.3 billion Chinese people are confidently moving toward the great rejuvenation of the Chinese nation under the guidance of the great banner of socialism with Chinese characteristics.”

On July 23, 1921, 13 representatives of the CPC gathered for a tense and secret meeting. With the convening of the 1st National Congress of the CPC, and thus the CPC was born. Mao Zedong later used “an epoch-making event” to describe the founding of the CPC, and later the development of Chinese history also made a good interpretation of this description.

From 1921 to 1949, the CPC led the Chinese people on the road to break through the

Figure 91.
On July 1, 2011, the conference to celebrate the 90th anniversary of the founding of the CPC was held in the Great Hall of the People in Beijing.

Knowledge about CPC History
Hu Jintao's speech at the conference celebrating the 90th anniversary of the founding of the CPC for the first time summarized the connotation of socialism with Chinese characteristics into three aspects: road, theory, and system. He said: "We have embarked on the path of socialism with Chinese characteristics, formed a system of theories of socialism with Chinese characteristics, and established a socialist system with Chinese characteristics. These achievements made over 90 years of endeavors, innovation, and enrichment should be valued, upheld on a long-term basis, and continuously built upon by our Party and people."

darkness, gain light, and overthrow the "three mountains of imperialism, feudalism, and bureaucrat capitalism" that lay on the Chinese people. It was a difficult and rugged road, through the Northern Expedition, the Agrarian Revolutionary War, the War of Resistance against Japanese Aggression, and the War of Liberation, and through 28 years of bloody battles, the Japanese imperialists were defeated, the reactionary rule of the KMT was overthrown, and the PRC was established. On October 1, 1949, Mao Zedong declared to the world with his powerful voice: the Chinese people have stood up! Later, we creatively achieved the transition from New Democracy to socialism, leading one-fifth of the world's population onto the path of socialism. China had transformed itself from an ancient oriental country with a lot of difficulties and weaknesses waiting to be addressed to a promising and dynamic socialist country.

After the Third Plenary Session of the 11th CPC Central Committee, the CPC summarized the experience of China's socialist construction and opened a new chapter of reform and opening-up with great courage. After the reform and opening-up, the Chinese people performed the music of the new era under the leadership of the Party. Tall buildings, factories, and enterprises sprang up like bamboo shoots after a spring rain, and the national economy rose rapidly and lifted. We cannot forget the excitement when Hong Kong and Macau returned to the embrace of the motherland; we cannot forget the upright steel bodies standing up in the flood rescue; we cannot forget the angels in white guarding people's safety in the fight against SARS; we cannot forget the military soldiers rescuing people in danger in the Wenchuan earthquake; and we cannot forget the pride of the Olympic rings rising in the Bird's Nest in Beijing. The Chinese people, under the leadership of the CPC, entered a glorious era that had not existed in a century.

History and the people chose the CPC, and the CPC led the Chinese people to change the fate of the whole nation. The 90 years of the CPC was the history of the Party's unremitting struggle, theoretical exploration, and self-construction.

2012 The Chinese Dream of National Rejuvenation

Keyword: the proposing of Chinese Dream

On November 29, 2012, Xi Jinping, General Secretary of the CPC Central Committee, visited the exhibition The Road to Rejuvenation at the National Museum of China. The large-scale exhibition, which attracted thousands of visitors, told the story of the great changes the country had undergone in the past 100 years since the Opium Wars, from which people could appreciate the struggle of the Chinese nation. After the visit, General Secretary Xi Jinping said with deep feelings, "Everyone is discussing the Chinese Dream. I believe that achieving the great rejuvenation of the Chinese nation is the greatest dream of the Chinese nation since modern times."

In fact, the proposition of the Chinese Dream had a profound historical origin. After the Opium War in 1840, China was forced to open its doors and began to become a country swallowed and divided by foreign invaders. From this time on, the Chinese people began to pursue the dream of national rejuvenation. In the later historical process, many people of insight had the dream of national rejuvenation. Sun Yat-sen was the first to shout the slogan "rejuvenating China." After the founding of the CPC, it undertook the sacred mission

Figure 92.
The Chinese Dream is the dream of the Chinese nation and the dream of every Chinese.

of leading the Chinese people to achieve national rejuvenation. It can be said that the Chinese spent more than a hundred years from 1840 to 1949 completing the first task of the Chinese Dream—to achieve national independence and national liberation. By this time, had our Chinese Dream come true? Obviously not, as the realization of the Chinese Dream still faced a second task—to achieve the great rejuvenation of the Chinese nation. This task can be divided into two goals: to build a moderately prosperous society in an all-round way by the 100th year of the founding of the Communist Party of China and to build a great modern socialist country in all respects by the 100th year of the founding of New China.

Knowledge about CPC History

The core content of the "Chinese Dream" can be summarized as the goal of "two hundred years," that is, to build a moderately prosperous society in an all-round way by the 100th year of the founding of the CPC, and to build a great modern socialist country in all respects by the 100th year of the founding of New China, and to achieve the great rejuvenation of the Chinese nation on this basis.

The seemingly grand Chinese Dream, scattered in each of us, has become a simple and practical dream. For example, we all expect better education for children, better medical conditions for the elderly, more satisfactory income from work, more comfortable living, a more beautiful environment, etc. Only when these are realized can the Chinese Dream be truly realized. Since the reform and opening-up, through constant exploration, we found a path belonging to the Chinese people—the path of socialism with Chinese characteristics. Our living standards have been constantly improving, and the Chinese nation also made great strides to catch up with the trend of the times. History had proved that the path of socialism with Chinese characteristics is the right path that conforms to China's national conditions and makes people rich and powerful. Only by holding high the great banner of socialism with Chinese characteristics can we unite and lead the whole Party and the people of all ethnic groups to achieve the "two centenary goals" and win a happier and better future for the Chinese people and the Chinese nation.

Looking at China today, we have already said goodbye to the humiliation of the past. The Chinese nation has stood firm among the nations of the world, and the Chinese people have their own dignity in the world. However, China needs to redouble its efforts if it is to become a more respected country and if the Chinese nation is to make more contributions to world development and human progress. Along the path of socialism with Chinese characteristics, we will eventually realize the Chinese Dream. The Chinese Dream is the dream of every Chinese. We all share the opportunity to make our lives brilliant and to make our dreams come true. Every Communist and every Chinese should be aware of their responsibilities and make their due contributions to the country, the nation, the family, and the children.

2013 The Roc Will Soar up Ninety Thousand Miles and Nine

Keyword: a general design for comprehensively deepening reform

At the root of the old city wall in Beijing, there was an old man who sold *Tanghulu* (sugarcoated haws on a stick). He grew up in Beijing and shuttled in hutongs since he was young. He could be said to be the most authentic "old Beijinger." The old man liked to chat with tourists passing by. He often talked about his childhood. He said, "When I was young, my siblings and I lived in a hutong. Although it was difficult to feed and clothe ourselves, we flew kites and caught birds in the park during the day and watched the stars and the moon in our own yard at night, thus having a lot of good memories of old Beijing." Then in the 1980s, when the country started to reform and open up, the old man said, "That was a big change! The small hutongs and courtyards of the past were turned into high-rise buildings, and it was easy to get around, with more and more subways being built in Beijing. Everyone wore colorful clothes and was happy, they could eat whatever they wanted, and they didn't have to do any work at home, it was all done by electrical appliances." But after a while, the old man said with a sad face, "Everything is fine now, but look, everyone is in a hurry on the street, and many people are wearing masks. Why? For no other reason than the fact that Beijing has had a bit of smog lately."

Beijing, in the old man's words, seemed to be a microcosm of modern China before and after reform and opening-up. Reform and opening-up that began in 1978 had brought about

Figure 93. The Third Plenary Session of the 18th CPC Central Committee was held in Beijing from November 9 to 12, 2013. The main agenda was to study the major issues of comprehensively deepening reform.

Knowledge about CPC History
The overall goal of comprehensively deepening reform is: to improve and develop the socialist system with Chinese characteristics, and promote the modernization of the national governance system and capacity. Some people in academic circles refer to the modernization of the national governance system and capacity as the "fifth modernization."

earth-shaking changes for modern China and had made remarkable achievements. However, after more than 40 years of reform and opening-up, we were still facing some problems such as unbalanced and uncoordinated development, destruction of resources and environment, a large income gap between residents, moral anomie in some fields, lack of integrity, etc. At such a key historical point, the Third Plenary Session of the 18th CPC Central Committee held in November 2013 made an important judgment: "In the face of new situations and new tasks, to realize the Chinese Dream of the great rejuvenation of the Chinese nation, we must comprehensively deepen reform at a new historical starting point." Therefore, the plenary session deliberated and adopted the *Decision of the CPC Central Committee on Several Important Issues of Comprehensively Deepening Reform*. The CPC Central Committee made a breakthrough in upgrading the reform and put forward the idea of "deepening reform in all aspects."

The trumpet was blowing, and the drums of war were urging people; the tide was surging, and the wind was blowing. The *Decision of the CPC Central Committee on Several Important Issues of Comprehensively Deepening Reform* closely revolved around the six major reform themes of economy, politics, culture, society, ecological civilization, and party building, covering 15 fields and 60 specific tasks. Among these tasks, the reform of the economic system was the key, and the core issue was to properly handle the relationship between the government and the market so that the market could play a decisive role in resource allocation and the government could play its role better. It could be said that only by comprehensively deepening reform could we solve a series of major problems facing China's development, maintain the momentum of sustained and healthy economic and social development, and provide strong impetus and vitality for upholding and developing socialism with Chinese characteristics and realizing the Chinese Dream of the great rejuvenation of the Chinese nation.

Li Qingzhao, a famous poet in the Song Dynasty, said in her poem "Pride of Fishermen," "The roc will soar up ninety thousand miles and nine,"[*] which describes that in the sky of 90,000 miles, the majestic roc is soaring high into the sky. We are convinced that the comprehensive deepening of reform will be like a roc spreading its wings, soaring in the wind, and taking solid steps toward the general goal of improving and developing the socialist system with Chinese characteristics and promoting the modernization of the national governance system and capacity.

* Xu Yuanchong, *Literature and Translation* (Beijing: Peking University Press, 2003), 490.

2014

The "Four Comprehensives" Supported the Chinese Dream

Keyword: the proposition of the "Four Comprehensives"

In 2016, an "earworm" suddenly became popular in the streets and alleys, and both the elderly and children could hum some of it: "One is the point, two is the line, three is the plane, and four is Comprehensives ..." What was this song? It turns out that this was the latest popular mix and match of the current politics song "Four Comprehensives" released by Xinhua News Agency. This song combined dance music, rap, chorus, and other musical forms. It interpreted the "Four Comprehensives" with simple lyrics, with a catchy melody. After listening to it several times, people couldn't help singing along.

What are the "Four Comprehensives" in the song? The "Four Comprehensives" are the strategic layout and overall framework of the CPC Central Committee's governance, with Comrade Xi Jinping as the core. It refers to a four-pronged strategy of deepening reform, advancing law-based governance, and improving Party conduct in an all-round way. Such a simple and understandable framework set the direction for China's future development.

In terms of time, the "Four Comprehensives" was gradually proposed by the Party leaders on different occasions: in November 2012, the 18th National Congress of the CPC proposed to build a moderately prosperous society in an all-round way; in November 2013, the Third Plenary Session of the 18th CPC Central Committee proposed to comprehensively deepen reform; in October 2014, the Fourth Plenary Session of the 18th CPC Central Committee proposed to comprehensively promote the rule of law; in October 2014, the summary meeting

Figure 94.
"Four Comprehensives" is the unity of strategic objectives and strategic initiatives.

of campaigns for advancing study and implementation of the Party's mass line proposed to strengthen Party self-discipline. In December 2014, General Secretary Xi Jinping proposed during his research in Jiangsu to "make coordinated and comprehensive efforts to finish building a moderately prosperous society in all respects, deepen reform, advance the rule of law and strictly enforce party discipline, and promote reform and opening-up and socialist modernization to a new level." This was the first time mentioning the "Four Comprehensives" was at the same time.

Knowledge about CPC History

According to the report of the 18th National Congress of the CPC, the tasks and requirements for building a moderately prosperous society include sustained and healthy economic development, continuous expansion of people's democracy, significant enhancement of cultural soft power, overall improvement of people's living standards, and significant progress in building a resource-saving and environment-friendly society. The realization of these specific goals means the overall improvement of China's modernization degree and level and becomes an important step to realize the Chinese Dream of the great rejuvenation of the Chinese nation.

According to "Four Comprehensives," building a moderately prosperous society in an all-round way is the strategic goal placed in the central position; comprehensively deepening reform, comprehensively promoting the rule of law, and comprehensively governing the Party with strict discipline serve the strategic goal and are strategic measures. The strategic goal and measures are organically combined to form a whole.

Since the 18th National Congress of the CPC, Comrade Xi Jinping, as the core of the CPC Central Committee has made a series of major decisions, especially the "Four Comprehensives," making us feel the role of history more and more genuinely and excitingly, and feel the hope of approaching our dream and more clearly. The "Four-pronged Comprehensiveness," which is interrelated and organically integrated, is the pillar that will lead us to continue our efforts and struggles to achieve the dream of the great rejuvenation of the Chinese nation. As the song "Four Comprehensives" says: "In 'Four Comprehensives'—the building of a well-off society is the goal, reform is the driving force, the rule of law is the guarantee, and party building is the key." The "Four Comprehensives" was put forward by the CPC Central Committee from the reality of China, with a long-term perspective, a foothold in China, and a global perspective. It is the creative achievement of the Chinese Communists who deeply grasped the law of social development and correctly applied law of development.

In 2020, the Fifth Plenary Session of the 19th CPC Central Committee proposed to coordinate and promote the strategic layout of the comprehensive construction of a socialist modern country, comprehensively deepening reform, comprehensively governing the country according to law and comprehensively governing the Party with strict discipline. The strategic layout of the "Four Comprehensives" evolved from "building a moderately prosperous society, deepening reform, advancing law-based governance, and strengthening Party self-governance in an all-round way" to "building a socialist modern country, deepening reform, advancing law-based governance, and strengthening Party self-governance in an all-round way."

2015 "Ballast" of the Honors System

Keyword: the first law on national medals and national honorary titles

The CPC has a fine tradition of selecting advanced models and honoring meritorious deeds. For example, the titles of "Combat Hero," "Model Party Member," and "Model Militia Member" were established during the War of Resistance against Japanese Aggression, and the titles of "People's Hero," "Medal for the Hero Supporting the Front," "Mao Zedong Medal" and so on were awarded during the War of Liberation. Since the 18th National Congress of the CPC, the CPC Central Committee has attached great importance to the commendation of meritorious deeds and honors and gradually improved the national honors system.

On December 27, 2015, the Eighteenth Session of the Standing Committee of the 12th National People's Congress passed the *Law of the People's Republic of China on National Medals and National Honorary Titles* (hereinafter referred to as the *Titles Law*) by a high vote. This is China's first specialized law on national medals and national honorary titles, which provided a basic legal text for the improvement of the national honors system and is known as the "fundamental law" and "ballast stone" of China's honors system. The birth of the *Titles Law* was not smooth. As early as the end of 1986, the Legislative Affairs Commission, the Legislative Affairs Bureau of the State Council, and other relevant central departments began to study and draft the *Titles Law*. In October 1993, during the deliberation of the draft of the *Titles Law* at the fourth meeting of the Standing Committee of the 8th National People's Congress,

Figure 95.
On September 29, 2019, the winners of the national medal and national honorary titles were at the awarding ceremony.

Knowledge about CPC History

On February 27, 2014, the seventh meeting of the Standing Committee of the 12th National People's Congress voted to designate September 3 as the "Victory Memorial Day for the Chinese People's War of Resistance against Japanese Aggression." In 2015, in order to commemorate the 70th anniversary of the victory of the Chinese People's War of Resistance against Japanese Aggression and the World Anti-Fascist War, the CPC Central Committee and the State Council decided to carry out a series of commemorative activities with the theme of "bearing history in mind, honoring all those who laid down their lives, cherishing peace and opening-up the future."

the Law was put on hold for a time due to different opinions on whether to grant posthumous awards to deceased persons and on the definition of the time frame for granting such awards. Until the report of the 17th National Congress of the CPC and the report of the 18th National Congress of the CPC successively proposed the establishment of the national honors system, and then the Fourth Plenary Session of the 18th CPC Central Committee decided to "formulate the 'Law of the People's Republic of China on National Medals and National Honorary Titles', and commend outstanding persons with outstanding contributions." The *Titles Law* was passed by vote at the end of 2015, which was really "a sword forged in three decades."

The *Titles Law* made scientific specifications on the subjects, categories, time, and objects of national honors, effectively ensuring the authority and credibility of meritorious honors. For example, the law specifies that the national medals include "the Medal of the Republic" and the "Friendship Medal," and the national honorary title is titled with the name "People"; the Medal of the Republic is awarded to "outstanding persons who have made great contributions to the country and established outstanding achievements"; the national honorary title is awarded to "outstanding persons who have made significant contributions in various fields and industries and enjoyed a high reputation." With regard to the issue of whether the deceased should be awarded titles posthumously, which caused disagreements at previous meetings, the *Titles Law* made specific provisions that "persons who made outstanding contributions during their lifetime and met the conditions for awarding national medals and national honorary titles under this Law may be awarded national medals and national honorary titles posthumously if they die after the implementation of this Law," fully demonstrating that the Law is a vivid text that responsible for the people, the state and history.

Since the implementation of the *Titles Law* as of November 2020, 46 people had won national medals and national honorary titles. Among them, there were soldiers who sacrificed their lives and died in the front, medical and nursing personnel who put life first and loved without boundaries, grassroots cadres who were willing to dedicate themselves and work silently, and scientific researchers who were pioneering and innovative and dared to be the first. Their outstanding achievements and advanced deeds will further promote the cultivation and promotion of the national spirit and the spirit of the times, will lead young people in the new era to shoulder the mission bravely in the great practice of socialism, and will certainly gather great strength for the realization of the Chinese Dream of the great rejuvenation of the Chinese nation.

2016 The Universal Two-Child Era Began

Keyword: the universal two-child policy

"It's the Spring Festival again, and the time has passed quickly. Last year we were having a parents' meeting for our first child, and this year we're about to have our second child." In 2017, the language programs on the stage of the Anhui TV Spring Festival Gala focused on social hot spots, in which the opusculum about the universal two-child policy started with this limerick, which won a smile from many of the audience. Since January 1, 2016, the socially anticipated comprehensive two-child policy has been in place, marking the end of the 35-year-long one-child policy in China and heralding the advent of the universal two-child era. For a long time, the public opinion caused by the universal two-child policy remained high, forming a heated atmosphere of national discussion and becoming a real hotspot of people's livelihood.

As we all know, China has the largest population in the world. Although China had steadily promoted family planning since the 1970s, the trend of rapid population growth in the country didn't change at that time, with a population growth of 100 million in five to seven years. Considering that too fast population growth would bring heavy pressure on economic and social development, the CPC Central Committee issued *An Open Letter to All Communist Party Members and Communist Youth League Members on Controlling Population Growth in China* in 1980, advocating that a couple should only have one child. Subsequently, the 12th National Congress of the CPC determined the family planning policy as the basic state policy.

Figure 96.
Implementing the universal two-child policy and promoting balanced population development

> **Knowledge about CPC History**
> In February 1957, Comrade Mao Zedong first proposed "family planning" at the 11th Supreme State Conference. Subsequently, the struggle against the Rightists and the "Great Leap Forward" craze led to twists and turns in China's exploration of population issues. Until December 1962, the CPC Central Committee and the State Council issued the *Instruction on Seriously Promoting Family Planning*, and population and family planning issues were put on the agenda again.

Since then, slogans such as "fewer children and a happy life," "build roads first, and have fewer children and more trees if you want to get rich," and other publicity slogans had spread all over the cities and countryside. The fertility concepts such as "late marriage and childbearing" and "sound maternal and child care" had been deeply rooted in the hearts of the people, and a path with Chinese characteristics to solve population problems as a whole gradually took shape.

However, as China entered the 21st century, especially since the 12th Five-Year Plan period, the internal dynamics and external conditions of population development changed significantly. The imbalance of the labor force structure and the increase in an aging population triggered calls for adjusting population policies. Some scholars even put forward the assertion that "China's population is approaching its peak and will face an avalanche decline in the long run." Therefore, since Shandong, Sichuan, and other places took the lead in implementing the two-child policy for couples from one-child families at the end of the 20th century, passed the policy of two children in total in 2013, and clearly put forward the policy of "one couple can have two children" at the Fifth Plenary Session of the 18th CPC Central Committee in 2015, China's family planning policy was in an "ongoing" dynamic adjustment. As a "policy gift" in response to social concerns and in line with national conditions and public opinion, the universal two-child policy could encourage people to form a more mature and rational fertility concept. "Three people in one family" was no longer a "standard configuration," meeting the happiness pursuit of some parents that "the best gift for children is brothers and sisters." One mother of two children said in an interview: "The happiest moment in my life is when I take my two children out to play. Watching them playing and laughing, I can imagine how wonderful it will be when they grow up to discuss things together and rely on each other."

The opening of a universal two-child era is conducive to the formation of a new round of demographic dividends and the development of China's economy and society in the long run. In the medium and long run, it will help to alleviate the degree of social aging and improve the supply of labor. In the short term, it will also directly promote the development of maternal and child health, childcare services and other industries. At the same time, however, the social public service system is also facing a series of challenges such as "second child" enrollment for kindergartens and schools, as well as medical treatment. In the next step, the state will strengthen the supply of public services, accelerate the improvement of family welfare policies, steadily release policy dividends, and ensure that the two-child policy, which is beneficial to the people's livelihood and long-term interests and popular among the masses, is carried out well.

2017 The First Flight of Domestic Large Aircraft Succeeded

Keyword: domestic large aircraft

At about 2:00 p.m. on May 5, 2017, the normally busy Shanghai Pudong International Airport held its breath and ushered in a historic moment: a large passenger plane decorated with blue sky and green earth patterns on its tail wing was like a giant dragon lying on the fourth runway, ready for departure. "Agree to fly!" At the command, the "giant dragon" took off and soared into the sky and flew in a leisurely fashion along the coast of the East China Sea, winning cheers at the scene. The successful first flight of the large domestic aircraft C919 fulfilled the dream of large domestic aircraft of several generations of Chinese aviation personnel. There was finally a large Chinese passenger plane with independent intellectual property rights in the blue sky, which was completely developed in accordance with the world's advanced standards. "Made in China" once again amazed the world!

An elderly man stood on the runway and watched the whole process of C919 takeoff. The big plane took off to form a strong wind, and the old man's gray hair fluttered with the wind, but he didn't care. He just waved to the big plane again and again, and he was excited and proud. The old man, named Cheng Bushi, was the first-generation aircraft designer in

Figure 97. China's large aircraft C919 flying in the blue sky

New China. "Y-10," the first large jet passenger plane in New China designed by him, was the only domestic aircraft to arrive in Lhasa, Xizang in the 20th century. As the technical consultant of the large domestic aircraft C919 this time, he had too many expectations and feelings for this large aircraft, which was a milestone in the history of China's civil aviation.

Knowledge about CPC History
Compared with Western countries, China's large aircraft research and development did not start late. As early as August 1970, the country officially launched the development of a large civil aircraft project code-named "Y-10," which later became known as project "708." At present, there is still a white-painted passenger plane in the factory of Shanghai Aircraft Manufacturing Company, that is, the "Y-10," which achieved its first flight in 1980.

In the era when technology was strictly blocked by Europe and the United States, Cheng Bushi led a group of young researchers with an average age of less than 22 to start from scratch and work hard. It took only eight years to complete the design of the "Y-10," and the first flight was achieved in 1980. Later, during a long period of the low ebb of "buying was better than building" and "renting was better than buying" large passenger aircraft, they never forgot their dream of "letting the large aircraft made in our country show its majesty in the blue sky." In 2007, the C919 project was officially approved as a new journey for domestic large aircraft. The process from its design, development, and testing to the first flight was like "ten years' sharpening of a sword," after which the plane took off to the high sky. Each step in the journey of C919's flight witnessed the progress of independent innovation in China's aviation industry, which demonstrated China's strength and boldness in competing for the international aviation market, and demonstrated China's institutional advantage in concentrating its efforts on major issues.

Advanced equipment of the country was the wing for fulfilling dreams. As a commercial airliner, the C919 reached the world's advanced level in terms of safety performance, passenger carrying experience, economic cost, and late development advantages and had broad market prospects. As a shining Chinese business card, the overall layout design of C919 is completely independent, and the aircraft's "nerve center"—avionics system is provided by a company in Shanghai, equipped with tens of thousands of components with a localization ratio of up to 60%, which is a vivid epitome of the transformation and upgrading of "Made in China" and its advancement to the middle and high end. As a general-purpose platform, the C919 drove the development of the entire industrial chain and also had the ability to serve the national defense, on the basis of which military transport aircraft, early warning aircraft, and even aerial refueling aircraft could be developed in line with the urgent needs of China's Air Force modernization. It was a well-deserved "jewel" in the crown of manufacturing.

The sky of dreams is still calling for people to never stop and actively explore. The domestic C919 large aircraft was not the endpoint. The technical scheme of the larger CR929 long-range wide-body passenger aircraft development project had been determined, and the preliminary design work was started. "Made in China" is bound to continue to work hard, make breakthroughs and create first-class products, and continue to demonstrate China's strength, spirit, and efficiency. The future of large domestic aircraft is promising.

2018 "Super Bridge" Cast Miracles

Keyword: Hong Kong–Zhuhai–Macao Bridge

"With a total length of 55 kilometers, it is the world's longest sea-crossing bridge; the submarine immersed tube tunnel has a total length of 6.7 kilometers, which is the world's longest submarine immersed tube tunnel; the submarine tunnel has a maximum depth of 48 meters, which is the world's deepest immersed tunnel ..." The Hong Kong–Zhuhai–Macao Bridge officially opened at 9:00 a.m. on October 24, 2018, and became famous in the world because of its huge construction scale, unprecedented construction difficulties, and top construction technology, setting a number of world records in the history of bridge construction, and was known as the "Everest of Bridges," and was called one of the "Seven Wonders of the Modern World" by the British newspaper the *Guardian*.

This "super project" was like a light and elegant ribbon across the Lingdingyang waters at the estuary of the Pearl River. Among them, the landscape design of the waterway bridge clearly showed Chinese characteristics, Chinese style, and Chinese manner: the knot-shaped support on the top of the tower of Qingzhou Channel Bridge absorbed the cultural elements of the "Chinese knot," "curving" the original right angle shape, making the bridge tower appear delicate, flexible, exquisite and elegant; the crown of the main tower of the Jianghai Direct Shipping Channel Bridge was shaped like a dolphin, combining with the marine culture of the Chinese White Dolphin Sanctuary, and emphasizing the harmony between man and nature; the main tower of the Jiuzhou Channel Bridge was shaped from the element of "sail," with the ancient rhythm of "A time will come to ride the wind and cleave the waves,

Figure 98.
Hong Kong–Zhuhai–Macao Bridge

I'll set my cloud-like sail to cross the sea which raves." This perfect unity of architectural beauty, artistic beauty, and cultural connotation benefited from the design goal of Meng Fanchao, the chief designer of the bridge, and his team, which was "Not only to build a bridge that can run a car on it but also to build an important humanistic landscape; integrating architectural structure and landscape art to achieve the perfect combination of force and beauty."

Knowledge about CPC History

2018 marks the 40th anniversary of China's reform and opening-up. On December 18, the conference celebrating the 40th anniversary of reform and opening-up was grandly held in the Great Hall of the People in Beijing. Comrade Xi Jinping delivered an important speech at the conference, pointing out that the great concept of "one country, two systems" has great vitality and that it is necessary to support and promote the better integration of Hong Kong and Macao into the overall development of the country.

It was approved to carry out preliminary work in 2003, started construction in 2009, and officially put into operation in October 2018. After 15 years of cultivation and pouring, the Hong Kong–Zhuhai–Macao Bridge was finally completed with 12 subsystems, including toll collection, communication, power supply, drainage, and lightning protection, which could withstand a magnitude 8 earthquake, a magnitude 16 typhoon, a 300,000-ton impact, and a once-in-300-years flood at the Pearl River estuary. At the same time, completing the "Super Bridge" created 454 invention patents and seven world records. For example, to protect Chinese white dolphins, the "pandas in the water" in the construction area, the research team developed a scientific and effective repellent program based on the habits of the white dolphins, which ensured "zero casualties" during the construction period and was granted a patent; and the team innovated the construction method of the super-long offshore immersed tube tunnel, the technical path of the immersed tube adjustment device, and the design and construction technology of the offshore artificial island, all of which reflected the craftsmanship of China's bridge builders in their pursuit of excellence and perfection, and all of which reflected China's rising capacity for independent innovation and its national ambition to create a world-class bridge.

The Hong Kong–Zhuhai–Macao Bridge is a super project, advanced equipment of the country, and well-deserved symbol of the national image. As a landmark project of infrastructure connectivity in the Guangdong-Hong Kong–Macao Greater Bay Area, it greatly facilitated the exchange and economic and trade exchanges among residents of the three regions, provided new opportunities for the Guangdong-Hong Kong–Macao Greater Bay Area to further complement their advantages and achieve mutual benefit and win-win results, created new conditions for "one country, two systems" to radiate more powerful vitality, and accumulated new practical experience for promoting the formation of a new pattern of comprehensive opening-up.

This "Super Bridge," which carries the beautiful expectation of "Dream Bridge, Concentric Bridge, Confidence Bridge, and Revival Bridge," once again proved the Chinese power of "chopping the waves" and demonstrated the Chinese people's struggle spirit of "building bridges when meeting water."

2019 National Day Celebration Showed National Prestige

Keyword: the military parade celebrating the 70th anniversary of the PRC

On the occasion of National Day, the mountains and rivers were magnificent, and people were jubilant, and the sky was clear in Beijing, the capital. In Tiananmen Square, flags were flying, people were crowded together, and the large "Red Ribbon" landscape sculpture was symmetrically surrounded, gorgeous, and dynamic; in front of the Monument to the People's Heroes, the huge three-dimensional words of "National Day," "1949" and "2019" stood out in the sunlight. In the expectation of everyone, 70 salutes rang through the sky, and the grand ceremony of "celebrating the 70th anniversary of the founding of the PRC" came as scheduled.

The grand ceremony, the country showed the world a new look at China's vigor and progress in the new era. "Today, socialist China is standing rock-firm in the east. No force can ever shake the status of China or stop the Chinese people and nation from marching forward." General Secretary Xi Jinping fondly saluted China's great leap from standing up, and getting rich to getting strong with powerful and resounding words that signaled the glorious future of the nation and echoed for a long time in the minds of the participants and the audience.

Figure 99.
National Day military parade on October 1, 2019

Knowledge about CPC History

The military parade at the 2019 National Day Ceremony was the first National Day military parade in the new era of socialism with Chinese characteristics and the first overall appearance of the Republic's armed forces after their reform and reshaping. In the Foot formations, formations, such as peacekeepers, rocket forces, civilian personnel, and scientific research institutes, were reviewed in the National Day military parade for the first time, demonstrating the new composition and style of the peoples's army.

The grand ceremony of the country demonstrated to the world China's firm confidence in building a world-class army in the new era. On the wide Chang'an Street, iron armor glowed, and warriors gathered. The parade had a total size of about 15,000 people, more than 160 aircraft of all types, and 580 sets of equipment. From the imposing leadership command formation to the heroic servicewomen formation, from the "Land Tiger" to the "Sea Dragon," from the joint air defense "Strong Shield" to the strategic strike "Dongfeng Family" ... the scale of the full type, the new equipment, the number of senior commanders on parade were the largest in history, centrally demonstrated the independent innovation capability of China's national defense science and technology industry and the level of weapons and equipment development. "In the founding ceremony military parade 70 years ago, 95% of the reviewed equipment was captured from the battlefield, which is really 'a flick of the finger, the old looks new.'" He Xiaoming, the daughter of Marshal He Long, said with emotion, "Seeing the majesty of the People's Army in the new era and remembering the 70 years of the extraordinary history of the Republic, I can't help but burst into tears."

The grand ceremony of the country made the world feel the Chinese people's passionate patriotism and positive spirit in the new era. When the resistance against Japanese aggression veterans who had experienced the baptism of the battlefield of blood and fire passed by Tiananmen Square by car, their steely gaze and standard military salute made people pay endless respect. They dedicated their most beautiful youth to the country and used their lives to interpret their pure hearts to defend their country. As the representative of the new era and new occupation, the "take-away boy" appeared in the parade team with a confident smile, wearing eye-catching work clothes and riding a familiar "small electric donkey," winning applause and cheers from the crowd. All walks of life were making contributions to the construction of the motherland with practical actions, and they were unique "dreamers"!

Seventy years of hardships and 70 years of great achievements, from seeking independence to becoming rich and strong, from seeking survival to rejuvenation: under the leadership of the CPC, the Chinese people constantly strove for self-improvement, forged ahead, staged many amazing national ceremonies, ushered in a new era of the great rejuvenation of the Chinese nation, and wrote a magnificent chapter in the history of the development of the Chinese nation.

2020 The Dream of a Moderately Prosperous Society in All Respects Finally Came True

Keyword: completion of building a moderately prosperous society in all respects

In 2020, a rampant COVID-19 epidemic swept across China, and 2020 was the closing year for building a moderately prosperous society and winning the battle against poverty. Under the leadership of the CPC Central Committee, the people of the whole country overcame all kinds of adverse effects caused by the epidemic and finally won the great victory of poverty alleviation.

Since ancient times, "a moderately prosperous society" had been the common dream of the Chinese nation. Three thousand years ago, "a moderately prosperous society" was the dream of the laboring people in *The Book of Songs* to reduce taxes; more than 100 years ago, "a moderately prosperous society" was the innovation dream of Kang Youwei and other people with lofty ideals; more than 40 years ago, "a moderately prosperous society" was the dream of the CPC represented by Comrade Deng Xiaoping. From "solving people's food and clothing" to "achieving a moderately prosperous society in all respects," to "building a moderately prosperous society in all respects," and then to "realizing a moderately prosperous society in all respects," the CPC led the people of all ethnic groups across the country to embark on the journey of pursuing their dreams, leaping over numerous peaks and mountains, and reaping fruitful results and witnessed for the first time the realization of the true meaning of "building a moderately prosperous society in all respects," and embarked on a key step to realize the Chinese Dream of the great rejuvenation of the Chinese nation.

"When defining a moderately prosperous society, the key is to observe the condition of farmers." "Without prosperity in rural China, particularly those impoverished areas, we can't complete building a moderately prosperous society in all respects." At the end of 1978, there were about 770 million people living in poverty in China's rural areas, with the incidence of poverty there as high as 97.5%, accounting for nearly 40% of the world's poor people at that time. Since the 18th CPC Party Congress, the CPC Central Committee, with Comrade

Knowledge about CPC History

In the face of the sudden outbreak of the COVID-19 epidemic in early 2020, a unified and efficient command system was established under the strong leadership of the CPC Central Committee with Comrade Xi Jinping at the core, providing a strong guarantee to win the battle of epidemic prevention and control. The tremendous achievement in fighting the epidemic highlights China's strong comprehensive national strength and the remarkable advantages of the socialist system with Chinese characteristics.

Xi Jinping as the core, took poverty eradication as the bottom-line task for building a moderately prosperous society and made every effort to fight the battle against poverty. In the mountainous areas where resources were scarce, and disasters frequently occurred, poverty alleviation by relocation opened a new life for people in need; in remote mountainous areas with a certain accumulation of natural resources, poverty alleviation by developing industries and e-commerce poverty alleviation opened up a road to prosperity for people in need; in areas with beautiful mountains, waters, and distinctive landscapes, tourism poverty alleviation turned lucid waters and lush mountains into invaluable assets. It took eight years for nearly 100 million poor rural people in China to get rid of poverty under current standards, and all 832 poor counties and 128,000 poor villages were removed from the list. The goal of poverty reduction in the 2030 Agenda for Sustainable Development was completed 10 years ahead of schedule, and the United Nations Secretary General Guterres praised it as the "world record-holder in the field of poverty reduction," creating the Chinese miracle in the history of human anti-poverty.

"The quality of the ecological environment is the key to a moderately prosperous society in all respects." A sound ecological environment is a bright backdrop for building a moderately prosperous society in all respects, and it is also the commonwealth of the people. During the 13th Five-Year Plan period, China's goal of building a moderately prosperous society in all respects with a high-quality ecological environment was realized scheduled, which laid a good foundation for the in-depth battle against pollution during the 14th Five-Year Plan period. At present, China's environmental protection work sticks to the "same direction and unabated intensity." The state has taken action from sand control, watershed management, guarding green hills, energy saving and emission reduction, and animal protection, making the image of a beautiful China where nature is well treated, blue water flows forever, green hills are always present, the air is always fresh, and people and nature live in harmony more and more clearly.

Those seemingly ordinary things are extraordinary, and those seemingly easy things are arduous. The century-long journey of the CPC in leading the nation to moderate prosperity can be described as a heavy task and a thorny path. The impressive report card and historic leap achieved in this dream-fulfilling trip once again let the world feel the strong development pulse of Chinese society and witnessed the extraordinary courage of a great country to overcome difficulties.

Figure 100.
The agricultural market, the first place for precise poverty alleviation, in Shibadong Village, Xiangxi, Hunan Province